Faith and Reason from Plato to Plantinga

Faith and Reason from Plato to Plantinga

An Introduction to Reformed Epistemology

Dewey J. Hoitenga, Jr.

STATE UNIVERSITY OF NEW YORK PRESS

Published by
State University of New York Press, Albany

© 1991   State University of New York

For information, address State University of New York
Press, State University Plaza, Albany, N.Y. 12246

Production by Ruth East
Marketing by Fran Keneston

Library of Congress Cataloging-in-Publication Data

Hoitenga, Dewey J., 1931–
    Faith and reason from Plato to Plantinga : an introduction to
Reformed epistemology / Dewey J. Hoitenga, Jr.
        p. cm.
    Includes bibliographical references and index.
    ISBN 0–7914-0590–7 (alk. paper) . — ISBN 0–7914-0591–5 (pbk. :
alk. paper)
        1. God—Knowableness—History of doctrines. 2. God—Knowableness.
3. Reformed Church—Doctrines—History. 4. Reformed Church-
-Doctrines. 5. Plato—Contributions in doctrine of knowableness of
God. 6. Augustine, Saint, Bishop of Hippo—Contributions in
doctrine of knowableness of God. 7. Calvin, Jean, 1509–1564—
Contributions in Reformed epistemology. 8. Plantinga, Alvin—
Contributions in Reformed epistemology. I. Title. II. Title:
Reformed epistemology.
BT98.H58 1991
231'.042—dc20   90–37214
                                                                CIP

10 9 8 7 6 5 4 3 2 1

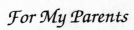

For My Parents

Contents

Preface

The late twentieth century revival in philosophy of religion continues in full force. Positivism, with its antireligious and antimetaphysical onslaught, although not dead, no longer struts on center stage as it did at midcentury when it roundly declared religious language meaningless. The revival in philosophy of religion has many facets, ranging from a renewed investigation of such traditional Western Judaeo-Christian doctrines as God, creation, incarnation, atonement, and bodily resurrection to an exploration of the religious confrontation of East and West.

One conspicuous element in the revitalized investigation of Judaeo-Christian themes is the discussion of Reformed epistemology. The central claim of Reformed epistemology is the immediacy of our knowledge of God. No one a generation ago could have anticipated the controversy over this claim that has arisen among contemporary philosophers of religion. The term *Reformed epistemology* itself does not seem to have existed before Alvin Plantinga introduced it in 1980, in the paper he read for the American Catholic Philosophical Association, "The Reformed Objection to Natural Theology." In the book *Faith and Rationality: Reason and Belief in God* (1983), which Plantinga edited with Nicholas Wolterstorff, he, Wolterstorff, and others articulate the main contours of the Reformed approach to faith, knowledge, and belief. In his "Introduction" to the book, Nicholas Wolterstorff suggests that the new term *Reformed epistemology* is "infelicitous" (7). It is quite well founded and altogether correct, nonetheless.

The word *Reformed* identifies the theological tradition inspired by John Calvin and the epistemological claim derives from Calvin's famous words near the beginning of his *Institutes of the Christian Religion:*

> There is within the human mind, and indeed by natural instinct, an awareness of divinity. . . . To prevent anyone from taking refuge in the pretense of ignorance, God has implanted in all men a certain understanding of his divine majesty. . . . Since, therefore, men one and all perceive that there is a God and that he is their Maker, they are condemned by their own testimony

because they have failed to honor him and to consecrate their lives to his will. (I, iii, 1)

This conviction, namely, that there is some God, is naturally inborn in all, and is fixed deep within, as it were in the very marrow. . . . It is not a doctrine that must be first learned in school, but one of which each of us is master from his mother's womb and which nature itself permits no one to forget, although many strive with every nerve to this end. (I, iii, 3)

Thus, although the term *Reformed epistemology* is new, its central claim lies at the heart of a modern theological tradition.

During the 400 some years since Calvin wrote these words, his claim about the immediacy of our knowledge of God has been reiterated mainly by Reformed theologians. Consequently the claim has often been perceived as a narrowly theological doctrine. Now, however, Reformed philosophers are defending the claim as a *philosophical claim*, and it is being examined by non-Reformed philosophers of every stripe, Christian and secular alike. The theological origin of Reformed epistemology in John Calvin's *Institutes* signifies, of course, that the claim is a theological thesis, but not that it is therefore irrelevant to philosophy. Those who, like Wolterstorff, Plantinga, and myself, were reared and educated in the Reformed tradition stemming from the Netherlands have known from the beginning of our intellectual reflections that the Reformed articulation of Christianity is rich with philosophical implications. What is clearer today than perhaps ever before is that the Calvinist claim about our knowledge of God is also a *philosophical* claim in its own right.

Nevertheless, the recent spectacle of Calvinists marching into philosophical territory without leaving their Calvinism to one side has given rise to serious misconceptions about the the nature of Reformed epistemology. It is said that *Reformed* thought is, properly speaking, *theological* thought that arose as a narrowly religious and ecclesiastical protest against the thought and practice of late medieval Christianity. The adjective *Reformed* has no business, therefore, modifying the noun *epistemology*, which refers to a subdivision of philosophical inquiry. Epistemology is the province of philosophers—of Platonists, Aristotelians, Cartesians, Kantians, or positivists, if you will, but not of Calvinists; they should be studying their John Calvin, Benjamin Warfield, Abraham Kuyper, and Karl Barth.

A closely connected misconception is that, because Reformed epistemology derives from Calvin and Calvinism, its claim about knowing God is a typically *modern* claim, one without the force of an

ancient or medieval tradition behind it. This impression is reinforced by
the fact that Plantinga and Wolterstorff do their Reformed epistemology with the new tools of modern logic and in a way that engages contemporary philosophers, many of whom are under the spell of modern
Cartesian assumptions. Hence their thinking (so goes the impression) is
doubly modernistic, for they are not only protesting against the authority of the Catholic Church and its official Thomistic approach to philosophy, but also embracing the essential skepticism that has characterized
modern philosophy since the seventeenth century.

The clearest expression of these misconceptions I have seen can
be found in several of the essays recently collected in the volume
Thomistic Papers IV, edited by L. A. Kennedy. The contributors to this
book join in a concerted response to Plantinga's and Wolterstorff's
Faith and Rationality: Reason and Belief in God. To take one example, in
"'Reformed' Epistemology," T. A. Russman expresses his reaction to
Reformed epistemology as follows:

> The *raison d'etre* of any project whose title carries the adjectives
> "Reformed" or "Protestant" is that which is to be "reformed" or
> "protested against." In a theological context, what was histori-
> cally to be reformed or protested against was "Catholic Chris-
> tianity," to speak broadly, or "Medieval Christianity," to speak
> more narrowly. To take an epistemological stand against these is
> presumably to stand with the "moderns," to stand fundamental-
> ly with the philosophies which arose from the 16th Century
> onward. (185)

There it is in a nutshell. One cannot be Reformed without being either
narrowly *theological* or dangerously *modernistic* or (probably)
both—not only religiously opposed to medieval and to Catholic
Christianity but also philosophically opposed to the wisdom of
ancient philosophical traditions that (for Russman, it becomes clear
later in his essay) culminates in Aristotelian-Thomistic philosophy.

From contemporary analytic philosophers of religion comes the
related misconception that Reformed epistemology is best understood
as a form of *fideism*, the view that religious faith not only needs no
support from reason but may even stand in judgment on the claims of
reason. Thus, in *God and Skepticism*, Terence Penelhum, one of these
philosophers, interprets Plantinga as an "evangelical fideist" in the
tradition of Pascal and Kierkegaard. Penelhum observes that, in coun-
tering the critics of his Reformed epistemology, "Plantinga makes use
of arguments which, though original and contemporary, inevitably
call to mind Skeptic attacks on the doctrines of infallible representa-

tions and Skeptic discussions of the criterion of truth" (147). Penelhum is careful not to charge Plantinga with skepticism and believes that Plantinga successfully "fend[s] off the charge of irrationality" against his views (154); still, his analysis of Plantinga's position and his associating it with Wittgenstein's approach (148–151) can only lend aid and comfort to the suspicions of both traditional Thomists and contemporary secular philosophers that Reformed epistemology is probably irrational and skeptical after all. Even Reformed philosopher Jay Van Hook argues, in "Knowledge, Belief, and Reformed epistemology," that Plantinga's version of Reformed epistemology is in danger of collapsing into "fidestic skepticism" (17).

One aim I have in writing this book is to remove such misconceptions. Traditionalists tend to regard Plantinga's Reformed epistemology as lining up with the moderns against the ancients in that very important debate which has been going on since Jonathan Swift's "Battle of the Books." But this simplistic reaction obscures a far more important issue that Calvinists want to engage, namely, the issue over the nature of our knowledge of God. Furthermore, by fixing attention only on the fact that Plantinga's and Wolterstorff's epistemology is Reformed, such critics have overlooked the ancient philosophical roots of their thought as well as those of Calvin, their most conspicuous mentor on this issue. To be sure, Russman recognizes this ancient philosophical pedigree of Reformed epistemology. Commenting on Calvin's *sensus divinitatis*, he writes: "Like Augustine, Calvin appears to be appealing to the Platonic tradition of 'innate ideas' to explain how one comes to know of God's existence" (195). Exactly! Russman's problem, however, is that he ignores the philosophical significance of Calvin's appeal to Plato. That very appeal undermines Russman's complaint that Reformed epistemology is mainly *Protestant*. It also undermines his complaint that Reformed epistemology is modern, that it is, as he colorfully puts it, some kind of "new bird" that its advocates have provided with "its own preening branch to stand on" (185). So what really seems to upset him, as it does some of the other contributors to *Thomist Papers IV*, is that Reformed epistemology is Platonic and Augustinian instead of Aristotelian and Thomistic. Yet he fails to concentrate his criticism of Reformed epistemology on that (clearly ancient and philosophical) issue; instead, he studiously avoids considering Reformed epistemology exactly for what it is, a serious philosophical theory with an ancient philosophical pedigree.

As I hope to show, Reformed epistemology is not a new bird at all, but a wise old owl whose lineage can be traced to Athena herself, or at least to her ancient city, and to Plato, its first great philosopher. If this lineage is the salient fact, any criticism of Reformed epistemology that ignores it will be superficial criticism indeed. Whoever thinks that *Reformed epistemology* signifies mainly a sixteenth century religious protest or that, because it has been revived in the language of contemporary analytic philosophy, it is hopelessly contaminated by the winds of "modern philosophy," cannot expect to see its abiding philosophical significance.

I do not intend, however, primarily to address the objections that have recently been raised against Reformed epistemology. My purpose is mainly expository and historical. I want to show that Plantinga's epistemological position is very traditional, expressed though it is within the framework of contemporary analytic philosophy. Only those who know the philosophical tradition will be able to see and appreciate this fact, although even some of them have missed it; and so I want to address them as well as those who have neglected the history of philosophy, influenced by the modern prejudice that such ignorance is innocent.

Accordingly, my topic is Faith and Reason from Plato to Plantinga. It will be obvious that I do not intend to provide a grand tour of faith and reason from the Greeks down to our day; far from it. I will largely ignore the Aristotelian and Thomistic tradition, except where it is necessary to refer to it as the most important alternative to the Platonic and Augustinian tradition. I do not even intend to give a comprehensive account of the Platonic-Augustinian-Calvinist development of epistemological ideas. I want rather to focus upon the main landmarks along the way of this lengthy and complex development. These landmarks provide the essential conditions of Reformed epistemology, and include, as I see it, just Plato, the Bible, Augustine, and Calvin. I shall also largely ignore the skeptical tradition, except where it bears directly and significantly on the interpretation of Augustine and Plantinga. In moving from landmark to landmark, I hope to highlight the central continuity that defines the main components of Reformed epistemology, while taking due account of the discontinuities and differences in emphasis, terminology, and overall context between these landmarks.

The main components of the Reformed view of our knowledge of God are two: its *immediacy* and its *vitality*. Calvin is utterly clear that human knowledge of God is originally immediate and direct, based neither on inference and argument nor on human testimony. And he is utterly clear that our knowledge of God makes a vital difference to us, according to whether we live in conformity with that knowledge or try to ignore it. For Calvin, that choice, whether to live in conformity to our knowledge of God or ignore it, is the ultimate religious choice of every human being. In the language of William James's *Will to Believe*, that choice is the most important "living, forced, and momentous" (3) option a human being can face. I will show that the seeds of these two characteristics of our knowledge of God are present already in both Plato and the Bible, that they are developed by St. Augustine, and that they are still alive and well in Plantinga.

I should explain why I devote three chapters to Augustine instead of just one. First, Augustine represents the original definitive and therefore most influential synthesis of Greek and biblical ideas. He is, moreover, the Church Father to whom both Catholics and Protestants appeal in the midst of their most fundamental and ongoing theological and philosophical disagreements. Furthermore, he is enormously interesting in his own right as a person and as a thinker. Finally, his formative ideas on faith and reason harbor some of the critical ambiguities that continue to plague the theory of knowledge down to this day. A large part of epistemology consists in a defense of how these ambiguities are best resolved, ambiguities not only of the term *knowledge* but also of many other terms that compose our epistemic vocabulary: *faith, belief, opinion, certainty*, and *trust*.

It should go without saying that Reformed epistemology cannot be understood except in the context of general epistemology, for knowing God cannot be wholly different from knowing anything else—physical objects, mathematical entities, moral values and obligations, other persons, and our very own selves. Knowledge, like its objects—the universe and everything in it, is a "many-splendored thing" (in Francis Thompson's familiar phrase), and perhaps just as complex and mysterious. Therefore how we know one kind of thing may well shed light on how we know another kind of thing. In any event, one of Plantinga's important contributions to the subject is that he shows the kinship between epistemological issues as they arise in religion and as they arise everywhere else.

An adequate introduction to epistemology should acquaint us with the main approaches to the nature of knowledge, and to the main issues that divide these approaches from skepticism. As I hope to show, Plato already addressed the central issues, so that it is entirely appropriate to begin our study of general epistemology with him. Not only does Plato constitute one of the ancient roots of Reformed epistemology, he also provides the first important (and altogether engaging) introduction to the whole subject of knowledge. One of the most important things Plato does is to explore two main alternative approaches to the nature of knowledge. In one of these approaches, knowledge is a direct acquaintance of the mind with an object, and to be contrasted sharply, therefore, with belief about it. In the other approach, knowledge is actually a form of belief, "true belief accompanied by an account."

Although I argue that Plato's final view is that knowledge is true belief accompanied by an account, I am not concerned to resolve that question. I am more interested in using his thought as a springboard to outline my own theory of knowledge as a form of belief, "justified true belief" (in the language of contemporary epistemologists). Knowledge, I argue, is true belief justified by an account (Greek *logos*), and such an account can consist in the narration of an experience (a claim to an acquaintance), the offer of premises in an argument, the citation of testimony, or a combination of two or all three of these. This theory has the advantage of incorporating into a comprehensive view both knowledge by acquaintance, which so impressed Plato at certain points of his discussion, and faith as trust in testimony, which is so dear to Augustine. Augustine's great contribution, inspired by the Christian religion, was to rescue faith, that is, belief on testimony, from the prejudice of Platonic rationalism against it and to emphasize its importance not only for religion but for all of life. But Augustine fails to work out a view that embraces both reason *and* faith in the theory of what it is for human beings to *know*. The cogency of my own theory of knowledge is a secondary matter, however. My main purpose is to affirm the "justified true belief" framework that it assumes to set the stage for a favorable exposition of Plantinga's justified true belief theory of knowledge; for in that theory lies his most significant digression from the language and framework of the Augustinian and Reformed tradition.

I close the book with a chapter on apologetics. This seems appropriate for several reasons. Most conspicuously, the times require it. Christian theology and Christian philosophy face more widespread and far-reaching objections from secular thought these days than ever before. Second, differences over the nature and scope of apologetics increasingly have divided religious thinkers, both Protestant from Catholic and Protestant from Protestant. Finally, no other subject perhaps brings out so clearly the intrinsic connection between theology and philosophy, as well as the need to question the sharp lines that so often have been drawn between natural and revealed theology. My conclusion in this chapter is that Christian thinking about God and about the knowledge of God should be of one piece, that it should integrate important things that are often too easily kept separate by their various medieval and modern practitioners and advocates: philosophy and theology, reason and revelation, knowledge and faith. Such an integration of faith and reason is one legacy of Reformed thought.

I base my exposition of the origin and development of Reformed epistemology on the primary sources themselves—the writings of Plato, of biblical authors, of Augustine, and of Calvin; and I cite standard, readily available English translations. Where it seems helpful to refer to the texts in their original languages or to scholarly commentaries on them, I have done so. Still, it is not my aim to contribute to this specialized scholarship but to use it for the purpose of illuminating the primary sources of Reformed epistemology, all the while concentrating on these sources themselves.

The introductions to the epistemological ideas in each of these sources are my own, and I occasionally pursue fresh possibilities of interpretation. For example, I argue that Plato's theory of knowledge as acquaintance does not really conflict with his theory of knowledge as true belief accompanied by an account, because the former can be incorporated into a version of the latter. Elsewhere, I argue that Augustine's *Soliloquies* and *Confessions* suggest a theory of our knowledge of God that has been unduly ignored and that is quite opposed to the claims for natural theology which arise in the later medieval thinkers who otherwise owe much to Augustine. Finally, I argue that, in ignoring natural theology, Calvin does not ignore a *natural knowledge* of God and that this natural knowledge has to be considered among the grounds for faith and revelation in a way that has been obscured by narrowly theological preoccupations with Calvin's doctrines of faith and revelation. Whether these interpretations are warranted by the texts is a question on which I welcome the comment of those specialized scholars who are prompted by them to respond.

Acknowledgments

I am grateful to the following friends and colleagues who have read one or more of the chapters in draft form: Frederick Crosson, George Mavrodes, Clifton Orlebeke, Alvin Plantinga, Kenneth Sayre, Jay Van Hook, Arvin Vos, Nicholas Wolterstorff, and the members of the Calvin College Philosophy Department Tuesday Afternoon Colloquium. Each of them has either helped me to improve my approach to an issue or corrected mistakes or both. Of course, I alone am responsible for the final version that follows. I also profited from conversation and correspondence with Christopher Kirwan about Augustine's refutations of skepticism, from discussions with my fellow participants in Philip Quinn's Workshop on Skepticism and Fideism at Notre Dame in May 1986, from correspondence with Henry Veatch on Plantinga's epistemology, and from discussions over many years with my philosophy colleagues at Grand Valley State University, Thomas Cunningham, Stephen Rowe, Irving Wasserman, and Theodore Young. I also want to thank my colleague Benjamin Lockerd, Jr., and my daughter Noralyn Masselink for their careful editing of certain sections of the draft. Finally, I owe a special debt of gratitude to Henry Stob, my first teacher in philosophy, my mentor and friend, for his abiding interest in my work.

I am also obliged to Grand Valley State University for granting two sabbatical leaves, during which I did most of my reading and research. One of these leaves I spent at Oxford University, and I am indebted to the Fellows and Tutors of Mansfield College for providing hospitality, intellectual stimulation, and library opportunities during Hilary Term, 1980. During the other leave, 1987–88, I enjoyed the same splendid conditions for scholarly pursuit as an Adjunct Fellow in the Center for Philosophy of Religion at the University of Notre Dame, for which I want to thank its Director and my friend, Alvin Plantinga.

Much of the material in Chapter 6 on John Calvin appeared earlier as "Faith and Reason in Calvin's Doctrine of the Knowledge of God" in *Rationality in the Calvinian Tradition*, ed. H. Hart, J. Vander Hoeven, and N. Wolterstorff (Lanham, MD: University Press of America, 1983) and is reprinted here with permission of the publishers.

My greatest debt of gratitude I owe to my wife, Kay. She heartened me with her cheerful disposition, wise counsel, and loyal support. She knows (on any credible theory of knowledge whatsoever) what it is for a husband to seek, in season and out of season for over a decade, the nature of what it is to know.

Dewey J. Hoitenga, Jr.

1 Knowledge and Belief: Plato

Two Theories of Knowledge and Belief

Ever since Plato proposed them, there have been two main theories of knowledge and belief. One of them, presented in his *Republic*, is that knowledge and belief are two different and opposite states of mind, similar in some formal respects, but with knowledge in no way being definable in terms of belief. The second view, suggested already in the *Meno* but explored in detail later in the *Theaetetus*, is that the difference between knowledge and belief is not so absolute, that knowledge is actually a form of belief, so that it must be defined in terms of belief. In this view, knowledge is *true* belief accompanied by an *account*, as Plato puts it, or, in the language of contemporary philosophers, knowledge is *justified true belief*.

The two views are incompatible with each other, for in the former, knowledge is not only not definable in terms of belief; it is not definable at all. Instead, in this view, knowledge is like some ultimate notions such as being, space, and time or like some elemental sensations such as the sense of pain, the taste of salt, and the sight of the color red—notions and sensations that are primitive and ultimate and therefore not definable in terms of anything else. Like them, knowledge is sui generis, in a class all by itself. We can call this first view the *indefinabilist* view of knowledge. By contrast, the second view is a *definabilist* view; according to it, not only can knowledge be defined, but it must be defined, if we are to understand its nature at all. It must be defined in terms of truth, belief, and the ability to give an account.

In this chapter I will develop an outline of my own view of knowledge as true belief with the ability to give an account—justified true belief. In pursuing this aim, however, I will emphasize a very important point in the alternative view, viz., its focus on a unique component in one *kind* of human knowledge. This component is commonly called *experience*, although I shall usually call it *acquaintance*. Knowledge by acquaintance may even be the ultimate source of everything we know, and thus, in that way, too, it may be sui generis, in a class by itself. Even if this is so, it does not follow that knowledge by acquaintance is, as the indefinabilist approach affirms, the only kind of knowledge we possess. I hope to show instead that human knowledge, in religion as in all of life, includes also those many things we learn by testimony and by inference. Indeed, it will become evident that knowledge by acquaintance even presupposes testimony and inference, in such a way that we cannot even account for knowledge by acquaintance as the ultimate origin of all our knowledge without considering its dependence upon on them. In short, I will defend a theory of knowledge on which acquaintance is to be incorporated, along with testimony and inference, in an analysis of knowledge as justified true belief. Being acquainted with something, though in itself something ultimate and undefinable, is just one of three main ways—the others being testimony and inference—by which we *come* to know and, thus, by which we can *justify* our true beliefs. Not only is the justification of belief thus inseparable from considering the origin of belief, but the definition of knowledge is also inseparable from understanding how it originates.

Beginning with Plato. I begin my study with Plato, not only because he is the first philosopher to elaborate the two views but also because he discusses knowledge and belief in a way that makes it both interesting and relatively easy to discover the issues that need to be addressed. Furthermore, Plato is important for his enormous influence on the entire history of the topic. The history of philosophy, as Alfred North Whitehead reminds us in his *Process and Reality,* "consists of a series of footnotes to Plato" (63); we do well then to begin with the original text: the Platonic dialogues. If one thing is clear in the footnotes to these dialogues that constitute the history of philosophy, it is that these notes elaborate one or the other of the two main views of knowledge that are to be found in the original text. This will become evident in the chapters that follow. St. Augustine insists, as we shall see, on the *difference* between knowledge and belief, and he quite ignores the possibility that knowledge can be defined in terms of belief; hence he perpetuates the indefinabilist view. The view has been revived in recent times by such philosophers as John Cook Wilson (*Statement and Inference,* 1926) and H. H. Prichard (*Knowledge and Perception,* 1950). Alvin Plantinga, on the other hand, has developed a specific theory of knowledge as justified true belief in the context of a plethora of justified true belief theories that have dominated the epistemology of the last several decades. And so Plato's quest for knowledge as justified true belief is still very much alive; indeed, at the moment it occupies center stage.

Which of the two views is Plato's own view? We can hardly accept the thought that he meant to teach two incompatible views of knowledge at the same time. It may look as if he did, and even that he leaves them unreconciled; but that would be a strange conclusion to reach about the thinker who, inspired by the great Socrates before him, took pains to find the truth on any topic by first clearing away the inconsistencies in the thinking of those who claimed to have already found it. I shall argue that Plato does not really embrace both views, that his more settled view is that knowledge is true belief accompanied by an account, even though he never explicitly rejects what he says about knowledge being quite opposed to belief. But I am less concerned to discover what Plato really thought—a very complicated question—than to show that the indefinabilist approach to knowledge is mistaken and that knowledge correctly understood is defined as justified true belief.

How Each View Arises.   Before turning to Plato, it will be useful to indicate how each view arises and makes some sense. I will do this by considering briefly the discussion of one recent influential writer, H. H. Price, who seems quite consciously torn between the two views. Actually, Price moves from an indefinabilist view, under the acknowledged influence of Cook Wilson, to a definabilist view, observing that the latter view prevails among contemporary epistemologists. Still, in making this move, Price does not quite give up his penchant for indefinabilism. Thus in an early essay, "Some Considerations about Belief" (originally published in 1934), Price asserts that "knowledge is something ultimate and not further analysable. It is simply the situation in which some entity or some fact is directly present to consciousness" (1973, 41). Two considerations lead Price to this conclusion. First, knowledge is (as it seems to him in this essay) identical with direct acquaintance with an object, whereas "when I believe truly, there is a fact which makes my belief true. But this fact is not itself present to my mind" (42). Second, "knowledge is by definition infallible" whereas "belief on the other hand is always fallible" (41). Later, however, he recognizes two further points: first, that in this view, "we know very little indeed" (51); and second, that we can be be "reasonably assured" by evidence of many of our beliefs, even though this does not alter their essential fallibility (52). These two further points lead him to distinguish a "strict" sense of knowledge in which it signifies both direct acquaintance with an object and infallibility from "a wider sense, a sense in which it is *not* contrasted with belief" and with its connotation of fallibility (51). Still, in this essay Price stops short of developing a theory of *knowledge* based on all these points. He is content to develop only a theory of "proper belief": "Belief proper, the theory says, is reasoned assent to an entertained proposition; acceptance is unreasoned absence of dissent" (50). Here, then, he proposes only a theory of *rational* belief, as that is opposed to "acceptance" or "mere belief."

Decades later, however, in his book *Belief* (1969) Price develops this earlier theory of rational belief into a theory of knowledge, admitting "that there are some sorts of knowledge... which can be defined, with suitable precautions, in terms of belief" (91). These "precautions" actually yield a version of the justified true belief theory of knowledge: "(*a*) that the proposition believed is true, (*b*) that the believer has conclusive reasons for it, (*c*) that he believes it with full conviction" (91). Still, Price maintains that any knowledge so defined is "completely different" from knowledge as direct acquaintance with an object present to the mind, because "it makes no sense to ask for reasons" for the latter (90–91). Thus Price appears to offer two theories of knowledge, one in which it is identical with acquaintance and infallible and another in which it is justified true belief. This ambivalence about the nature of knowledge appears already in Plato, as we shall see. I will argue that we must, of course, recognize the difference between knowing by acquaintance and knowing in other ways, but that it does not follow from this that we need a theory of knowledge for each one. Price suggests that we do, as Plato did before him, because of a an alleged connection between acquaintance and infallibility—an issue to which we will return.

If the two theories are thus defended side by side today by an important philosopher who seems consciously torn between them, and each one originated side by side in Plato himself, the first great philosopher to theorize about knowledge and belief, there must be some lessons to learn. One of these is that the two views reflect what Price, in his early essay, calls a "muddle" deeply embedded in our language itself, in our everyday use of the terms *knowledge* and *belief*:

> Thus common usage seems to be simply muddled.... On the one hand it includes under the head of knowing the firm belief in a reasonably certain proposition; on the other, it refuses to admit that knowing can be mistaken. And yet if the proposition is only reasonably certain, there is the possibility that we may be mistaken in believing it. (50–51)

Let us elaborate upon this muddle. For it does seem clear that everyday use leads us in two opposite directions: that knowledge is not belief, and that it is.

Knowledge Is Not Belief.   First, it is clear that knowledge implies truth whereas belief does not. If I know that my desk is brown, it cannot turn out that my desk is a different color. If, however, it is the case that my desk is different color, then I cannot know that it is brown; and if I think it is, I am mistaken. What I am mistaken in, however, is not some knowledge I have, but a belief. People once believed that the earth is flat; indeed, some may even have claimed to know it. Now that we know it is not flat but round, we do not deny that people once believed it to be flat; rather what we say is that those who claimed to know it is flat were mistaken. What they had was a belief about the shape of the earth, and it was a mistaken belief. No one can know what is not so.

In view of this, it can be said—and Plato was the first to say it—that knowledge is infallible whereas belief is not. To be infallible is to be incapable of being mistaken. So knowledge is incapable of being mistaken, but belief can be mistaken. And from this it seems to follow that knowledge and belief must be two different and incompatible states of mind, the one irreducible to the other. For if knowledge cannot err, and belief can err, how can knowledge be a form of belief? And thus we are led to the first approach: knowledge is not a form of belief, but something unique and in a class by itself, not to be confused with or thought of in terms of belief.

Knowledge Is Belief. On the other hand, it also clearly seems absurd for me to know that my desk is brown but then to tell myself or someone else that I do not believe it. Most people today know that the earth is round; but if one of them were asked, not whether he knows it but whether he believes it, he would normally reply that he did. "Normally," I say, for there are special circumstances in which a person might deny that he believes it. For example, if a member of the Flat Earth Society has just asked me, "Do you really believe it?" I might well respond, with the appropriate emphasis, "I don't *believe* it; I *know* it." But with that reply I would be invoking the *difference* between knowledge and belief we noted earlier to convey to the Flat Earther that I am *not* mistaken; this consequence is clearly implied by my saying I know it, but not by my saying I believe it. Or again, I might sensibly say to a friend who visits me following a long absence: "Here you are; I can't believe it!" But then I am not really denying that I believe something I also know; I am only expressing my surprise and excitement over our meeting again, and what I mean is that the long absence of my friend hinders my calm acceptance of the pleasant turn of events. Therefore, unless there is some special point to be made that reflects the difference between knowledge and belief, I can quite correctly say that I believe the things that I know. I know that twice two is four. Do I believe it? Of course, I do. I can even say that if I did not believe it, I could *not* know it. Thus to know something is also to believe it. No one can know what he does not believe.

From this it follows that knowledge and belief are not different states of mind; quite the contrary, it looks very much as if knowledge is a form of belief itself. Instead of being a unique and indefinable state of mind, knowledge appears to be definable as a form of belief. Of course, it must be *true* belief, for we just saw that no one can know what is not so. But if knowledge is true belief, it is *belief*, and we have come out with just the opposite conclusion from the one we reached a moment ago. Then we concluded that knowledge is not belief, now we conclude that it is.

One of these conclusions must be wrong, and we should try to discover which one it is. Knowledge cannot be mistaken, belief can. But belief *need not* be mistaken, and so when it is not, there is nothing to prevent it from being at least a *component* of knowledge, which cannot be mistaken. When a true belief is also justified, the combination may produce the knowledge that cannot be mistaken. It may be difficult to locate in this combination just what creates its "infallibility"; but it could be there somewhere. A bulletproof vest is impenetrable by a bullet, but such a vest may consist of three different materials, none of which by itself makes it so, though all working together do. So it may be with belief. When belief is combined with truth and justification, something is created that makes the resulting state of mind infallible, even though belief by itself is not. With this sketch of a recent discussion of knowledge and belief in hand we are ready to turn our inquiry to Plato.

The *Republic* Approach

In Book V of the *Republic* Plato contrasts the infallibility of knowledge with the fallibility of belief, and from that contrast he derives his account of knowledge and belief as two essentially different states of mind (477). He reaches this conclusion in a curious way that, though not in vogue today, is instructive nevertheless. He holds that the *objects* in the universe come in two fundamental, mutually exclusive, and jointly exhaustive kinds. One kind of object is indivisible, eternal, unchanging, and ultimate; these he called the *Forms*. The other kind is divisible, temporal, always changing, and not ultimate; these are the physical objects in the material world about us. Furthermore, he held that we are in touch with both kinds of object, but that, unless we are philosophers, we are much more aware, by means of our senses, of physical objects that exist in space and time than we are aware, by means of reason, of the Forms. Now belief, in the *Republic* account, is the state of mind that results from our contact with physical objects, whereas knowledge is the state of mind that results from our contact with the Forms.

Plato's view here is that the infallibility of knowledge (its unchangeable relationship to truth) arises from the unchanging character of its objects (the Forms), whereas the fallibility of belief (its changeable character with respect to the truth) arises from the changing character of its objects (individual, physical things). Just as these latter objects constitute an intermediate reality between the Forms and nothingness, so belief is an intermediate cognitive state between knowledge and ignorance (478c–d). The key point is that each cognitive state, knowledge and belief, is caused by a certain kind of relationship of the mind to its object. The nature of this relationship is suggested by the terms we have already used: the mind is *in touch with* an object; it has *contact* with it. These terms are metaphors, of course, drawn from a relationship that can exist between physical objects.

It will be useful, perhaps, to use a different, more literal term. The term I will use is *acquaintance*. In *Plato's Republic*, R. C. Cross and A. D. Woozley observe:

> When [Plato] is talking of knowledge and belief the model of seeing or touching does seem to be prominent. Now, of course, in the case of sight and touch, the notions of acquaintance ... , of objects, of the reality of the objects, all have a place. If I am seeing or touching something, then I am immediately aware of, directly acquainted with, a thing or object, and it must be a real thing or object—there must be something there that I am seeing or touching. (176)

In *Plato's Theory of Knowledge*, F. M. Cornford translates a parallel passage in the *Sophist* as follows: "We have intercourse with Becoming by means of the body through sense, whereas we have intercourse with Real being by means of the soul through reflection" (248a). He comments on the term *koinonein*, "have intercourse with," as follows:

> *Koinonein* ('are in touch with,' Taylor) is chosen as a neutral word covering all forms of cognition, the usual words (*eidenai*, *gignoskein*, *epistasthai*, *aisthanesthia*, etc.) being too much specialized and associated either with knowledge to the exclusion of sensation and perception or *vice versa*. It is used of social and business intercourse, and also of sexual intercourse. (239)

The idea behind Plato's language is clearly the intimacy that characterizes the knowledge of something by direct experience of it.

The term *acquaintance* is derived from the Latin *ad* (intensive) and *cognoscere* (to know), which in turn is derived from the Greek *gignoskein*, mentioned earlier. The special kind of knowledge suggested is just that which results from direct experience of an object. This directness also connotes intimacy, closeness, especially as it pertains to the knowledge of other persons. The *American Heritage Dictionary* offers as the first meaning for *acquaint* v.: "to make familiar"; and *familiar* is derived from *familial*. Plato's view, then, is that when I am acquainted with a physical object which changes, either slowly or rapidly over a period of time, my mental state about that object (belief) must change just as it changes, with the consequence that there is no fixed truth in my mind; whereas when I am acquainted with an unchanging Form, my mental state (knowledge of that Form) will remain fixed and unchanged in truth, just as that Form remains fixed and unchanged in reality.

It is easy for us to think of some of our beliefs as being formed by a direct acquaintance with sensible objects, but not so easy to think of belief as a constantly changing "intermediate state" that has no fixity, or at least no fixed truth. This is because we think in terms of *particular beliefs*, each of which is true or false, depending on whether or not some object truly is *at the time* what we believe it to be at that time (or at any other time). But this view introduces a complexity into the nature of belief that is absent from the *Republic* account. This complexity becomes evident when Plato begins to explore his second approach to knowledge, viz., knowledge as true belief accompanied by an account.

The Meno.   Actually, Plato first takes this approach already in the *Meno*, which was written before the *Republic*. Although he mentions it at several points in the *Republic* (see 427–428, 506, 538), he does not elaborate on it; hence I do not take this approach as distinctive of the *Republic*. In this approach, Plato distinguishes knowledge, not from *belief*, but from *true* belief. This difference in starting point makes all the difference between the two accounts. Knowledge is still the more excellent mental state, but here it is more excellent than *true* belief, not belief as a general, changing state of the mind. Plato states the difference between knowledge and true belief: "And this is why knowledge is more honorable and excellent than true opinion, because fastened by a chain" (*Meno*, 98a, Jowett). So knowledge, on this account, has something that *true* belief ("opinion") does not have: it is "fastened by a chain."

Notice two critical differences between this account and that of the *Republic*. First, truth now enters the picture as a characteristic of belief, and without any special attention either to the question of the *object* of that belief or to the *relationship* of the belief to that object; this relationship was, according to the *Republic*, one of acquaintance with it. In *Plato on Knowledge and Reality*, Nicholas P. White comments on *Theaetetus* 201e, which picks up this account of knowledge. Observes White: "This passage, like the rest of *Theaetetus* 200–210, is plainly an attempt to say what knowledge is, *quite apart from* the question of what sort of objects it may be concerned with" (176). Here, then, Plato analyzes mind in its state of belief quite apart from the changing nature of the real object of that belief.

Second, the *Meno* account focuses not upon belief as a general mental state of mind that changes over a period of time, but upon a *single* belief as a *particular* mental state that is *true*. This new focus implies, significantly, a fixity about belief that was lacking in belief as a changing mental state. A *true* belief does not change *its* truth status, although, of course, the true belief about the weather in Athens today may have to be *replaced* by a different true belief about the weather in Athens tomorrow. But this way of changing our *particular* beliefs was as commonplace to Plato as it is to us. By changing our belief about the weather as it changes we do not think the truth of any one of the beliefs we have along the way changes. The truth of a given belief about a temporal state of affairs is as fixed and eternal as the truth of the knowledge of any of the eternal Forms. Truth is fixed and eternal, even when it refers to noneternal things.

The question now arises, Why are these true beliefs about temporal things not *knowledge*, solely in virtue of their being true? In the *Meno*, Plato suggests the answer in a simile. A true belief is like an image of Daedalus: it is "beautiful and fruitful," but there is the problem of making it *stay put*. According to the myth, Daedalus was so skillful an artisan that he could make images of living things that moved. So, too, true belief is "beautiful and fruitful," for it is as good as knowledge as a guide to life. Unlike knowledge, however, and like an image of Daedalus, it can get away from us, it can be lost. So true belief, even though in one sense fixed by truth, is not fixed in some other sense. It is not fixed, it seems, *in our minds*, although knowledge is. The reason for this is, says Plato, that these true beliefs, like the images of Daedalus, are not "fastened by a chain." Here the Jowett translation gives us a metaphor. The Grube translation says that "true beliefs are not worth much until one ties them down by [giving] an account of the reason why" (98a). The Greek is *deō aitias logismos*; the idea is that a true belief will be knowledge, will be *fixed in our minds*, whenever it is "bound" (in our minds, presumably) by an "account or reasoning out of the cause or origin" of the belief.

The *Theaetetus* Approach

Plato elaborates this approach to knowledge in the *Theaetetus*. In this dialogue, he first argues that knowledge is not to be identified with the appearances of sensation because these, though they are like knowledge in being infallible, are unlike knowledge in always changing; thus they are like belief in the *Republic* account. He next argues that knowledge is not just true belief because, although true belief is true like knowledge, it is unlike knowledge in that it is acquired by persuasion and hearsay, not by instruction or eyewitness experience. Plato had earlier made this contrast in the *Republic* when he distinguished between lower education, which inculcates true belief by the persuasion of good examples, and higher education, which aims at knowledge by reason and reasoning.

Finally, Plato explores the proposal that knowledge is true belief "tied down" with an *account* (201d–210a). In contemporary terms, I know something whenever I believe it, it is true, and I am justified in (or can give a justification for) my belief. In "Concepts of Epistemic Justification," W. P. Alston observes that this distinction between *being justified* and *being able to give a justification* has been neglected in many recent accounts of justification. He argues that the former is the fundamental one for the sake of a justified true belief approach to knowledge, because the latter presupposes abilities on the part of the knower that the knower may not and even need not possess (58). Plato does not make the distinction, but his discussion in *Theaetetus* 206d–210b clearly implies that the knower must be able to give the account.

In the last section of the *Theaetetus*, Plato examines three possible interpretations of "giving an account," only to reject each one. He thereby gives the impression that he is not very committed to, or even that he is abandoning, the whole approach; we may therefore be tempted to conclude that his settled view is that of the *Republic* approach. Against that conclusion, however, are two pieces of evidence. First, the *Theaetetus* definition of knowledge as "true belief with an account" appears at too many critical points in Plato's dialogues for us to dismiss it simply because he fails in the *Theaetetus* to elaborate it to his satisfaction. I quote some of the most important of these:

> Socrates.   If a man knows certain things, will he be able to give
>   an account of them, or will he not?

Simmias. Unquestionably he will, Socrates. (*Phaedo* 76b, Hackforth)

Diotima. Do you not see that there is a mean between wisdom and ignorance?

Socrates. And what may that be?

Diotima. Right opinion, which, as you know, being incapable of giving a reason, is not knowledge (for how can knowledge be devoid of reason?) (*Symposium* 202a, Jowett)

Timaeus. Now we must affirm that they [intelligence (*noesis*, another word for knowledge) and belief] are two different things, for they are distinct in origin and unlike in nature. The one is produced in us by instruction, the other by persuasion; the one can always give a true account of itself, the other can give none; the one cannot be shaken by persuasion, whereas the other can be won over; and true belief, we must allow, is shared by all mankind, intelligence only by the gods and a small number of men. (*Timaeus* 51e, Cornford)

Second, we must add to these references some key passages in the *Republic* itself. Even though Plato in a critical passage there gives us the acquaintance theory of knowledge that I call the *Republic* account, at other points he describes one who has knowledge as being able to give an account. For example, "And have you not noticed that opinions not based on knowledge are ugly things? The best of them are blind; or do you think that those who express a true opinion without knowledge are any different from blind people who yet follow the right road?" (506c, Grube). Significantly, Socrates draws this contrast between knowledge and true belief in the context of his search for the highest knowledge of all, knowledge of the Good. True, presently, when Glaucon asks Socrates to give an account of the Good, Socrates begs off (506d). But it does not follow from this momentary refusal by Socrates that knowledge of the Good, when sought and found, does not consist of true belief with an account.

Even knowledge of the Good consists in being able to give an account, as Socrates later confirms after twice repeating that knowledge requires giving an account:

Further, I said, do those who cannot give and exact a reasoned account of what is said know anything at all of the things we say they must know? (53le, Grube)

And you also call a dialectician the man who can give a reasoned account of the reality of each thing? To the man who can
give no such account, either to himself or another, you will to
that extent deny knowledge of his subject? (534b, Grube)

Immediately upon this second repetition of the view, Socrates applies
it to the knowledge of the Good itself, which he has just said is
"beyond my powers to express"—presumably because of its transcendence. The passage is as clear as it is dramatic in its declaration that
knowledge—even of the Good—requires an ability to give an account:

And the same applies to the Good. The man who cannot by reason distinguish the Form of the Good from all others, who does
not, as in a battle, survive all refutations, eager to argue according to reality and not according to opinion, and who does not
come through all the tests without faltering in reasoned discourse—such a man you will say does not know the Good itself,
nor any kind of good. If he gets hold of some image of it, it is by
opinion, not knowledge; he is dreaming and asleep throughout
his present life, and, before he wakes up here, he will arrive in
Hades and go to sleep forever. (534b–c, Grube)

I conclude, therefore, that it would be a mistake simply to regard
Plato's identification of knowledge with acquaintance—what I have
called his *Republic* account—as his definitive theory of knowledge and
belief. My own view is that we should do what Plato clearly did not
do, that is, incorporate his acquaintance approach to knowledge into
his more complex approach that knowledge is justified true belief.

The Meno, *Again, on True Belief.*   I noted earlier that Plato introduces the notion of true belief in the *Meno* without any special attention the *object* of belief. Implicit in this approach, I said, was its
attempt to discuss how true belief might be knowledge without
connecting such true belief to a special kind of object. I need now to
elaborate and clarify what this approach further implies. Just before
making his claim that true belief must be accompanied by an account,
Socrates gives an example of the difference between knowledge and
true belief:

S.   . . . A man who knew the way to Larissa, or anywhere else
you like, and went there and guided others would surely
lead them well and correctly?
—Certainly.

S. What if someone had had a correct opinion as to which was the way but had not gone there nor indeed had knowledge of it, would he not also lead correctly?
—Certainly. (97a–b, Grube)

The example embodies the Platonic theme that true belief, no less than knowledge, can serve as a reliable guide in human life. Why is this so? The answer, of course, is because true belief, like knowledge, is *true*. How then do they differ? We have already seen that they differ, according to Plato, by knowledge staying *fixed in the mind* whereas true belief does not, because knowledge is, and true belief by itself is not, *accompanied by an account*. The function of the account, therefore, is to give the mind *control* over its true beliefs, so that they will stay fixed and not "run away" when challenged by opposing beliefs.

Acquaintance vs. Testimony. The example, however, points up a second difference. The person who knows the way to Larissa has taken the way himself, and so is acquainted with it; whereas the person who believes truly has not taken it, and so is not acquainted with what he believes. And so the *Meno* discussion involves the object of knowledge after all, but suggests by its example that the believer whose belief is true is *disconnected* from the object of his belief because he is not, like the knower, acquainted with it.

This difference between knowledge and true belief invites both a comparison with and a contrast to the *Republic* account. In line with that account, the guide in the *Meno* account who knows the way to Larissa knows it in virtue of his having taken that way; he is an eyewitness, who has seen the object on which he reports. Unlike the *Republic* account, however, the guide here who has only true belief, and no acquaintance with the way to Larissa, seems to have no object at all for his belief, even though his belief is true. But is that really so? No, and we can see that it is not so by asking how *this* guide—the guide who has only true belief—acquired his belief. Plato does not go into this question, but we can easily supply the answer. Either the believer was told the way to Larissa or he was not. If he was told, it was either by someone who *had* taken the way himself or by someone else who, like himself in his present state, possessed the true belief. If he was not told, he probably saw a sign or read a map. In all these cases, however, he acquired his belief by the *testimony* of someone else. Such testimony is the only other way to find anything out (except for inference, which we will discuss later), if one is not, or cannot become, acquainted with it for oneself.

We can now begin to see that true belief as well as knowledge *has* an object and what that object must be like. If one who believes truly does so by having seen a sign or a map, it may look as if the object of his belief is that sign or that map, for either of these is a form of testimony and illustrates clearly something of the nature of the *object* of a true belief. A sign or a map that shows the way to Larissa, as an object of belief, is not the way to Larissa itself. It is rather a *substitute* for the way, and if the sign is a good one or the map is accurate, it *represents* the way. If, however, the sign is not a good one, or the map is inaccurate, it will mislead the believer and induce a *false* belief. Hence the object of a belief is a substitute for what the belief is about; and it can be a good substitute or a bad one. When it is a good substitute, it represents what it purports to represent; when it is a bad substitute, it fails to represent what it purports to represent.

Propositions

What then is a true, or a false, *belief?* A sign or a map that leads to a belief is not a belief nor are the words in which a belief can be expressed. There are many different possible signs, many different possible maps, and many different possible words and possible forms of words, in which the same belief can be expressed. No two signs need to be alike in shape, color, or how they reveal that they are signs; no two maps need to agree in the graphic symbols used to show the routes from city to city. Both signs and maps will likely use some language (though not necessarily: a sign or a map can portray a city with a nonlinguistic, graphic symbol that identifies it) and there need be no uniformity in just what language is used or how much. Likewise, no two Greeks will use precisely the same Greek words to describe the way to Larissa to a fellow Greek who asks; and a Persian may be able to describe the way only in Persian words. Yet there is only one shortest, direct way to Larissa from a given point on which all these users of signs, linguistic and nonlinguistic, agree. So there is also only one true belief that *represents* that way. There must be, therefore, some *one thing* amidst all the variety of signs and symbols that eliminates the accidental differences between these signs and symbols that purport to represent the reality, but that still purports to represent that reality. That thing must be the *proposition*.

It does not seem that Plato had the concept of a proposition as so defined. This fact leads to a number of difficulties in his theory of knowledge that he might otherwise have avoided (N. P. White 176, 204; Cornford 1957, 113, 264). In *Plato's Theory of Understanding*, Jon Moline argues that what Plato means by *epistēmē* "differed in fundamental ways from the concept of knowledge as it is now employed" and that we should therefore translate it as "understanding" (6). Moline suggests that contemporary epistemology is unduly restrictive in its preoccupation with propositional knowledge, with the result that "it has obscured some of Plato's more interesting philosophical aims, methods, assumptions, and contributions" (x–xi). His book makes a good case for the latter thesis; but I am not convinced by his suggestions that propositional knowledge is not a very important (albeit implicit) component of Plato's *epistēmē*. I agree with other scholars that the concept of a proposition is not only helpful but also essential for interpreting Plato's theory. The concept will not only help us to explain how beliefs can be true or false, as Plato claims they can be, but also to focus on the important similarities and differences between the *Republic* and the *Theaetetus* approaches to knowledge. Indeed, the concept of a proposition will help us to bring the two approaches together in a way that illuminates the importance of each.

To accomplish all this, I begin with an account of knowledge and belief by another contemporary philosopher. In his "Marks of Distinction between Belief and Knowledge," Kenneth Sayre takes us from Larissa in ancient Greece to Denver in modern Colorado. He asks us to consider two individuals, N who *believes*, because he has looked at a map, that Denver is the capital city of Colorado, and M who *knows* that Denver is the capital of Colorado, because he is a veteran of Colorado state politics. Now it looks from the grammar, says Sayre, as if the objects of N's belief and M's knowledge are one and the same object ("that Denver is the capital of Colorado"), until we discover that the similarity in grammar conceals an all important difference. For

> if what N believes is identical with what M knows, then both the following should be true:
> (1) N believes what M knows
> (2) M knows what N believes.
> But (1) as it stands is unintelligible (or incomplete—N might believe what M knows to be irrelevant, etc.); and (2) has M knowing quite a different thing—not that Denver is the capital of Colorado, but that N believes this of Denver. (1)

Having analyzed the different functions of noun clauses, Sayre argues that this difference can be explained only by acknowledging that the two cognitive attitudes, belief and knowledge, have different objects. The object of a belief is a *proposition*; the object of knowledge is a *state of affairs* (Sayre's term for fact or reality).

Sayre's argument is less conclusive than it appears to be. He claims that the two "what" phrases in (1) and (2) *must* be taken differently in the way he points out. If this claim is true, then it follows that "what N believes" and "what M knows" are not identical as the antecedent states. But this claim is not true; what is true is only that the "what" phrases in (1) and (2) *can* be understood differently in the way Sayre points out. The strength of his argument, however, lies right here. In order to explain how the two phrases can be understood differently, there must be such things as propositions. To make the argument stronger than that is to put more weight on usage than usage by itself can bear. The ambiguities of usage suggest at best the need to develop a theoretical position; in the present instance, the position is that both belief and knowledge by acquaintance must have objects and that these objects must be different from each other. The ambiguities of usage do not by themselves dictate the correctness of a theory, however; that is a philosophical, not a linguistic matter. Earlier we saw the importance of this limitation on arguments from usage in our discussion of Price's analysis of knowledge and belief; it will come up again when we find Augustine making a distinction between the ordinary usage of the term *know* and what he wants to preserve as its "strict" sense.

We can now explain, in terms of propositions, how Plato's *Republic* approach differs from his approach in the *Theaetetus*. "What M knows in knowing that Denver is the capital is not a proposition but a SOA [state of affairs]" (4). What the believer believes, however, is not a state of affairs, but a *proposition*. Sayre suggests that the reason why many philosophers ignore this difference is precisely the "grip on our thinking" of the view that knowledge is justified true belief, going back as it does to the *Theaetetus*: "If we assume that the objects of beliefs are propositions (which seems correct), and think that belief becomes knowledge with the accumulation of evidence, then we may naturally (albeit incorrectly) assume that the object remains the same while the attitude changes" (4). Sayre reminds us (following Plato), that knowledge by acquaintance is acquired by "palpably experiencing" a state of affairs, whereas belief (in his example about Denver's being the capital of Colorado) is acquired by looking at maps or listening to what others tell us (2). So the *object* of the mind when it knows, for Plato in the *Republic*, is reality; the *object* of the mind when it believes, in the *Theaetetus*, has to be a proposition—a substitute for, a (purported) representation of reality.

The Ambiguity of Belief. Having introduced the concept of a proposition, we need now to point out an important ambiguity in the term *belief*. For if a true belief is the same thing as a true proposition, then a belief is its own object; for propositions were introduced to show that *they* were the *objects* of beliefs, even though at first (on the *Meno-Theaetetus* account), it looked as if beliefs had no object. For recall that, in the *Republic* account, belief is a *mental attitude* which has a proper object, the concrete, individual, changing things in the sensible world around us, whereas in the *Theaetetus* account, we saw Plato concentrate on the *truth* of the belief, ignoring the question of its object. We shall have knowledge, he says there, when we have true belief *accompanied by an account*. In his search for an account to accompany true belief, Plato seems to say that true belief is the *object* of our thinking, in addition to which we need an account. But how can true belief be at once the *object* of a mental attitude and the *mental attitude* itself?

The answer is that it cannot, and we must dispel the paradoxical implication that it is. To do this, we need to distinguish belief in its new sense of *proposition* from belief in its original sense as a *mental state or attitude*. As a proposition, a belief is the *object* of a mental attitude; as a mental attitude, a belief is an attitude toward a proposition. Furthermore, this attitude is an affirmative attitude, "to think with assent," in the famous definition of Augustine (*On the Predestination of the Saints* v). Disbelief, thinking with dissent, is the opposite attitude. There is no good pair of terms with which to characterize these opposite mental attitudes. True and false they are not; but one is favorable (belief) and the other is unfavorable (disbelief). If I believe that Homer wrote the *Iliad* and you do not (you disbelieve it), I have a favorable attitude toward and you an unfavorable attitude toward the proposition that Homer wrote the *Iliad*. The proposition is one that comes to us from the testimony of scholars. Now that proposition is true or false quite independently of your and my opposite attitudes toward it; this fact shows how very important it is to distinguish between belief in its sense of being a proposition from belief in its sense of being a mental attitude.

We have thus found something (a true proposition) that will serve as the object of belief (as a mental state or attitude) in the *Theaetetus* account of knowledge and that does not need to be (and indeed *is not*, following Sayre's distinction) the object of knowledge on the *Republic* account. The price on its head, however, is that the proposition, even the true proposition, is not a *reality* but a *substitute* for reality. Plato, we noted, does not talk of propositions; and it is tantalizing to conjecture that he does not see any difficulty in his *Republic* approach to knowledge as *acquaintance* with reality precisely because he lacks the concept of a proposition. It seems obvious to him that, if we are *acquainted* with reality, nothing comes between the mind and its object. Some may even wish to conjecture that he abandons his *Theaetetus* approach to knowledge because he suspects that belief, even *true* belief, is always an acquaintance with nothing more than a shadow, a copy, an image of reality—which is his view of it in the *Republic* account. Be that as it may, we can draw an analogy between the physical objects of the *Republic* and the true beliefs, that is, true propositions, as we are employing them here to interpret the *Theaetetus*. Just as physical objects are halfway between reality and nothingness, so true propositions are "abstract entities"—not full-blooded, concrete entities, but not simply nothing either.

Today, of course, we have a stronger sense of the reality of physical things than Plato did, and against this sense of reality, perhaps the reality of propositions pales. But it does not disappear entirely; the more we reflect, the more we see that propositions have *some* kind of reality, even though we may find it as difficult to give an account of that reality as Plato did of the reality of physical objects. Just as it helped Plato to see physical objects as intermediate realities, unreal in their coming to be and passing away but real in so far as they participate in the Forms, so it may help us to see true propositions as intermediate realities, unreal in that they are only substitutes for reality but real in so far as their elements are derived from reality and their truth or falsity is determined by reality.

Logoi has been translated variously as "discussions" or "words" (Grube), "conceptions" (Church), "the world of mind" (Jowett), and even "propositions" (Hackforth). On one occasion Plato compares his *logoi* to images. The occasion occurs in the *Phaedo* (99d–100a), when Plato has Socrates describe his conversion from natural science to philosophy. Socrates turns from seeking the truth in *things* to seeking it in *logoi*. Just as the scientists protect their eyesight by looking at an image of the sun-eclipse, so Socrates will seek truth in logoi. Socrates questions the analogy, however: "For I certainly do not admit that one who investigates things by means of words is dealing with images, any more than one who is looking at facts" (100a). So *logoi* for Plato have a special connection to reality, even closer than the connection of images to their objects or (we may add) physical objects to the Forms.

Ambiguity of Truth.   This a good place at which to point out another critical ambiguity that can confuse the effort to understand Plato's two accounts of knowledge and belief. Truth comes into the mind of one who believes truly quite differently from the way in which it comes into the mind of the one one who knows by acquaintance. Plato, we said, seems to think that nothing comes between the one who knows the way to Larissa, as the map (or the proposition) comes between one who believes what the map tells him about about the way and the way itself which he has never taken. That is because the knower is acquainted with the way itself, whereas the believer is acquainted only with a map (or, more precisely, with the proposition that the map signifies). Now to know the way to Larissa is to know the truth; however, to believe a true proposition of which an accurate map is a sign is to believe the truth. Therefore it seems as if the object of knowledge and the object of true belief is one and the same object, the truth.

But *truth* here is critically ambiguous. It can be used as a synonym for *reality*. In the *Republic*, for example, Plato has the philosopher seeking both truth and reality in the same breath, as it were (475–477, 485, 490), although he falls short of explicitly identifying them. At one point, where Plato says it is *reality* that knowledge seeks, Cornford (the paraphraser) translates the passage as follows: "And knowledge has for its natural object the real—to know the truth about reality," even though the word for "truth" is not even in the Greek text (477a). We, too, still talk about reality and truth as if they were one and the same thing. *Truth*, however, can also signify a property of propositions. In *that* sense the term cannot be synonymous with *reality*, for as we have seen, the propositions it characterizes are themselves something less than full-blooded reality. Hence the believer who has only the proposition as the object of his or her mental state has truth all right, but only in the same substitute sense as the proposition that it qualifies is a substitute for reality.

The relationship between the two senses of truth seems to be this. When *truth* is synonymous with *reality*, it refers to the *standard* for *truth* when it denotes the characteristic of a proposition. A proposition is true when it correctly represents reality. Thus truth for the believer who believes truly is, like the proposition which is the object of that belief, a step away from the reality the believer seeks to know; and the believer will know that reality (on the *Republic* account) only upon getting *acquainted* with the reality itself.

In the light of these distinctions, we can now focus more clearly upon the difference between the *Republic* and *Theaetetus* accounts. In the former, one knows only when one is acquainted with reality; otherwise one has only belief. In the latter, one knows also when one can give an account of one's true belief about that reality. And the question is, Can these two apparently incompatible views of knowledge and belief be reconciled in a single approach that does justice to each? I believe they can, but some other points need to be explored first.

Acquaintance and Infallibility

We have now seen Plato give two different explanations for the fallibility of belief. In the *Republic* account, belief is fallible because, as a general mental attitude, it will *change* as its *objects*, physical things, change. In the *Theaetetus* account, belief is fallible because its object is a proposition, which is a *substitute* for the reality it purports to represent and, as such a substitute, it may *fail* to *represent* reality accurately; that is, the proposition may be false. Even "true belief" signifies only a "true proposition," and true propositions, although they correctly represent reality, are still less than fully real entities; they are a step away from the reality they represent. Because of this gap between true belief and the reality it represents, the seeker after knowledge must fix this belief in mind, presumably because it is not fixed there by the mind's own direct acquaintance with reality. As we have seen, that is the function of the account that the believer must give of the true belief.

Can a true belief with an *account* ever be as convincing to the mind as the mind's own direct acquaintance with an object itself? That is the question that emerges at the end of the *Theaetetus* when it is read against the background of the *Republic* approach. Even during the *Theaetetus* discussion, Plato expresses his preference for such direct acquaintance when he shows his prejudice against whatever is not an eyewitness account:

> **Socrates.**   And when a jury is rightly convinced of facts which can be known only by an eye-witness, then, judging by hearsay and accepting a true belief, they are judging without knowledge, although, if they find the right verdict, their conviction is correct?
>
> **Theaetetus.** Certainly. (201c; cf. *Timaeus*, 51d–e)

Plato here suggests that the jury cannot *know* the facts of a case by weighing the testimony of witnesses; instead, even when the jury is persuaded to believe the truth, it acquires a mental state that falls short of the knowledge that "only" the eyewitness can possess. But a trial is an unusual situation, of course. The testimony of different witnesses may conflict, in which case some uncertainty, however slight, may accompany the jury's true belief. Thucydides, in *The Peloponnesian War*, had earlier noted that the historian, too, is faced with this fact: "Different eyewitnesses give different accounts of the same events, speaking out of partiality for one side or the other or else from imperfect memories" (I, 22). Still Plato's analysis does not go deep enough, for the possible conflict between eyewitness reports should have indicated to him that *acquaintance*, on which an eyewitness report is based, is as insufficient a condition for knowledge, and hence for its infallibility, as believing the *testimony* that expresses it.

Why does Plato nevertheless continue to suggest the privileged status of acquaintance as the clue to the nature of knowledge? The answer is, because he thinks that nothing comes between the knower who knows by acquaintance and the object of that acquaintance, and that this is the reason why the eyewitness cannot be mistaken in identifying that object. What the knower knows by acquaintance is what it is and cannot be something else; whereas what the believer believes (the map or the proposition) is something else. What the believer believes is both a *substitute* for the reality, and it may be a *mistaken* substitute, a misrepresentation. Plato thinks, therefore, that the infallibility of knowledge arises from the direct acquaintance of the mind with reality.

Knowledge as Union. It is an appealing view, which appears to find support in the knowledge of sexual intercourse and the knowledge manifested by skill. Although the *New American Heritage Dictionary* regards *to know* in its sense of "to have sexual intercourse with" as archaic, the RSV Bible (1952) still translates Genesis 4:1, "Now Adam knew Eve his wife." The same dictionary, however, defines *carnal knowledge* as "sexual intercourse" without designating it "archaic." *Carnal knowledge* denotes the physical union of two human beings; nothing intervenes between them; they become "one flesh," as the ancient text puts it (Gen. 2:24). Insofar as they *are united* with one another, sexual partners cannot help but *be united* with each other; their mutual "knowledge" is necessarily successful. They are literally *in touch* with each other, to use the phrase discussed earlier. Similarly, Jubal, whose skill consists in *knowing how* to play the pipe, unites himself with the pipe in the act of playing it; insofar as he knows the pipe, he is united with it and cannot but have the relationship *correct*. There is an ancient link between knowing and being able to do, as the *Oxford English Dictionary: The Compact Edition* explains: "*Know.* . . . Generally held to be from the same root (*gen-, gon-, gn-*) as CAN v., and KEN" (I, 1549). Jon Moline reminds us of a related archaic sense of "know": "Homer employed it [*oida*, used by Plato as a synonym for *epistamai*] with nouns and adjectives in the accusative neuter plural to ascribe to people what we can conceive of only as emotional states, states of character, and dispositions to act" (14). Moline cites such examples as people knowing gratitude, knowing friendly things toward each other, and Achilles, who is said to "know fierce things"

(*Iliad* 24.41) and Polyphemos, to "know lawless things" (*Odyssey* 9.189). In these related archaic senses, too, to know is for the knower to be one with what is known.

Now Plato often thinks of intellectual knowledge, and the search for it, on an analogy with sexual love. He begins what I have called his *Republic* account by defining one who seeks knowledge as a *philosopher*, a "*lover* of wisdom [who] has a passion for wisdom," having just reminded Glaucon of the nature of pederasty. His more well-known and extended analogy between sexual eros and the nature of the knower is found in the *Symposium*. Like love itself, the philosopher is an *offspring* of the union of poverty (ignorance) and plenty (wisdom) (202–204). Now the lover (and the player of the pipe) has something like infallibility in the union that constitutes his knowing. By analogy, Plato seems to think, the philosopher who seeks to know reality is seeking knowledge, an infallible state of mind consisting of the union of his mind with reality. This analogy of knowledge with sexual union, combined with the dialectical "way of ascent" (which we discuss later), is the source of the claims for Plato's mysticism. It is true that Plato's ideas have influenced several mystical traditions; however, as Paul Friedlander argues in *Plato: An Introduction*, "Plato, after all, is not a mystic" (77) The reason is that for the mystic, reason eventually breaks down in a "rejection of knowledge," whereas for Plato knowledge of ultimate reality, on the model of the mathematics that is its prerequisite, is the highest accomplishment of reason (77–80).

The problem arises from Plato's own suggestions that knowledge can be understood by analogy with sexual union. The analogy fails, however, because the literal union of lover and beloved (and of player and pipe) contains a bodily (carnal) element that has no counterpart in the relationship of mind and reality. Indeed, the analogy invites a confusion of noetic with ontological union. For the mind to know an object is for it to be united with its object in a quite different way from the way in which two beings are united with one another in sexual intercourse. For, as we have seen, the knower has to *express* the knowledge of reality in a proposition; this proposition then comes between the knower and the reality that is known in a way that *nothing comparable* intervenes between lover and beloved in their sexual union (or between player and pipe when playing it or between Achilles and his fierce actions).

The union of all these involves a physical *intimacy* of the knower with the object known: Adam with Eve, Jubal with his pipe, and Achilles with his pursuit of Hector. The union of the intellectual knower and the reality thus known, however, is precisely not that of physical intimacy between the mind and reality; the mind does not literally *touch* the reality it knows, but represents that reality in propositions. Because these propositions can be mistaken, the mind that expresses its acquaintance with reality does not possess an automatic guarantee that this expression is correct in the same way that the union of sexual lovers is its own guarantee that the union exists. Propositions can prevent the acquaintance of the mind with reality and will do just this when they are false. Nothing comparable can prevent the union of Adam and Eve. Hence the acquaintance of mind with reality can go wrong in a way that Adam's acquaintance with Eve in their sexual union cannot. Hence, too, the infallibility of intellectual knowledge cannot arise from the mind's acquaintance with reality. Such acquaintance can be the source of its knowledge, but not of its knowledge's infallibility.

The Uniqueness of Acquaintance. Propositions, then, make knowledge by acquaintance possible. They also make it possible for one who knows by acquaintance to *share that knowledge* with others who lack such acquaintance. One does not, of course, share one's *acquaintance* with those others. Indeed, one who has taken the way to Larissa *cannot* share *such acquaintance* with that way with those who in ignorance ask the way, any more than Adam can share his intercourse with Eve with anyone else. Knowledge by acquaintance belongs solely to the one who has it, in virtue of the unique and privileged position that person is in. Here the analogy between carnal and intellectual knowledge by acquaintance holds. In each case the knower is in a privileged position which cannot be shared with others. This privileged position explains the uniqueness and priority of knowledge by acquaintance.

Discourse. But one who has such knowledge *can tell* someone who does not have it *what it is that he or she is acquainted with*—for example, the way to Larissa. The inquirer can then *believe* on the testimony of the one who is acquainted with it that the way to Larissa is as the proposition represents it to be. Thus (as I hold, at any rate) the believer also comes to *know* the way to Larissa, without being acquainted with it. But the believer can do this only if the one who knows the way to Larissa by acquaintance expresses this knowledge in a (true) proposition for the inquirer to believe. This is the essence of what goes on in communication and discourse, not only when it expresses what people know by acquaintance but also when it expresses what they hear on testimony (and what they have inferred from either or both of these).

Plato is keenly aware of *discourse*; without it, he says at one point in the *Sophist* (260a), philosophy itself would be impossible. His explanation for the possibility of discourse, and hence of philosophy, however, breaks down. He says: "Any discourse we can have owes its existence to the weaving together of the Forms" (259e). The explanation founders on the fact of false beliefs, which make up at least part of human discourse, an all too familiar part of it. The Forms, which are unchanging in their reality and in their relationship to one another, cannot be "woven together" in just any old way; they are what they are, and their nature and relationships are, in Plato's own view, fixed eternally by necessity. Therefore when in discourse we formulate and assent to false beliefs, what we must be doing is *misrepresenting* the Forms and their interrelationships, either in themselves or as they are participated in by physical objects.

To understand how we can misrepresent them (at least in the case of physical objects), Plato explains the difference between the true statement, "Theaetetus is sitting," and the false statement, "Theaetetus is flying," by describing the former as stating something about Theaetetus that is and the latter as stating something about Theaetetus that *is not*—actually, as Plato explains, something about Theaetetus that is *different* from what is (*Sophist* 263). We said earlier that Plato does not seem to have the concept of a proposition. But here he comes as close as anywhere else to having such a concept, or at least to requiring it. For, to explain speaking falsely, we need something that *misrepresents* the Forms or the way in which physical objects participate in them. This explanation is most easily accomplished by attributing falsity to propositions. A similar explanation is needed to explain speaking truly; we need something that *represents* the Forms. This is accomplished by attributing truth to propostions. Thus to speak at all with other human beings, whether truly or falsely, there must be things that purport to represent the way the world is. These things are propositions. Without them, but wishing to communicate with others, we would be at the same disadvantage as those successful men of business who had to carry in a bundle on their back all the things they would otherwise talk about and sell, owing to the scheme of some Professors in the Academy of Lagado to abolish all language (*Gulliver's Travels*, III, v). (The advantage of their scheme for the reduction of error in trade seems to have escaped the Professors: the object the buyer would buy would be identical with object the seller would sell; no sales pitch could intervene.)

Acquaintance and Propositions. We cannot overemphasize the point that all knowledge by acquaintance (as well as by testimony and inference), even when it is not being communicated to others, requires propositions for its conscious realization. It is the point that

Plato entirely overlooks in his *Republic* account of knowledge and belief. The man who knows the way to Larissa by becoming acquaint-ed with it needs to *express* that knowledge *even to himself*. We can believe he knows the way if he is able to *tell* us; but what about him? Can he suppose he knows it unless he can tell himself? It is difficult to think that a man who cannot tell *himself* the way to Larissa, even though he has taken it, *knows* the way. Even if he could follow the way as a matter of some instinct, like a homing pigeon, but could not articulate the way to us or to himself, we would rightfully doubt whether he really *knew* what he was doing, whether he knew the way. To know by acquaintance just is to be able to *say* what one knows, not only to others but even to oneself. And there is no way to do that without expressing the acquaintance in a proposition that one affirms.

The Role of Reason. Plato often refers to reason (*nous:* intelli-gence) as the faculty that defines human beings and that is necessarily involved in knowledge. To know the Forms, to know the way to Larissa, to know that Theaetetus is sitting, the knower has to *formulate* (or be able to formulate) a proposition in which the acquaintance with each of these objects will be represented. Not that these propositions are objects of belief for one who is acquainted with some reality in the same way that they are objects of the believer's belief. For in the case of the former, reason comes to formulate them in a critically different way, from being acquainted with the reality itself rather than from the testimony of someone else. This acquaintance distinguishes one's noetic state from that of the one who believes the same proposition on testimony, and that is a central point of the *Republic* account which should not be lost. The one who knows by acquaintance has *reality itself* as the *object* of one's mental state, even though one must also be able to express this reality in a proposition. The one who believes, by contrast, has the proposition *alone* as the object of one's mental state. The faculty of reason that formulates the proposition serves them both.

It is this faculty of reason that distinguishes a human being, both as knower and as believer, from a beast. The earthworm is in touch with the earth, but it does not *know* the earth it is "acquainted" with. The birds and the beavers know how to build their nests and their dams, but they do not know *what* a nest or a dam *is*; they do not even know what they themselves, birds and beavers, are. Why not? The animals have no language with which to express the propositions that are necessary for knowing *what* the earth that they are "acquainted" with is, or even *that* it is. Nor can they believe on testimony what they do not know; for belief on testimony also presupposes reason, as much as knowledge by acquaintance. Thus reason is essential for knowledge by acquaintance, if such acquaintance is to be more than that of brute, ignorant contact of one being with another, if it is to be more also than the functional sensitivity (which, of course, all living things have in one degree or another) that results in the orderly and self-rewarding, but *inarticulate*, responses of nonrational living beings to objects around them.

Infallibility Again. If, then, propositions are as essential to the knower who knows by acquaintance as they are to the believer who believes on the testimony of another, the *infallibility* of knowledge cannot be traced simply to the fact that one who knows is acquainted with reality in a way that the believer on testimony is not. For that acquaintance is nothing to the knower, that is, the reality one is acquainted with is nothing *known* to one, until one expresses it (to oneself) in a proposition. And the proposition in which one expresses one's acquaintance is as fallible for one as it is when it becomes one's testimony to someone else who only believes it on that testimony. By its very nature, a proposition is a substitute for reality—whether it functions as the object of a believer's belief who believes it on testimony or as the expression of one's acquaintance with reality who seeks thereby to know that reality. What is sauce for the goose is sauce for the gander. The infallibility of knowledge must therefore lie somewhere else than in acquaintance with reality, contrary to the suggestion of the *Republic* account.

From this conclusion it does not follow, of course, that knowledge by acquaintance has no *priority* over belief on testimony. For it still seems to be the ultimate *source* of knowledge, both for those who have it and for those others who do not have it but who only believe truly on testimony. But if that priority, and not infallibility, is the significance of knowledge by acquaintance, the infallibility of knowledge will have to be traced to something else. And if it can be found somewhere else, just possibly it is an element in the justified true belief approach to knowledge as well. For consider: if the proposition in which someone represents his or her acquaintance with reality is false, what a believer believes on *this* person's testimony will also be false. If, however, the proposition in which someone else represents his or her acquaintance with reality is true, the proposition that a believer believes on *that* person's testimony will be true. Thus not only what is sauce for the goose is sauce for the gander, but also what is fish for the gander is fish for the goose. Indeed, if he who takes the road to Larissa tells me truly the road he took, and if I believe him, do I not as *infallibly know* the road without having taken it as he does who has?

Anyone who considers the matter will agree that what we believe on the true testimony of others can be just as certainly true, and thus infallible, as what we affirm on our own acquaintance with something. Hence belief on testimony can produce the mental state of knowledge as well as acquaintance. The point about infallibility, then, is clear. Once anything is known, regardless of *how* it is known, it is infallible simply in virtue of its being *known*. Whatever is known, however it is known, cannot be mistaken. And we can know by way of testimony as well as acquaintance. This is the point Plato misses in his *Republic* account.

Knowledge as Justified True Belief

We can now see how both acquaintance and testimony can be incorporated into a justified true belief approach to knowledge, into what Plato calls the need for the knower to be able to *give an account*. It is fairly clear that he means by this phrase the ability to give a *reason* (*logos*) that will hold up under questioning. As we shall see later when we turn to his methods of hypothesis and dialectic, this questioning comprises not only an ability to infer conclusions from premises, but also an ability to discover the ultimate premises from which all conclusions can be derived. This ultimate discovery, however, takes the form of some direct intuition of reason—what we have been calling its acquaintance with an object.

It is also fairly clear that Plato excludes from any account that makes for knowledge the citation of the testimony of others. The thrust of his thinking is that knowledge consists in coming to see the truth *for ourselves*—that is, by our own acquaintance with it. This is the case even for what we may believe on the highest authority, which Plato accords the poets and oracles. For an example of the former, the *Republic* is Plato's examination of Simonides' definition of justice. Plato gladly begins with this definition, but is not content simply to accept it on authority (331e). For an example of the latter, Socrates examines the oracle of Delphi, which said that no man was wiser than Socrates (*Apology* 21a)—an examination Plato certainly approved. According to Plato, authority can create only belief; knowledge requires an *account* by reason. In my view, however, citing a trustworthy authority may be an equally good way to give an account of any true belief we claim to know. Each way of giving an account can *justify* the true belief, can (in the language of the *Meno*) fix it firmly in the mind.

Plato's view falls short, then, of making room for what can appropriately be called *knowing by faith*, for that is certainly the way in which I know when I know by accepting the testimony of someone else whom I trust. In that sense, Plato is a rationalist, not a fideist who accords faith in testimony an essential role in the theory of knowledge. He is also a rationalist in the sense that he rejects the testimony of the senses. Thus he actually misses two important points in his *Republic* approach to knowledge and belief. The first point is that believing something about reality on the basis of one's own acquaintance with it is no more a guarantee of truth than believing something about reality on the testimony of someone else is a sign of falsehood. The second point is that the direct acquaintance of reason with the Forms (their rational "self-evidence") is no more a guarantee of the truth of what reason *formulates* about them than the "evidence of the senses" of physical objects to reason is a sure sign of the falsity of what reason *formulates* about them. That Theaetetus cannot be flying and sitting at the same time is evident to reason alone, on the assumption that its *definitions* of flying and sitting are true; but that he is sitting and not flying at a given moment can be just as evident to reason from the senses. Plato's assumption that reason is always infallible in its own world of the Forms is as tenuous as his assumption that it is always fallible in the world of the senses and in the world of human testimony.

A justified true belief approach to knowledge can thus include knowledge by acquaintance as one of its several kinds. Indeed, if I have established this point, it offers two main reasons to prefer a justified true belief to an acquaintance theory of knowledge. First, it shows how knowledge as justified true belief can incorporate knowledge by acquaintance as one of several kinds (whereas the converse is quite implausible). Second, knowledge as justified true belief includes far more in the scope of human knowledge than the knowledge we have by acquaintance, which is very little indeed. This, of course, accords with our initial impression of the matter as well as the way in which we generally use the word *know*. And although initial impressions and usage are by no means completely reliable guides, a theory should try to "save the appearances" of things in its effort to see more deeply into them.

Knowing as Inference. We turn now to what I want to call the third way of giving an account. Sometimes what I believe is true, and I know it because it *follows* from something else I know. This is the way of knowing by proof or inference. It constitutes the third way—in addition to acquaintance and testimony—of giving an account of what I believe truly such that what I possess is knowledge and not merely true belief. If it follows from the fact that there are groceries on the counter that my wife has returned from shopping, then I can know that she is home by inferring that proposition from the proposition that the groceries are on the counter (plus some additional propositions that have to be true, of course). Thus to know something by inference (that my wife is home) is to know something else first (there are groceries on the counter), on the basis of which I come to know what I know by *inference*. It is important to note about both the former (the basis) and the latter (the inference) that each expresses my knowledge in *propositions;* for inferences can be made only from propositions and can themselves be expressed only in propositions. The phenomenon of inference reveals thus a network of *propositions* that are related to each other in a special sort of way. This is the way of logic, the way (among others) of premises and conclusions. It is a way of relating propositions for which, of course, we have our reason to thank. Reason not only conceptualizes our acquaintance with objects and formulates propositions which express that acquaintance in a way that is true or false; it also *sees* a relationship between many of those propositions according to which some propositions *follow from* others.

If reason reflects reality in its reasoning, it is reality itself we ultimately have to thank for this network. The significant question is, however, At what point does reality initially enter into that network? Reflecting on the network itself, we discover a logical relationship in which some propositions (the premises) constitute the sources from which the others (the conclusions) follow. If we ask, What are these *sources* of our inferential knowledge? we ask about the *way* in which those propositions *first* enter our minds, that is, prior to the inferences we draw from them. We may designate such propositions the noninferential sources of our knowledge. Now Plato, as we have seen, tends to hold that the only reliable noninferential source of knowledge is acquaintance with an object. If he is mistaken about this, because the testimony of others can be an equally reliable noninferential source of knowledge, then there are two quite different noninferential sources of knowledge—what we know by our own acquaintance and what we know by the testimony of others.

Thus I could know that my wife is home by inferring it from my own acquaintance with the groceries on the counter (the evidence of my own sense experience) or I could know she is home by inferring it from the testimony of my son who tells me while I am working in the back yard that there are groceries on the counter. If the testimony of another can constitute knowledge as well as my own acquaintance, then the inferences I make from such testimony likewise can constitute knowledge as well as the inferences I make from what I know by my own acquaintance. Indeed, it is precisely a *combination* of testimony *and* inference that *extends* the scope of my knowledge beyond the extremely narrow confines of my direct acquaintance. Like testimony, inference extends my knowledge beyond my own immediate experience, though unlike testimony, my own reasoning, not the word of someone else, produces the extension. The combination explains how knowledge as we understand it in everyday life includes much, much more than just that which we know by our own direct and immediate acquaintance.

I noted earlier that Plato resists taking testimony as a source of knowledge. Perhaps, however, he would be more open to reasoning as a way of extending our knowledge by acquaintance, for reasoning avoids the reliance on others that he distrusts. But does Plato himself allow even that way of extending our knowledge beyond acquaintance? He does, of course; still it will be instructive to review his account of inferential knowledge, for it will help us to focus on a central point of the entire Platonic tradition, viz., the priority of knowledge by direct acquaintance. The priority of such knowledge constitutes one of the main threads of this book and will reappear in the thought of Augustine, Calvin, and Plantinga.

The Vision of the Good

Plato's view of the role of reasoning and inference in human knowledge is embodied in his discussion of two distinct but interrelated methods of seeking the truth: *hypothesis* and *dialectic*. In Book VII of the *Republic* Plato characterizes the method of hypothesis (the "downward way") as making inferences from widely accepted and possibly true beliefs (such as the axioms of mathematics) without, however, having *given an account* of these beliefs themselves and therefore without *knowing* them. The method of dialectic (the "upward way"), by contrast, seeks a first principle beyond these widely accepted beliefs that *can* be known by giving such an account and from which the widely accepted beliefs themselves will follow as inferences (533b–c). The method of hypothesis thus presupposes the legitimacy of reasoning but leaves open the question of how the premises are to be known. The premises will be refuted if the proposition that follows from them either contradicts the premises or is known independently to be false (the way of *elenchus*, which follows the argument form *modus tollens*). If the premises survive refutation, it does not yet follow that they are known. They can be known only if they are inferred from a higher principle that has itself been discovered by the upward way of dialectic.

In what does this upward way consist? Plato is not entirely clear in his various but brief elaborations of an answer to this question. In *Plato's Earlier Dialectic*, Richard Robinson discusses several interpretations that have been offered by Plato scholars. I follow Robinson's own interpretation as the most plausible of these, which he calls the "intuition-theory of the upward path" (Ch. 10). In this interpretation, there are two ingredients in Plato's "upward way." First, dialectic presupposes the training of the mind gained from extensive engagement in the methods of hypothesis and *elenchus*, in other words, in the reasoning and search for truth that these methods involve (533a). Such reasoning is necessary for what Plato calls the *arousal* of reason (532c), but it is insufficient. Second, therefore, dialectic yields a direct, noninferential vision of reality that reason attains in the course of its reasoning about reality. This is a vision of the Forms themselves, and ultimately of the Form of the Good (518c–d, 532a–b, 534b–c).

Knowledge by Acquaintance—Once Again. For Plato, then, there are principles, the Forms, and ultimately a first principle, the Good, from which all that we know can be inferred, but that themselves cannot be known by inference. They can only be *seen* by the mind. This teaching is identical with what I have called his *Republic* approach, viz., that knowledge consists ultimately in one's own direct acquaintance with the mind's proper objects. Apart from such acquaintance as our starting point, all inferences we make at best will follow from hypotheses that, no matter how widely they are accepted and testified to by others, fall short of what is required to give them the status of knowledge in our own minds. In other words, there is a knowledge that is *basic* to all that we know either by inference or by testimony, and we must acquire it by our own acquaintance, intuition, or insight.

Now Plato, in his *Republic* approach, limits such knowledge to the abstract, impersonal, unchanging Forms and to the necessary relationships that can be seen to exist between them. He thereby excludes the possibility of knowing sense objects, the soul, and the gods. Sense objects, the objects of the physical world exist without the permanence and necessity that characterize the Forms; acquaintance with these leads, therefore, to the inferior, fallible mental state he calls *belief*. Second, Plato seems to exclude from knowledge by acquaintance the rational souls of human beings; for he also finds it necessary to give proofs for their true nature as immortal, according to which they emerge not as contingently existing entities but as necessary realities akin to the gods and to the Forms themselves (*Republic* X 611; *Phaedo* 105c–106e). Finally, Plato's theory of knowledge by acquaintance seems to exclude, significantly, knowledge of the gods. For although the gods are not physical entities, they are individual beings; thus they share (it seems) in the contingency of all such beings, in spite of the traditional Greek view of their immortality. At any rate, Plato portrays our knowledge of them (except perhaps for that of the poets) as arising not from the vision that is the result of dialectic but from proofs drawn from the orderliness of the world (*Laws* X 893–907, XII 966–968).

Of most interest to us here is Plato's exclusion of the gods from being known by direct acquaintance of the mind. For if the direct awareness of God is one of the hallmarks of Reformed epistemology, how can Plato be counted among its sources, as I count him? The answer to this question is that Plato ascribes some central characteristics of God to the form of the Good. The Good is the ultimate cause of both the being and the intelligibility of the world, and as such it *transcends* the world (*Republic* 509b, 517c). But as Etienne Gilson observes in *God and Philosophy*, "nothing more closely resembles the definition of the Christian God than this definition of the Good" (25). H. D. Lewis, in "History of Philosophy of Religion," calls Plato's discussion of the Good "the first formulation in Western thought of the idea of transcendence as it came to dominate much subsequent thinking" (278). If Plato fails to identify the Good with God, he does not fail to think of it in a way that resembles the thinking about God both in the Old Testament writers before him and in all religious and philosophical writers in the West after him. The important point for our purposes is that, for Plato, *knowledge* of the Good in those respects in which the Good resembles God is not inferential but immediate and direct.

Three Ways of Giving an Account.   In conclusion, our study of Plato has led us to a view of knowledge as justified, true belief. I know something whenever I believe it, it is true, and I can give an account of it. Unlike Plato, who narrows down such an account either to being acquainted with an object or to whatever can be inferred from what is known by such acquaintance, I have argued that an adequate justification of true belief can also include what comes to us on the testimony of others. In short, my true beliefs constitute knowledge when I can give an account of them in any one of three possible ways. If someone asks me, How do you know? I can answer by saying either "I saw it" (acquaintance), "I heard it" (testimony), or "It follows from what I saw or heard" (inference). Whether my account in each case holds up as I elaborate it under questioning is a further question, of course, one that invites a more detailed analysis of veridical experience, reliable testimony, and correct reasoning than I offer here.

Actually, of course, what we know is a complex product of all *three* ways of knowing working together. In "Religion: Reality or Substitute," C. S. Lewis writes: "Authority, reason, experience, on these three, mixed in varying proportions, all our knowledge depends" (41) George Mavrodes elaborates on the point in *Belief in God:*

> For apprehending an experience, inferring from data and premises, and assessing testimony are not mutually distinct and isolated activities in the life of a rational man. We make use of all of them in all of the important endeavors of our cognitive life. Any really significant belief is almost sure to have its roots, good or bad, weak or strong, in many areas of our lives. If the belief has reasons at all, those reasons are likely to form a web woven of experience, inference and testimony (and perhaps other factors also)—a web whose scope and complexity will tax and perhaps defy our powers of analysis. (88)

Chief among those "other factors" to which Mavrodes alludes, no doubt, is memory. For apart from memory, whatever we know at a given moment by any of the other three ways will be nothing to us a moment later. Memory, too, is a large and complex topic, one I will not explore. It is to be distinguished from reason and reasoning, even though it is closely related (and even essential) to reason and being rational; indeed, it is essential to what it means to be a person who has an identity that persists through time. The whole "web" of knowledge that is formed from our experience, our beliefs on testimony, and our inferences is available to us only through our memory, and then just in various segments at one time.

In the next chapter, I will consider belief on testimony, for Christianity rests in a special way on the testimony of a book. But according to Christianity, belief also arises from divine testimony, from faith in the word of God himself. Thus no Christian account of knowledge can overlook the nature and role of faith.

2 Faith: Abraham

Faith as Trust, Belief, and Obedience

The concept of faith as we know it in the West derives not from ancient Greece but from still more ancient Israel. To understand it we must enter the world of the Bible, and when we do this, we find ourselves in a different world indeed. For Plato, the difference between knowledge and belief is center stage; for Judaism and Christianity, it is the difference is between faith and unbelief. In the Bible knowledge recedes somewhat into the wings, although (as we shall see) it remains an altogether essential player. Still, faith takes over as the more prominent player, with unbelief as its chief antagonist. The fundamental constituent of faith is trust, although it also includes belief and obedience. Religious faith, in the Judaic-Christian religious tradition, is trust in God.

Now trust is not entirely missing in Plato. On the human level, we may trust the guide who has true belief about the way to Larissa; he is as trustworthy as the guide who knows. Still, as impressed as Plato is by the reliability of true belief, he nowhere considers that the trust in human testimony on which such true belief can be based should figure in an account of knowledge. True belief is knowledge only when those who have it can give an account of it by combining hypothetical reasoning with dialectical vision of what is real. By contrast, in the Bible it is not knowledge so defined that is to be sought over belief, but faith over unbelief. And faith, although it includes belief, is more than just belief; it is belief that arises from trust. And the most significant object of trust is not our fellow human beings, but God. For the Greeks, as Benjamin Warfield points out in *Biblical Doctrines*, the biblical notion of trust is "too strong a term" to characterize their attitude toward the gods, which is more accurately denoted by the Greek term *nomizein*, translated usually as "reverence" or "respect" (472). For biblical religion, properly to reverence and respect God is, among other things, to trust him.

Of course, in the biblical record human beings are also the objects of faith, or the lack of it. Trust in their testimony is a conspicuous and necessary part of their daily life. For example, Jacob believed the testimony of Joseph's brothers that Joseph was still alive in Egypt—though only after initial disbelief (Gen. 45:26–28). For another, an example of distrust, Thomas did not trust his fellow disciples who said they had seen the risen Lord (John 20:25). What is more interesting, faith in human beings is also the way in which faith in God is propagated to others. This is evident from the missionary activity of the first Christian believers and the spread of the gospel ever since. Christians are keenly aware of the function of such religious witness and testimony. Paul asks, "How are they to believe in him of whom they have never heard?" and answers, "So faith comes by what is heard, and what is heard comes by the preaching of Christ" (Rom. 10:14, 17). Nor is the spread of Christian faith limited to the conspicuous, public, and dramatic activity of preaching. It occurs also in the privacy of a family setting. Thus Paul affectionately remembers that the faith of his young friend and fellow missionary, Timothy, had been handed down from his mother Eunice and grandmother Lois (2 Tim. 1:5). For not only can beliefs be taught and thereby handed down, so can attitudes, including the attitude of trust. Thus trust in the testimony of others has played, and continues to play, a central role in the spread of Christianity.

Believing on Acquaintance vs. Believing on Testimony.   Still, biblical faith is set forth, not as faith in the prophets or in the apostles or in believing parents but as faith in God and in Jesus Christ. This progression of faith from faith in other human beings to faith in Christ himself is portrayed in the story of Jesus and the Samaritan woman. Many of her neighbors, we read, "believed in him because of the woman's testimony, 'He told me all that I ever did.'" Later, after these neighbors had met Jesus personally and visited with him for two days, they said, "It is no longer because of your words that we believe, for we have heard for ourselves, and we know that this is indeed the Savior of the world" (John 4:39, 42). Thus the crucial distinction emerges already in the pages of the Bible itself between believing in God (or in Christ) on the basis of the testimony of other believers and believing in him by "hearing for oneself."

Indeed, in the Samaritans' hearing for themselves that Jesus is the savior, John actually combines knowlege by acquaintance and belief on testimony, for the acquaintance with Christ himself combined with *his* testimony about himself leads them to *know (oidamen)* something—that he is the Messiah—that they formerly believed only on the testimony of others. In this story we can see the heart of biblical epistemology, that human beings can, upon hearing about God from their fellow human beings, come to know God themselves, both by being acquainted with him and from his own testimony about himself. In other words, if on the pages of Scripture knowledge recedes into the wings (as I said earlier), it does not follow that it is less important than faith. On the contrary, knowledge—the knowledge of God—is actually the essential condition for everything the Bible says about faith and unbelief; without it the drama (the *agōn*) between faith and unbelief would be unintelligible.

The Biblical Paradigm of Faith. A good way to explore the nature of biblical faith, which will also lead us into the biblical view of what it is to know God, is to consider the story of Abraham. Abraham is significant because, according to Paul, he is the "father of all who believe" (Rom. 4:11). As such, Abraham is not only in some sense the progenitor of faith but also its paradigm (Rom. 4:12). His story even contains the first occurrence of the word *faith* in the Bible: "And he believed the Lord" (Gen. 15:6; the Hebrew *emunah*, in its active form, occurs only once again in the Old Testament, Habakkuk 2:4).

The story of Abraham is a dramatic story indeed. It begins as follows: "Now the Lord said to Abram, 'Go from your country and your kindred and your father's house to the land that I will show you. And I will make of you a great nation, and I will bless you, and make your name great, so that you will be a blessing. . . .' So Abram went, as the Lord had told him" (Gen. 12:1–4). So far, no mention of faith; but already two ingredients in faith are implicit, trust in God and obedience to God's command. The trust becomes explicit in the account of the fourth recorded appearance of the Lord, in which Abram asks the Lord concerning his childlessness. The Lord responds that Abram's own son, not his servant Eliezer, will be his heir. "And," continues the narrator, "he believed the Lord; and he reckoned it to him as righteousness" (Gen. 15:6). Abram then asks the Lord, "How am I to know that I shall possess it [that is, the land to which he has come, which the Lord has promised him]?" In answer, God gives Abram a mysterious sign, adding another verbal assurance: "Know of a surety that your descendants will be sojourners in a land that is not theirs . . . [but] shall come back here in the fourth generation" (Gen. 15:13, 16). To assure him, God gives him a sign—the sign, in ancient near Eastern cultures, of a *covenant* (verse 18). Thus, all Abram really has to go on is God's word. What would ordinarily count as evidence for what Abram is to believe seems to be lacking, because the land is occupied by Canaanites, and Abram and Sarai are childless. If anything, the weight of the normal evidence available to him counts *against* his belief.

In the next major appearance, God renews his promises to

Abram, changes his name to Abraham and Sarai's to Sarah, but this time Abraham (and later Sarah, too) responds to the promise of a son with laughter, for the evidence against its fulfillment has become overwhelming: "Shall a child be born to a man who is a hundred years old? Shall Sarah, who is ninety years old, bear a child?" (Gen. 17:17) But God reassures him, and a year later, Isaac is born. The climax of the story of Abraham comes, of course, when God commands him to offer up his son Isaac "as a burnt offering upon one of the mountains" in the land of Moriah (Gen. 22). Abraham's response is one of simple obedience; of his thoughts and feelings there is not a trace in the Genesis account. For what these may have been, we can read Sören Kierkegaard's commentary in *Fear and Trembling.* The Genesis record gives us no more than Abraham's affirmation of faith that "the Lord will provide" (Gen. 15:8). Kierkegaard concludes: "No one is so great as Abraham! Who is capable of understanding him?" (15)

Three Elements of Faith.   From the story of Abraham, we can distinguish three elements in biblical faith: trust, belief, and obedience; a volitional-emotional, an intellectual, and a moral element. One of these ingredients, trust, as we noted a moment ago, is conspicuously absent from Plato's theory of knowledge and belief. Another, the moral component, is very much present in Plato's theory of knowledge, though not in the form of obedience but in the form of virtue, in his doctrine that knowledge is virtue; but, as I left that important (and complicated) teaching to one side in Chapter 1, so here I do the same with obedience, the moral ingredient in faith. Finally, there is belief, the intellectual element. In a curious and uniquely modern reversal, many liberal theologians ignore or even reject this element as essential to biblical faith; it is fashionable in their quarters to expound on the "nonpropositional" character of religious faith. The fashion finds no support in the Bible. Abraham believes *that* he will have a son, *that* the land of Canaan will belong to his descendants, *that* these descendants will be many, and *that* the world will be blessed through them. All of these beliefs are propositions; they can be true or false. When Abraham believed them, he of course believed them to be *true;* that is just what it is to believe what someone says. Abraham's faith is unintelligible if these beliefs are ignored.

Did Abraham then also *know* the realities represented by these beliefs? Clearly not, if knowledge is restricted to a direct acquaintance with those realities or to an inference to them from such acquaintance with other realities. All Abraham had to go on was the say so, the testimony, of God. Indeed, as we have noted, the rational evidence for the truth of the propositions in this testimony, as people normally count rational evidence, not only was lacking but actually counted against it. Abraham was old, Sarah was beyond her childbearing years, and Canaanites dominated the land that God said would belong to him and his descendants. Only when the first promise came true, and Isaac was born of Sarah, was there a state of affairs that Abraham could know by his own experience. But later he was commanded to offer up his son Isaac without the slightest evidence that God "would provide." He simply trusted God.

If, however, as I proposed in Chapter 1, knowledge as justified true belief includes what we believe on reliable testimony, then Abraham *knew* the things he believed on God's say so. The author of *Hebrews*, in his great chapter on faith, celebrates Abraham's *faith*. He defines faith as "the substance of things hoped for, the evidence of things not seen" (11: 1). As this King James translation of the text reveals, although faith does not rest on the evidence of one's own acquaintance or reasoning, it is not therefore without its *evidence* (Greek: *elenchos*). The evidence derives from the *person* whose testimony one believes. The mark of biblical faith is trust in God; that trust provides the basis for believing what God says. Asked why he believes what God says, Abraham would certainly have said, because it is God who says it. That will be the *account* which justifies his belief.

Belief In *vs.* Belief That.   Let us look more closely at this trust, for it is clearly the *basis* not only for Abraham's beliefs, but also for his obedience. He would not have believed or acted as he did had he not trusted God. So, too, we can generalize to all cases of believing (and acting) on the basis of testimony. *Belief that* what someone says is true presupposes *belief in* that person (likewise, *disbelief that* what someone says is true presupposes *disbelief in* that person). We must observe here that the phrase *belief in* is distressingly ambiguous. Sometimes (as I have just used it) it is a synonym for *trust*. To say that "Abraham believed in God" can mean that "he trusted God." Sometimes, however, to *believe in God* means "to believe that God exists." What, then, does Paul mean by calling Abraham the "father of all *believers*" (Rom. 4:11, 16)? The term *believers* here is open, technically, to three interpretations: Abraham is the father of all those who believe *what* God says (i.e., *that* what God says is true), or of those who *trust* God (as the basis for believing what he says), or of those who believe *that* God exists. The question, What *does* Paul mean here? is the very question, What is the nature of biblical faith?

Believing What *and* Trusting.   I shall argue that biblical faith is (besides obedience, already mentioned) a combination of the first two of these three senses of belief, *belief* (in the testimony of God) and *trust* in God. Abraham *believed what* God said *because* he *trusted* God. That is biblical faith. Biblical faith consists, thus, only of *belief*, which has as its object the propositions that God speaks, and *trust*, which has as its object God himself. It does *not* include the *belief that* God exists; it does *not* have as its object the proposition, "God exists," but only the propositions that God speaks; and the proposition "that he exists" or, more correctly, "I exist" (spoken by God) is not one of these.

Two passages in Scripture might suggest the contrary, that biblical faith does include the belief *that* God exists. One is Exodus 3:14: "God said to Moses, 'I am who I am.'" But here I take God to be reminding Moses of his "covenant faithfulness," not to be testifying to his own existence (Berkhof 1949, 49; G. Vos 1948, 134). The other passage is Hebrews 11:6: "For whoever would draw near to God must believe (*pisteusai*) that he exists." This text seems to incorporate the belief that God exists into biblical faith, especially as the author has just said, "And without faith (*pisteōs*) it is impossible to please him." Such an interpretation is technically possible, for as we have seen, *faith* as *belief in* is ambiguous and can mean "belief that something exists." I think, however, that the author either writes loosely here, not paying attention to the ambiguity, or is expressing only the logical point that to be pleasing to God presupposes the recognition that God *exists*. If he had meant to incorporate *this* belief into faith, he would certainly have mentioned it again in his portraits of the heroes and heroines of faith. But he does not do this; instead, as he tells their stories, what makes them all heroic is that they believed the divine promises (11:39) and obeyed the divine commands. Not once does he commend any of the heroes or heroines for his or her belief that God exists. I conclude, therefore, that the text does not count against my thesis that biblical faith excludes the belief that God exists and includes (in addition to trust and obedience) only believing what God says on other matters about himself, about us, and about the world.

Faith: Human and Divine

This thesis finds support along another route, namely, the analogy between faith in God and faith in human beings. Like the belief component of faith, trust has an *object*. Abraham trusted God. Human beings trust each other, or do not trust each other as the case may be. Jacob trusted his sons; the Samaritans trusted the Samaritan woman; Thomas did not trust his fellow disciples. In all these cases, the object of trust (or distrust) is an object that is *believed* to exist by the one who trusts or distrusts. The question is, How does this belief in the existence of the object of trust arise? As I hope to show presently, in the biblical picture, the belief that God exists arises not by testimony nor inference but by a direct acquaintance with God himself, just like the belief that our fellow human beings whom we know personally exist arises by a direct acquaintance with those human beings.

We can first observe, incidentally, that the possible objects of trust include other things besides our fellow human beings. These objects can be impersonal things, as, for example, an animal: one cannot trust a wild ox to bring home the grain to the threshing floor, when it is wild; but if it is trained, one can (Job 39:12); or again, one can trust in the continuance of one's earthly life (Deut. 28:66). Examples could be multiplied, from the Bible and from all of human life. In *Belief,* H. H. Price mentions many different things that can be the object of human trust (some of which are not known to exist by direct acquaintance): animals (the blind man in his guide-dog); plants (the gardener in her chrysanthemums); artifacts (all of us in machines); natural objects (Englishmen used to believe in the sea); events (the victory of one's country in a war); institutions (the school or university one attends); and procedures, methods and policies (equal pay for both sexes); and even theories (scientific and philosophical). Price concludes: "Indeed, it is not easy to set any limits at all to the types of 'objects' which may be believed in" (428–430). Thus faith as trust can have as its object *anything* at all upon which we *rely*. The role of trust in human experience is as wide as such experience itself. To live is to trust—other people, animals, plants, physical objects in the world, the laws of nature, and much, much more.

But we are interested in trust in so far as it bears directly on knowledge and belief. Let us then restrict our attention to human beings trusting one another for what they *say* (ignoring their trust in each other for what they can do, although that too, of course, is a major aspect of human life). What they say to one another includes both information (testimony) and advice or commands. To believe the former and to follow the latter both require trust. We will also leave aside advice and commands, in order to focus on testimony, the source of many, perhaps most, of our beliefs. Indeed, it should be observed that, although obedience is a necessary constituent of divine faith, it is not so of human faith; in many human relationships faith includes only believing testimony on trust.

"What is it to believe someone?" Elizabeth Anscombe asks this question in her essay by this title. She expresses surprise that the topic is so neglected in epistemology, for "the greater part of our knowledge of reality rests upon the belief that we repose in things we

have been taught and told" (142). Compare Price, in *Belief*: "Epistemologists do not seem to have paid much attention to the evidence of
testimony" (113) and Alvin Plantinga in "Reason and Belief in God":
"One *prima-facie* justification-conferring condition [for belief] that
does not get enough attention is *training*, or *teaching*, or (more broadly) *testimony*" (85). One reason for the epistemological neglect of faith
and testimony is the deep-seated attitude of modernity against tradition and authority. What people do not highly value will not be a
topic of their serious investigation. Perhaps Christian epistemologists,
for whom faith and testimony are fundamental, will lead the way in
overcoming this neglect. Indeed, it was the Church Fathers—and
especially Augustine—who originally injected faith into philosophy. I
here discuss Anscombe; I could have discussed Wolterstorff, who
points up the significance of what Thomas Reid calls the "credulity
principle." In his recent "Evidence, Entitled Belief, and the Gospels,"
Wolterstorff accords Reid "the honor of first questioning the thesis" of
the Enlightenment that we must be guided in all our believing by reason and experience alone (427).

Anscombe answers the question, What is it to believe someone?
concisely: it is "to take something on faith." She notes, however, that
this phrase no longer carries its full-blooded sense of *having faith in*
our fellow human beings (or in God). It has become vestigial in the
language, so that the phrase "You merely took it on faith" nowadays
"is only actually *said* as a reproach." She wants us to note, however,
that "it is often true when it is not blameworthy" (141). She deplores
the fact that we no longer speak of faith as "human and divine:
Human faith was believing a mere human being; divine faith was
believing God" (142). That sense was very much alive in St. Augustine's day, as we shall see when we discuss him. If it has all but disappeared in modern times, this is in large part because of the modernist
attitude against authority just mentioned. The attitude is one of the
springs of modern culture, a culture that largely rejects *divine* faith, if
not *human* faith as well. Already in 1637 Descartes sets the tone,
explicitly for the latter and probably implicitly for the former, when
he writes in his *Discourse on Method*: "My plan has never been more
than to try to reform my own thoughts and to build upon a foundation which is completely my own" (II, 15).

Anscombe also laments that the phrase *belief in God* has been
reduced to *belief that God exists* and complains of the "rubbish about
'believing in' as opposed to 'believing that'" in the writing of contemporary epistemologists (142). It is not rubbish, however, to avoid the
confusions created by ambiguous meanings of important terms; Price,
for example, takes an entire chapter in *Belief* to sort out the ambiguity

(Part II, Lecture 9). In fact, as Anscombe's own thesis points up, it is necessary to cut through these ambiguities to *illuminate* what it is to *believe someone*, which we do everyday with one another, and which Christians do everyday with God. What we have seen is that faith (whether Abraham's faith in God or Jacob's in his sons) consists of belief (*that* some propositions are true) on the basis of trust (*belief in* the person who expresses them). Thus Anscombe also concludes that, when all the qualifications have been acknowledged, believing someone comes down to "relying on *x* for it that *p*," "trusting him for the truth" (145, 151). In her example: "A witness might be asked 'Why did you think the man was dying?' and reply 'Because the doctor told me.' If asked further what his own judgment was, he may reply 'I had no opinion of my own—I just believed the doctor'" (145). Thus believing someone can actually result in acquiring a belief of *one's own*, if one does not already have any on the subject: "What someone's saying a thing may bring about, is that one forms one's *own* judgment that the thing is true" (145).

One cannot (I point out by the way) even understand the *Apostles' Creed* without distinguishing "belief in" from "belief that." "I *believe in* God the Father, almighty, maker of heaven and earth. . . . I *believe in* the Holy Spirit." If Christians mean, in confessing these first eight articles only that they believe *that* God exists, and so on, they do nothing more than the demons (James 2:19). What they mean when they confess the first article of the Creed, therefore, and what the demons could not mean, is that they *trust* God, the Father, almighty, even as Abraham did before them. It is remarkable that the Creed is precisely a *creed*, in which nothing is said to the effect that God exists, or that its confessors *know* that he does. That they *know* God and believe with justification *that God exists* is simply *presupposed* by their confessing the creed, even as it is by the authors of the Bible and by the people whose stories they tell on its pages.

The Objects of Belief and Trust. This presupposition—that God exists—is crucial for any account of "biblical epistemology." It is the presupposition of biblical faith. To see that this is so, let us return to our model of faith in human testimony. First, of course, the attitude of *belief* one forms on the basis of human testimony has its object. This object is a *proposition*, which is a substitute in the mind of one who believes it for the direct acquaintance the believer lacks with the reality that it purports to represent. Likewise, *trust* has an object. What, in cases of believing on human testimony, is the object of trust? The answer, of course, is the very *person* who conveys the proposition one believes. The object of trust is, thus, a real object in the world and not a propositional substitute. It is not propositions we trust in cases of human testimony, but the people who convey them. Moreover, the relationship between belief and trust is that believing propositions is *based upon* trust in the persons who convey them. How then do we come to know *these* objects, the persons whose testimony we trust?

How We Know Those Whom We Trust.   The answer is, of course, that we do not know by acquaintance most of the human beings we trust; we do not know them "personally," as we say, at all. Some we do, and that is all-important. We know our wives, husbands, parents, children, friends, doctors, teachers, grocers, and so forth and trust them for what they say to us. Indeed, if we ever do not trust one of them, it will probably be because of something we know or believe about that one based on our own acquaintance or someone else's testimony about the person. But what is impressive, of course, is that we believe many more propositions on the testimony of people we do not know personally than we believe on the testimony of people we do. Anscombe gives some examples:

> You will take up a book and look in a certain place and see "New York, Dodd Mead and Company, 1910." So do you know from personal observation that the book was published by that company, and then, and in New York? Well, hardly. But you know that it *purports* to have been so. How? Well, you know that is where the publisher's name is always put, and the name of the place where his office belongs. How do you know that? You were taught it. . . .
>
> You may think you know that New York is in North America. What is New York, what is North America? You may say you have been in these places. But how much does that fact contribute to your knowledge? Nothing, in comparison with testimony. How did you know you were there? Even if you inhabit New York and you have simply learned its name as the name of the place you inhabit, there is the question: How extensive a region is this place you are calling "New York"? And what has New York got to do with this bit of a map? Here is a complicated network of information. (144)

Complicated? Yes, and the consequence is that what we know about anything at all consists, as George Mavrodes stated it for us at the end of Chapter 1, of "a web woven of experience, inference, and testimony." Anscombe has her own picturesque simile: "Nor is what testimony gives us entirely a detachable part, like the thick fringe of fat on a chunk of steak. It is more like the flecks and streaks of fat that are often distributed through good meat; though there are lumps of pure fat as well" (143–144). What is astonishing is the *anonymity* of thousands, probably millions, of individuals, past and present, whom we trust for most of what we believe about the world, past, present, and future. And it is all based on trust.

The Morality of Belief. This extensive and pervasive trust between human beings points up the deeply moral dimension of human testimony. Not only do those who give it have the duty to be honest, but those who hear it (read it, etc.) have the duty to believe. The latter duty even discourages taking the preliminary precautions of investigating the reliability of the source of the testimony. As Anscombe puts it: "It is an insult and it may be an injury not to be believed. At least it is an insult if one is oneself made aware of the refusal, and it may be an injury if others are" (150). And Price: "Am I treating my neighbor as an end in himself, in the way I wish him to treat me, if I very carefully examine his credentials before believing anything he says to me?" (114). Of course this duty to believe does not imply there are no occasions where caution and even investigation are necessary, where disbelief may even be our duty; but our prima facie duty to believe one another remains. Furthermore, the trust such belief presupposes is also a practical necessity, because no human being is in a position, by experience or inference, either to investigate even a small fraction of all those other human beings who give testimony or to verify the testimony itself.

Testimony: A Vast Network.   Our main question still is, How do we know those whom we trust for so much of what we believe? How do we even know that they exist (or existed)? The answer to either version of the question is the same. We acquire such knowledge of all those human beings outside our personal acquaintance only by way of the testimony that they have left us (or leave us, if they are our contemporaries). We know they existed (or exist) on the basis of the same kind of testimony, handed down both through other persons and by various impersonal means (books, other written records, pictures, artifacts, etc.) as we know those other things about the world that they knew (or know) and of which they left (or leave) their testimony. So, we can know that Abraham existed only on the basis of human testimony—including that of the author of Genesis.

Such testimony, however, seems, mirabile dictu, to be for the most part reliable. We can believe it with a high degree of confidence. Why? The answer seems to be, in part, because we are *connected* with all those human beings whom we do not know personally, both in our past and present. The nearest connection we have, of course, is through persons we do know personally; my father tells me of my grandparents, who died before I was born, and of his friends in Montana whom I have never met. These nearby connections, however, account for a very, very small range of the many human beings we know about beyond our own experience—the people in the past on the pages of the Bible, of Thucydides, of Tacitus, and of Josephus; and in the present, on the pages of *National Geographic* or of any daily newspaper. This vast network of human testimony extending both into our past and into the present world serves not only as the *source* of most of what we know, but also as a *control* on the reliability of human beings and the truth of their testimony about themselves, about others, and about the events of their times.

Human Testimony and the Existence of God

We can now ask the question, Could such a network of human testimony be the source of contemporary Christian belief in the existence of God, just as, for example, it is the source of their belief in the existence of Abraham, Isaac, and Jacob? Does that network perhaps explain how Abraham himself arrived at his belief in the existence of God, so that not only Christians today, but also he long ago came to believe in the existence of God simply, and only, on the testimony of others who went before? So that Adam and Eve, let us say, were the only ones who knew God by personal acquaintance, and they passed this knowledge of God on to their children as testimony for them to accept (or reject, as the case may be), thus establishing the biblical tradition called *belief in God?*

Judging from our model of the many things we know by the vast network of human testimony, it certainly seems possible that many people acquire and continue their belief in God (i.e., that he exists) in the same way they acquire and continue their belief (if they have such a belief) in the existence of Abraham. It is unlikely, however, that every instance of belief in God can be accounted for in this way. For no other belief in the existence of something so important for human life has survived in this exclusively testimonial way. Such beliefs usually have disappeared when the objects they purport to represent have not also been known experientially by at least some of those who first accepted their existence on human testimony alone. Consider two examples: Zeus and the magnificent Greek and Roman pantheon or the substances of medieval alchemy. No one believes any more that Hephaistos still fashions military shields for his mother's favorite war heroes, or that a "philosopher's stone" can turn mercury into gold. But many human beings still believe in God, that is, that God exists, and particularly in the existence of Yahweh, the God of the Bible. It seems improbable that they have believed this from ancient times on and still do so today on the basis of the testimony of a merely human tradition alone.

The Biblical Picture. Be that as it may, the *picture* we get in and from the Bible itself of how things are is quite different. It is a commonplace that the Bible, beginning with its very opening verse, takes the existence of God for granted, takes for granted, that is, that its *readers* will already *know* the God whose words and deeds it reports. As we said earlier, the biblical record presupposes that God exists. It neither cites testimony to his existence of some aboriginal source nor offers any proofs that God exists. The miracles and fulfillment of prophecy are offered as signs of his power and trustworthiness, not of his existence. Furthermore, the people in the biblical stories are all taken to be people who either do trust God or do not. They all need to *deal* with *God;* they cannot escape his demands on their lives, because he is taken to be their creator, redeemer, and Lord. The first and foremost of these demands is faith, even as it was required of Abraham, the father of all those who believe.

Testimony: Of Strangers and of Acquaintances. As we have seen, we can believe in persons we do not know by our own acquaintance; most of what all of us believe has come to us ultimately from total strangers. But some central part of what we believe comes to us from people whom we do know. Our trust in these is, perhaps, the fundamental, primordial trust, and it is based on acquaintance; whereas our trust in strangers is derivative from it. In any case, biblical faith in God is nothing like the latter. Those who trust in God are represented in the Bible as trusting someone they *already know*, not someone they only *know about*, or believe exists on the testimony of other human beings whom they do know. Thus even if such testimony to the existence of God could be as reliable a way of knowing that God exists as it is of knowing that so and so were one's ancestors, it is not the way the heroes and heroines of bibical faith, sung or unsung, seem to know that he exists. The greatness of Abraham is not that he trusts Terah, his father, on whose teaching Abraham may well have at first believed that God exists (although that is questionable, given the polytheism of his family's beliefs), but that he trusts God who speaks to him directly. The story of Abraham has every earmark of a man who is personally acquainted with God. God is no stranger whose existence Abraham accepts on the testimony of others, either strangers, friends, or family. Quite the contrary, Abraham becomes known himself as "the friend of God" (2 Chron. 20:7; Isaiah 41:8; James 2:23).

If Abraham is the model of biblical faith, human beings must be capable of something more than belief that God exists on the testimony of others who believe it. They must be able to know God (or come to know him) in the same way that Abraham knew him. For biblical faith, as trust in God for what he says, promises, and commands, presupposes knowing God who is the object of such trust in some *other way* than by human testimony; and the only other way (beside inference) is by direct acquaintance with God himself. What makes Abraham a hero of faith, as I interpret his story, is not that he believed on human testimony *that God exists*, but that he believed *what God said* in spite of the evidence against it.

Was It Really God?   There is a third possible interpretation of the story of Abraham. What if Abraham is a hero of faith because he believed *that it really was God* who spoke to him and not the devil? This interpretation is suggested by the dilemma which Martin Luther sees in the story of the sacrifice of Isaac (Gen. 22):

> "Human reason concludes naturally that either the promise is falsely asserted or that the command is not from God but from the devil, for the contradiction is manifest. For if he ought to slay Isaac, the promise is in vain; but if the promise is certain, the command cannot be from God." (quoted in Keil and Delitzsche, *Commentary on The Old Testament*; Genesis 22; my translation; source not given)

On this Lutheran line of thought, Abraham's trial consists in making a far more fundamental decision than to take God at his word. Instead he has to decide whether it is even God who commands him or the devil. His crisis then lies not in whether to trust God whom he knows, but in whether it is the God whom he knows that gives him this new command. If we extend this interpretation to all the occasions on which God calls Abraham, we shall have to take his significance as the father of believers not that he believes (and obeys) what God says (and commands) because he trusts God, in spite of the evidence of "human reason," but that he judges that it is really God who speaks to him, in spite of the evidence he has against that. His trial in Genesis 22, in this reading, did not consist in having to weigh what

God commands over what God had previously promised him, or both of these over what he can believe from his own reason and experience apart from God, but in his weighing whether it is even God who speaks to him. His heroism consists not in his faith *in God*, but in his faith *that it is God who speaks to him*. This might actually be more like faith in *himself*, that he has properly identified God!

This "Lutheran" interpretation, however, is not supported by the biblical record. There is no hint in any of the Abraham stories that Abraham wonders whether it is God who speaks. Indeed, when he doubts, as his laughing at the promise of Isaac's birth suggests he does (Gen. 17:17), what he doubts is that he and Sarah shall have a child (i.e., he doubts God's *word*), not *that it is God* who promises (i.e., the identity of the speaker). Later, when Abraham has withstood the trial of sacrificing Isaac, God commends him for his obedience to his command, not for the correctness of his judgment that it is indeed God himself whose command he has obeyed (Gen. 17:12, 16). Nor does the author of Hebrews support the Lutheran line of thought (Hebrews 11:8–12, 17–22). Keil and Delitszche also reject it. Having quoted Luther, they reject the horn of his dilemma that suggests it:

> But Abraham brought his reason into captivity to the obedience of faith. He did not question the truth of the word of God, which had been addressed to him in a mode that was to his mind perfectly infallible (not in a vision of the night, however, of which there is not a syllable in the text), but he stood firm in his faith. (248–249)

They, too, take the Bible record to indicate that Abraham *knew* God *independently* of being asked by God to *believe* and *obey* him.

Kierkegaard agrees. This is significant in view of the widespread view that Kierkegaard shares Luther's deep distrust of reason. How deep is Kierkegaard's distrust of reason? Does he doubt the ability of reason to affirm the very existence of God or to identify God as the one who spoke to Abraham? It is clear from Kierkegaard's discussion in *Fear and Trembling* that he has no such doubt, nor does he entertain the possibility that Abraham did. Quite the opposite: "He [Abraham] knew that it was God the almighty who was trying him, and he knew that it was the hardest sacrifice that could be required of him; but he knew also that no sacrifice was too hard when God required it—and drew the knife" (28). In other words, by the light of his reason, Abraham might well have doubted the promises of God (in the earlier stories) or hesitated to obey what God commands (in the story of the sacrifice of Isaac), for these, according to

Kierkegaard, are "unreasonable," "preposterous," and "absurd." But he did not; these are what Abraham "believed," "accepted," "held fast the expectation" (20–26, 47–49). Nowhere does it occur to Kierkegaard that Abraham finds the very existence of God unreasonable, or that he questions the identity of the one whose voice he hears. The greatness of Abraham's faith lies, for Kierkegaard (as for the Bible), in his trust in God for *what God tells him*, not in his believing, in the midst of rational doubts, that God exists or that it really is God who speaks.

At one point Kierkegaard mentions that Abraham might have "misunderstood the deity" (90), but he does not pursue even this possibility as the source of his trial or of the greatness of his faith. Abraham's trial consists rather in his having to obey the command of God to slay Isaac, which not only conflicts with God's earlier promises but also contradicts his moral duty, a duty that is also from God, who prohibits murder and requires him to love Isaac as he loves himself. It is a trial that Kierkegaard takes as evidence for the possibility of a "teleological suspension of the ethical" (79). Throughout his commentary, then, Kierkegaard takes for granted that Abraham is in the immediate presence of God. Abraham is a man who "strove with God" (19); his trial "is a question between him and the Eternal Being who is the object of faith" (75); his faith arises from his being an "individual" who "as the particular stands in an absolute relation to the absolute" (82). The challenge to Abraham's reason lies in what God says, not in the existence or identity of God himself.

Divine Faith vs. Knowledge of God in the Bible

I conclude, then, that biblical faith is neither believing *that God exists* (either by human faith or divine) nor believing *that it is God whose voice one hears*, but believing *God when he speaks*. If this interpretation is correct, we must not focus on the concept of biblical faith in order to discover the biblical view of what it is to know that God exists, but we must focus on that knowledge itself, which is *presupposed* by biblical faith, in so far as the biblical record indicates what it is like. The record indicates that it is very much like an immediate and direct acquaintance with God. What is at stake for Abraham is whether he believes what God says, not whether he believes or knows that God exists; his story assumes that he is already acquainted with God.

As we saw from our analysis of knowledge by acquaintance in Chapter 1, it does not follow from the fact that Abraham was acquainted with God that he formulated every belief he had about

God correctly; acquaintance does not imply infallibility. But Abraham's acquaintance with God was a unique and original source of those beliefs about him that he did formulate correctly; it was the source, thus, of his *knowledge* of God. This knowledge included, according to the biblical record, that God is just one God, in sharp contrast to the polytheism of his Chaldean family, tribe, and ancestors (Joshua 24:2). Abraham knew also that this one God is "maker of heaven and earth" (Gen. 14:22), a hearer of prayer (20:17), a personal presence "before whom I walk" (24:20), just (18:25), provident and faithful (24:7).

What is the nature of this knowledge? In theological language, is it natural or revealed? The biblical picture, as I see it, is that such knowledge is natural, not revealed, or, as we come upon the story of Abraham, perhaps a mixture of both, but with a natural knowledge as the base. For much of the knowledge is presupposed by Abraham's faith—certainly the knowledge of God's existence. Abraham *believes what* God says because he *trusts* him; and he can *trust* him only because he *knows* him independently of believing what he says; otherwise his trust could not be the basis for his belief. Or, to argue the point differently, suppose Abraham knew these propositions about God (that he is one being, the maker of heaven and earth, etc.) by God's *revealing* these to him. Then the *basis* for his believing these propositions could not be his trust in God, for he would not yet *know* who it was who was revealing them to him. But Abraham does trust God as the basis for his believing what God says; hence he must know God himself independently of what God says—independently, that is, of his revelation to Abraham.* If this knowledge of God is not revealed, it must be a *natural* knowledge of God.

The Basis of Trust. It might be objected that, if Abraham already knew God in the natural way I claim he did, he should have found God's testimony (revelation) perfectly reliable simply in view of who God is. Why, then, it might be asked, is Abraham a hero of faith? How, it may be asked, could Abraham have done anything but believe? Why should he doubt the word of God, who is perfect, any more than we rarely doubt the testimony of our fellow human beings, who are not perfect? Why was there, as there clearly was, any unbelief mixed in with Abraham's faith?

---

*I argue in more detail for this way of applying the distinction between knowledge and faith in "Knowledge, Belief, and Revelation: A Reply to Patrick Lee," in *Faith and Philosophy*.

The answer to these questions should be clear. What we come to believe is often a matter of what we must *decide* to believe in the face of contrary evidence. So it was with Abraham. On some occasions Abraham just lacked sufficient trust in God to decide to believe him in the face of contrary evidence (Gen. 16:1–4, 17:17–18). However, it is not for those occasions that Abraham is remembered as a hero of faith, but for the other occasions, when he did believe God in the face of contrary evidence. He is a hero of faith because his faith was the result of a moral challenge, a trial, that required a decision.

If, as is often said, faith involves a leap, it is the leap from self-reliance to reliance upon God, precisely because what God says so often conflicts with the conclusions that human beings reach when left to their own experience and reasoning insofar as these leave out God. Abraham had no way of knowing from his own experience and reasoning that "God will provide"; he knew it only by faith in God. So it is with all the main propositions that Christians *know* only by *faith:* that Jesus is God incarnate; that he arose from the grave; that he forgives sins; and that he is coming again. By their own experience and reasoning apart from God, Christians have little evidence in favor of these propositions and much that counts against them. Without a prior, original knowledge of God revealing such things, Christians would face no genuine conflict at all between believing what God reveals and what their own experience and reasoning apart from such knowledge might lead them to think is the case about the identity of Jesus, his resurrection, his grace and forgiveness, and his coming again. But armed with this knowledge of God and His revelation, such a conflict may arise. Still, in proportion to the strength of their faith, believers will manifest what C. S. Lewis calls an "obstinacy in belief." As it turns out in Lewis's essay by this title, the obstinacy is more precisely one in trust or confidence: "You are no longer faced with an argument which demands your assent, but with a Person who demands your confidence" (26). The source of such confidence is that divine person, who is known (as I have argued) not by inference but by direct acquaintance. Says Lewis: "For it seems to us . . . that we have something like a knowledge-by-acquaintance of the Person we believe in, however imperfect and intermittent it may be" (25).

Another Paradigm: St. Paul.   This all-important difference between *knowing* by acquaintance the God who is the object of trust and *believing what God says* is nicely captured by Paul's declaration, "I know whom I have believed and I am sure that he is able to guard until that Day what has been entrusted to me" (2 Tim. 1:12). Paul uses the Greek verb *oida* for "know," which connotes the knowledge of personal acquaintance;

pepisteuka (from *pisteuō*) for "believed"; and *pepeismai* (from *peithō*) for "am sure." Each of these last two verbs includes both "believe" and "trust" in its meaning. The former (*pepisteuka*) has God as its object and can mean either "to trust God" or "to believe God" or both; the latter (*pepeismai*) has a "that" clause, and thus a proposition, as its object. On the certainty that the latter connotes, *The Expositor's Greek Testament* has this to say: "In all the places in which St. Paul uses *pepeismai* he is anxious to leave no doubt as to his own certitude" (vol. 4, 154). Another example of Paul's certainty is his well-known declaration "that neither death, nor life . . . , nor anything else in all creation, will be able to separate us from the love of God in Christ Jesus our Lord (Romans 8:38, 39). In summary, it is one thing for Paul to know the existence of God, another for him to believe with certainty that nothing will separate him from God. The first is knowledge by acquaintance with God; the second is (in my theory of knowledge as justified true belief) knowledge by faith, faith that trusts God for what he says. The first knowledge is natural; the second is revealed.

The Conflict Between Faith and Reason. It is often thought that faith and reason are in logical conflict with each other and that, if we begin with one, we are logically required to give up the other. "When faith and reason clash, let reason go to smash." The sentiment expressed in this waggish quip has led some rationalist skeptics to reject religious belief on behalf of reason and some incautious religious believers to reject reason on behalf of faith. They are equally mistaken. For there is nothing necessarily contradictory in the beliefs that believers accept on God's testimony or in the propositions by which they express their knowledge of God. *What God says* may, of course, conflict with what such believers (and others) would normally conclude from reflection on some of their experiences. For example, from reflection on certain tracts of human experience, both that of believers and of unbelievers, the evidence is compelling that human beings are morally unjust in a rather pervasive and deep-seated way. But God says that those are righteous who have faith in what he says and in what he does in Jesus Christ. There is here no contradiction, for there may be more than one way of being righteous. Again, the evidence is pretty strong that human beings do not live again after they die; but God says there will be a resurrection from the dead, and a new heaven and earth; and Christians believe it—with no contradiction that anyone has ever demonstrated convincingly.

Faith, Unbelief and Knowledge. I have discussed the nature of biblical faith and argued that it must be distinguished from a knowledge of God, which it presupposes. It is important to notice that *unbelief* (the *lack* of faith), which is the biblical antagonist of faith, presupposes just such a knowledge of God, in the same way as faith. The unbeliever, in the Bible, is *not* one who fails to "believe in the existence of God," that is, one who denies *that* God exists. Such a person is rather a fool, according to the Psalms (14:1 and 53:1). No, the *unbeliever* is one who fails to *trust* God or perhaps, more accurately, who actively *distrusts* God. As a consequence, he will not just fail to believe what God says; he will doubt or even disbelieve it. But distrusting God and refusing to believe what God says, the two essential ingredients of unbelief, also presuppose knowing God. You cannot distrust, you cannot disbelieve someone whose existence you do not know. In the Bible, unbelief, like faith, assumes a natural knowledge of God.

How, then, can we account for the fool, who denies that God exists? How can one deny what one knows? The biblical answer in each of the two Psalms cited earlier is that the fool is professedly ignorant because of his moral corruption. The classic New Testament text is Romans 1, which teaches that human beings "by their wickedness suppress the truth"; that is, they suppress "what can be known about God" from "the creation of the world" (1:18–19). Moral corruption, however, is owing to unbelief. If this all sounds paradoxical, so it is. For just as moral corruption stems from unbelief, so moral goodness stems from faith. But moral goodness is a condition of the knowledge of God. So the Bible teaches. "Blessed are the pure in heart, for they shall see God" (Matthew 5:8). Thus, it would seem that without faith, no one can know God; but I have argued that, without knowing God, no one can either believe or disbelieve what God says. Is there really such a knowledge of God that is presupposed by faith? And how is that knowledge possible, if it is a function of moral goodness, and if "there is none that does good, no, not one" (Psalms, 14:3; 53:3)? This problem is the biblical version of the Platonic paradox that knowledge is virtue, referred to in Chapter 1. We shall see that the paradox reappears in St. Augustine and John Calvin; this should be no surprise, for their thinking is rooted in Platonic and biblical ideas.

For now, the main epistemological question is, How do human beings, believers or unbelievers, *know* God, and more particularly, that he exists? The implicit biblical answer to this question is, I have argued, not by faith, that is, by believing what God or humans say, but by a direct acquaintance with him that faith and unbelief must both presuppose. In the biblical view, human beings, both those who believe in God and those who do not, know that God exists in the same natural way, finally, by which they know that there is an external physical world or that there is such a thing as justice or that 2 times 2 is 4. That way is by an *acquaintance* with these things that can only be called immediate and direct, by contrast with the knowledge of testimony and inference. If there is such a thing as a biblical theory of the knowledge of God, or if at least such a theory is implicit in the Bible, this is it, or at least a fundamental part of it.

For an elaboration of that theory of knowing God, we must, of course, turn to Christian philosophers. The philosopher who articulated the first significantly influential Christian theory of knowledge is St. Augustine. In the next three chapters I show how Augustine combines the biblical conception of knowing God that I have defended in this chapter with the Platonic theory of the knowledge of the Good.

3   Faith Seeking Understanding: St. Augustine

St. Augustine was the first great Christian thinker to bring together in a definitive way the biblical concept of faith with the Greek concepts of knowledge and belief. His epistemological synthesis of biblical and Platonic ideas is summed up in the famous formula associated with his name, "faith seeking understanding" (*fides quaerens intellectum*). The formula is not to be found in these exact words in Augustine's writings; it first appears as the original title that St. Anselm gave to his *Proslogion* (as he informs us in its "Preface") over six centuries after Augustine's death. Still, everyone agrees that the ideas captured in the formula not only originated in Augustine, but also characterize his thought. As Vernon Bourke states it, in *The Essential Augustine:* "Augustine's position on the relation of faith and reason influences all the rest of his thinking: it could be argued that Augustinianism is essentially a way of looking at these key notions" (19).

This epistemological synthesis in Augustine joins his ontological synthesis of the biblical God with the ultimate principle of reality (the *archē*), so eagerly sought by the ancient Greek philosophers. Etienne Gilson details the story in *God and Philosophy*. The conspicuous failure of the Greeks was their "failure ... to build up an all-comprehensive philosophical explanation of the world without at the same time losing their religion" (36–37). Plato, as we saw in Chapter 1, does not associate his Forms with the Greek gods. Although he continues to reverence the gods, he does not see them, as he sees the Forms, as ultimate principles of reality. Aristotle finally combines *his* ultimate Form, the prime mover of the universe, with God; the result, however, is a God who is quite unsuited for human worship (29–37). By contrast, "taken in itself, Christianity was not a philosophy. It was the essentially religious doctrine of the salvation of men through Christ" (43).

The Church Fathers put an end to this cleavage between the God of religion and the ultimate principle of philosophy. As Augustine, the greatest of the Fathers, combines faith and reason, so he is the first to combine, in a definitive way, the God of the Bible with the ultimate principle of the universe sought by the Greeks. In *Of True Religion* he writes: "One God alone I worship, the sole principle of all things, and his Wisdom who makes every soul wise, and his Gift whereby all the blessed are blessed" (lv). Here in one statement Augustine, the "Christian Plato," as he has been called, summarizes his metaphysical and epistemological vision. The God of the Bible is both the supreme object of worship and the creative source of all things other than himself; he is also the source, by his Wisdom (i.e., his Son, the *logos*), of all human knowledge and wisdom and, by his Gift (i.e., the Spirit), of human salvation and happiness.

The Problem of Interpreting Augustine

Augustine often distinguishes carefully in his metaphysical thinking what he owes to Greek philosophy from what he owes to Christian revelation in Jesus Christ and the Scriptures. A notable example is his account in the *Confessions* of what he learned from "the books of the Platonists" (VII, 9; 20; Neoplatonists, as they are referred to today). He is not nearly so careful, however, to make analogous distinctions for his epistemological concepts. These also constitute an original fusion of Greek and biblical themes, but a correct understanding of this fusion requires a more complete analysis than he undertakes. Such an analysis will reveal, as I hope to show, some pervasive ambiguities that must be faced on the way to discovering his permanent contribution to a Christian theory of what it is to know God.

Ambiguities. These ambiguities directly affect the meaning of the formula itself, faith seeking understanding. We can get a picture in advance of some of the possible meanings of the formula by applying what we have already learned about faith, knowledge, and belief in our consideration of Plato and the Bible. We have seen that faith is a complex mental state, made up of at least two distinct elements, trust and belief; and that the object of trust is, in the case of its primary occurrence in human testimony, a person who is someone known by acquaintance to one who trusts.

We have not yet examined the term *understanding* that appears in the formula, but we shall soon see that it, too, carries a range of different meanings in Augustine. Some of these reduce to "knowledge," either by acquaintance or by inference. Following what I have called Plato's *Republic* approach, Augustine expressly excludes belief on testimony from being knowledge, as we shall see. In addition, the sense of knowledge as "comprehension" takes on an increasingly larger role in Augustine's later writings, as we shall also see. This meaning of "understand" is quite prominent among in the listings in the *Oxford English Dictionary*; and even this meaning contains an ambiguity between understanding the *character* or *nature* of something like an *art* or a *person* and understanding the *meaning* of *words*, which is something else again. The Latin *intellectus* (and the Greek *epistēmē*) reflects a similar range of meanings. So what does Augustine mean, faith seeks understanding? Which aspect of faith seeks which kind of understanding? And what is it for one state of mind (faith) to *seek* another (understanding)? These are the sorts of questions we need to answer in order to understand (!) Augustine.

It is interesting to note that Augustine seems to have himself misunderstood (i.e., misinterpreted) one of the key texts in Scripture that he cites in support of his view of faith and understanding. The text is Isaiah 9:7, "If you will not believe, surely you will not be established" (R.S.V.), which translates the original Hebrew. The *Septuagint* mistakenly translates it: "If you will not believe, you will not understand." Although Augustine is aware of both the original Hebrew sense and the Septuagint translation, in *On Christian Doctrine* he adopts the latter, glossing the difference between them: "Both of them nevertheless contain something of great value for the discerning reader" (II, xii, 17). He misses what Keil and Delitzsche, in their *Commentary on the Old Testament, Isaiah*, call a "play on words" in the original (specifically on two forms of *emunah*, the Hebrew word for faith): "If Judah did not *hold fast* to its God, it would lose its *fast hold* by losing its country, the ground beneath its feet" (vol. 1, 212). Augustine thereby also fails to focus on faith as *trust*, which the term translated in most versions as "believe" here connotes. James Moffatt translates the verse: "If your faith does not hold, you will never hold out," which not only reflects the play on words but also more clearly suggests that it is the people of Judah's *trust* in God, their *belief in* him, that is the condition for their deliverance from the coalition of kings. Augustine's reading of the second verb in the text as "understand," combined with his use of "believe" instead of the more accurate "have faith" for the first verb, reflects his tendency when discussing faith to emphasize its intellectual element, belief, instead of its volitional-emotional element, trust. He certainly does not ignore the latter, of course, as we shall see.

Knowledge and Belief. The most obvious sense of the formula is precisely this intellectually oriented one, and we shall begin our effort to discover its various meanings in Augustine by exploring this sense. Augustine writes: "Now it is faith to believe that which you do not yet see; and the reward of this faith is to see that which you believe" (*Sermon 43*). In the terms we have been using, *faith* here means the belief on someone's testimony that some proposition is true, a proposition representing some event or object that we have not seen for ourselves. Understanding, by contrast, is knowledge by acquaintance—seeing an event or object for oneself. Here Augustine combines Plato's *Meno* account of belief based on testimony (as I interpreted it earlier) with his *Republic* approach to knowledge as acquaintance. This combination permeates the whole of Augustine's epistemology, and therefore also the several senses of "faith seeking understanding" in his writings. We should *seek* to know by our own acquaintance what it is we believe on the testimony of others.

Augustine also *opposes* belief and knowledge in just the way Plato does in the *Republic*. This opposition is very clear in *The Usefulness of Belief*, his most sustained discussion of the two ideas. Belief is fallible and knowledge is infallible: "There are... in men three mental activities, closely related but needing to be distinguished, viz., knowing, believing and holding an opinion. If these are considered in themselves the first is always faultless, the second is sometimes so, the third never" (xi, 25). Knowledge is thus always true, belief sometimes true, opinion never. Augustine evaluates holding an opinion harshly not because opinion is necessarily false, but because he means by *holding an opinion* "being opinionated," which he defines as the attitude of those who "think they know what they do not know." It is an attitude that, for Augustine as for Plato, manifests a fundamental error. Knowledge and belief, then, are the only two warranted cognitive states, for knowledge is always true, but belief is sometimes true as well.

In the same passage Augustine attributes knowledge to reason and belief to authority (what we have all along been calling *testimony*). Each of these—knowing and believing—requires clarification. Augustine gives an example of belief: "I believe that most wicked conspirators were once put to death by the virtuous Cicero. Not only do I not know that, but I am quite certain that I cannot possibly know it" (xi, 25). He cannot know it, of course, because it was an event that occurred 400 years before he was born. Clearly by knowing Augustine here means being an *eyewitness* to an event (which requires sensation as well as reason), in contrast with taking something on *the word of others*.

The contrast is present in numerous passages throughout Augustine's writings. A very important one of these is the section in his *Retractations*, in which he comments on the paragraph from *The Usefulness of Belief* quoted earlier. At the beginning of this paragraph Augustine refers to "those [in this life] who have already found the truth, whom we must judge to be entirely blessed" (xi, 25). In the *Retractations* Augustine corrects this by saying that only those who in the *next* life see God "face to face" are "entirely blessed." He carefully

points out, however, that he does not mean to deny that they have already seen God in this life; but such vision is "through a mirror in an obscure manner," in accord with St. Paul's description in 1 Corinthians 13:12, a text he is fond of discussing. Thus seeing God is possible in this life; it is the beginning, however faint, of the perfect vision of God in the next life: "For in this life knowledge, however extensive, does not constitute complete happiness, because that part of it which is unknown is by far incomparably greater" (I, xiii, 2). That there is knowledge of God already in this life is a claim of great importance to which we shall return. For the moment, the point is that, for Augustine, knowledge in its proper sense is *vision*, seeing for oneself (intellectually or by sensation), in contrast with belief, which is not.

This crucial difference between knowing and believing comes out in the following related passages from the same paragraph in *The Usefulness of Belief:*

> Suppose someone thinks he knows the fact I have just mentioned about Cicero. Nothing prevents him from learning it, though it cannot be a matter of knowledge strictly speaking. But if he does not know the difference between true knowledge, i.e., rational knowledge, and belief in what has been profitably handed down to posterity either by report or in writing, he certainly errs, and there is no error without disgrace.... But if one diligently considers the difference between thinking one knows, and believing upon authority what one knows one does not know, one will avoid the charge of error and of boorish pride. (xi, 25)

Thus, the difference between knowledge and belief is so important that failure to observe it may subject one to the danger of "error and boorish pride."

No Justified True Belief Approach in Augustine. The same paragraph also contains, however, the surprising claim that "knowledge always implies belief, and so does opinion" (as do at least two other passages: *Soliloquies* I, 3, 8 and *The Teacher* xi, 37). The claim immediately suggests that there might be a trace of the justified true belief approach to knowledge in Augustine's thinking. The suggestion is mistaken, however. Everything else Augustine says here and elsewhere contradicts it. What he probably means by the claim is that belief *precedes* knowledge; this would also accord with his claim about the temporal priority of belief. In other words, if I know anything, I must earlier have believed it. The formula, faith seeking understanding, also implies this temporal priority; *beginning* with faith, with something we believe on testimony, we then *seek* an understanding (or knowledge) of what we believe.

Nowhere does Augustine even consider that knowledge is a *form of belief*. The whole tenor of his thought is to distinguish sharply between them, in the way we have seen. It is important to keep this in mind in what follows, for I shall not always be making a point of it, that when Augustine talks of knowing he means knowing by acquaintance and when he talks of believing he means believing on testimony; and the latter is not another way of knowing, but a way of *not* knowing and to be contrasted with it. Augustine is oblivious to the Plato of the *Theaetetus*; instead, he is, par excellence, the channel to us of Plato's *Republic* approach to knowledge and belief. Very likely he was not a student of Plato's *writings*, but only of the Plato he found in the writings of the Neoplatonists. These are characterized by the aspirational and religious teachings of Plato, not his more analytic and epistemological investigations. The latter were picked up and advanced by the Stoics and the Academics.

Augustine recognizes, of course, that we often speak of knowing the things we only believe on testimony. In another *Retractation* to our paragraph in *The Usefulness of Belief*, he is very careful to recognize the common use of the term *know*; he is also very careful to resist this use as any kind of guide to his own theory of what knowledge "strictly speaking" is. In the paragraph he says: "Our knowledge we owe to reason, our beliefs to authority." In the *Retractation* he comments:

> In popular speech that would seem to mean that we shrink from saying that we *know* what we believe on the testimony of suitable witnesses. It should not be taken in this sense. When we speak strictly we mean, by *knowing*, certain rational comprehension. But when we are using words as they are used in ordinary parlance, as divine Scripture uses them, we do not hestiate to say that we *know* what we perceive with the bodily senses, or believe on the testimony of witnesses worthy of trust; and at the same time we understand the difference between the two uses of the word *knowing*. (I, xiii, 3)

Thus ordinary use of the term *knowledge* often conceals from us what knowledge really is and how it differs from belief. Unlike contemporary philosophers, such as H. H. Price whom we discussed in Chapter 1, Augustine is not impressed by the "muddle" of common usage nor inclined to take very seriously, for the purpose of a theory of knowledge, that in such usage knowledge sometimes implies belief.

Is Augustine a Rationalist?   While we have this *Retractation* before us, we should notice and clarify another important aspect of Augustine's epistemology that it reveals. "Strictly speaking," Augustine limits the scope of knowledge to "certain, rational comprehension," a limitation that betrays the influence of the rationalist aspect of Plato's epistemology. This limitation, of course, marks knowledge off, for Augustine as for Plato, not only from belief on the basis of testimony but also from "what we perceive with the bodily senses," as the passage clearly indicates. Thus, a case is to be made for the claim that Augustine is a rationalist who, like Plato, his philosophical mentor, denies the status of knowledge not only to belief on testimony but also to perception by the senses. Such a case can also be built on Augustine's account of sense knowledge in his *Literal Commentary on Genesis*. According to this account, the senses only "announce" physical objects to the mind, which knows them only by itself producing *images* of these objects as the only objects that it then knows (or sees) (XII, xi, 22).

Still, Augustine firmly rejects the skeptical implications that attend such rationalism. In *On the Trinity* he writes: "But far be it from us to doubt the truth of what we have learned by the bodily senses; since by them we have learned to know the heaven and the earth, and those things in them which are known to us, so far as He who created both us and them has willed them to be within our knowledge" (XV, xii; see also *The City of God* XIX, 18). It is essential for understanding Augustine's view of faith and reason *not* to confuse the very clear line he draws between knowledge and belief on testimony with the difference he acknowledges between rational knowledge and sense perception. As we have observed, Augustine (like Plato before him) even illustrates the distinction between knowledge and belief on testimony from within the realm of sense perception, when he distinguishes between seeing Cicero for oneself and believing that he lived on the testimony of others. He also (again like Plato) explains knowledge as mental vision on the model of our sensible vision of physical objects. If it is difficult to give a satisfactory account of physical vision (as indeed it is, no less for modern than for ancient epistemologists), this fact does not diminish the immediacy of such vision serving as a model for understanding the immediacy of rational knowledge.

So we can distinguish on *each level* (physical and intellectual), says Augustine in his *Letter to Paulina*, seeing for ourselves from believing on the testimomy of others:

> Is it enough to say that there is this difference between seeing and believing, that we see what is present and believe what is absent? Perhaps it really is enough, if by the word present in this

connection we understand what is an object of our bodily sense
or mental faculties. . . . The things which are not present to our
faculties are believed if the authority on which they are offered
seems trustworthy. (*Letter 147;* see also *The City of God,* XI, 3)

Thus the fundamental distinction in Augustine is not that between
reason and sensation, but between seeing and believing: seeing by
reason or sensation, and believing on the testimony of others who
have seen in either of those two ways.

The passage from *On the Trinity* cited earlier continues:

> Far be it from us, too, to deny that we know what we have
> learned by the testimony of others: otherwise we know not that
> there is an ocean; . . . we know not that those men were, and their
> works, which we learned by reading history; . . . lastly, we know
> not at what place or from whom we have been born: since in all
> these things we have believed the testimony of others. And if it
> is most absurd to say this, then we must confess, that not only
> our own senses, but those of other persons also, have added
> very much indeed to our knowledge. (XV, xii)

As Myles Burnyeat points out in "Wittgenstein and Augustine *De
Magistro,*" this passage is "in flat contradiction with" those other passages in which Augustine *denies* that we *know* what others tell us.
These other passages include the one about Cicero in *The Usefulness of
Belief* discussed earlier, one of his *Eighty-Three Different Questions* we
will discuss presently (48), and his pointed defense of believing the
testimony of others in *Confessions* VI, 5.

My own interpretation is that these other passages give us
Augustine's settled view that knowledge differs from belief in the
same way that seeing something for oneself differs from accepting it
on the word of others. The passages that make this point are numerous and they are found in contexts where Augustine's clear intent is
to distinguish knowledge from belief in just this way. In the passage
from *On the Trinity,* however, his purpose is rather the polemical one
of warding off the implications of skepticism ("the Academic philosophy"). Still, it must be conceded that Augustine cannot seem to ward
off those implications without granting to belief on testimony the
very status of knowledge he otherwise denies it. In ordinary language, of course, we do the very same thing, as Augustine recognizes
in the passage cited earlier from *Retractations* (I, xiii, 3). Now a *justified true belief* approach to knowledge is precisely the approach that
can accomodate this fact. As Burnyeat observes, however, Augustine,

unlike Plato, does not seem to be aware of knowledge as entailing justification (21). In any event, I conclude that Augustine is a rationalist only in the special sense in which a rationalist is one who limits knowledge to reason's seeing the truth of anything *for itself*, regardless of whether it sees it by itself alone or by way of the senses.

Three Levels of Vision.   For Augustine, then, *seeing for oneself* is the basic cognitive attitude. In the *Literal Commentary on Genesis*, he distinguishes "three levels of vision." By *corporeal* vision we see the words on a page that express the command to love our neighbor; by *spiritual* vision we have a mental image of our neighbor who at the moment is absent from us; and by *intellectual* vision we see with the mind incorporeal things, such as the love that is commanded us (XII, 6, 15). Because spiritual vision is simply corporeal vision retained in the memory, the three levels of vision reduce to two: corporeal and intellectual. (In Chapter 8 of the *Letter 147* just cited, Augustine explicitly extends knowledge to what we *remember* having seen.) Following Plato, Augustine affirms that there are also just two kinds of objects, "one of those things which the mind perceives by the bodily senses; the other, of those which it perceives by itself" (*On the Trinity*, XV, xii).

Temporal Priority of Belief, Qualitative Priority of Knowing.   We have now established the difference between faith as *belief* and understanding as *knowledge*, between taking on testimony and seeing for ourselves. In this sense, the meaning of *seeking* in the formula should also be clear. Augustine may well have *sought* to see Alexandria on the basis of reports about it. He certainly wants to see love, that is, to understand it, because he has heard (and believed) the command to love his neighbor. And he wants to see God, of whom he has also heard.

Why? Why do human beings want to see new places of which they have heard, to see the virtues to which they aspire, to see God? The motivation in every case is the same; to see for oneself is *better* than to believe on the word of another. In *Divine Providence and the Problem of Evil* Augustine writes: "Likewise, with regard to the acquiring of knowledge, we are of necessity led in a twofold manner: by authority and by reason. In point of time, authority is first; in the order of reality, reason is prior. What takes precedence in operation is one thing; what is more highly prized as an object of desire is something else" (II, 9, 26). This passage is one of several in which Augustine formulates his famous "twofold path" (see also *Answer to Skeptics* III, 20, 43; *Of True Religion* xxiv, 45). In each passage, Augustine nicely juxtaposes a *priority of faith* (in the order of time, believing others precedes knowing for ourselves) with a *priority of knowing* (which is "more highly prized as an object of desire"). The latter priority is a *qualitative priority* of knowing by acquaintance over belief on testimony (different from a *logical* priority to be discussed later). The qualitative priority of knowledge is an echo of Plato's evaluation of an eyewitness account as better than hearsay.

Like Plato before him (and unlike many philosophers who neglect the topic) Augustine spells out the implications of this priority of knowing for education. In *The Teacher*, for example, he asks the pointed question: "Who is so foolishly curious as to send his son to school to learn what the teacher thinks?" (xiv, 45). In true Socratic fashion, Augustine holds that the aim of teaching is not for the teacher to hand down his beliefs, let alone his opinions, but to get his students to *see* the truth which he, presumably, already sees; they must come to know reality for themselves, as he does already. Thus the formula, faith seeking understanding, contains Augustine's approach to education as well as to religion.

Applications of the Formula.   So far we have considered only an obvious sense of faith seeking understanding, that is, *belief* seeking *knowledge*; we *seek* to see for ourselves what we have believed on the testimony of others. We need now to probe the complexities and limitations of the formula to discover the various ways it can be applied and understood. I propose to do this by following the classification of beliefs that Augustine provides in one of his *Eighty-Three Different Questions*, according to "three kinds of objects":

> There are three kinds of objects of belief. One kind consists of those that are always believed and never understood: such as history in every case, running through the course of temporal and human events. Second, there are those objects which, as soon as they are believed, are understood: such are all human uses of reason, in the field of numbers or in any of the academic studies. Third are those objects that are first believed and later on understood: such are those items that cannot be understood about divine matters except by the clean of heart, a condition achieved by obeying the commandments which have to do with proper living. (Q. 48)

By "objects of belief" Augustine does not refer here, as we have done, to the propositions that represent realities, but to the realities themselves. Still, it will be easy (and even necessary, on occasion) to distinguish Augustine's "objects of belief" as real objects in the universe from the propositions that represent them.

"Objects Always Believed and Never Understood"

Historical Events.   Let us begin with the first kind of object of belief here identified, historical events. More exactly, these are the events prior to those past events in our own lives that we once saw and still remember. The striking, if obvious, point Augustine makes about such events is, as he says, that they can *never* be known. Here, then, is a large group of beliefs that we *cannot* seek to replace with the more desirable state of knowledge, that is, seeing them for ourselves. And so it is not the case that faith (in the sense of belief) *always* seeks knowledge; in some cases, the most obvious one being historical events, it is impossible. For these events, our dependence upon the testimony of others is absolute; and what we attain from them is never knowledge but belief.

For Christians, the implication of this dependence is startling, because Christianity is a religion rooted in historical events. Not only does history have a beginning, a middle and an end, but God also spoke in a special way in the past, to and through an ancient people, the Jews; and he acted through their generations in a special way, culminating in his own incarnation in Jesus Christ, who lived on earth many years ago. It is sometimes said that Augustine's great contribution to epistemology is to rescue the cognitive status of belief. Although inferior to knowledge, it is nevertheless *essential* to human life in general, but especially in religion. In an important way, Christianity rests on the testimony of those ancient authors of Scripture whom none of us can ever know, at least in this life.

Our essential dependence on the testimony of others for what happened in the past does not imply, of course, the irrelevance of reason and reasoning to what we thus believe—no more for Augustine than for us. For testimony handed down from the past needs to be evaluated and interpreted, especially because of its incompleteness and the conflicts that appear within it. Augustine recognizes this and affirms the need for a rational evaluation of such testimony. He himself offers an impressive model of such evaluation in the first ten books of *The City of God*, where he rejects the charge brought by pagan writers against Christianity that it was responsible for the fall of Rome and argues for an entirely different explanation of the events. Although there was no "quest for the historical Jesus" in Augustine's day, he would doubtless have endorsed the modern examination of the testimonial evidence in the Gospels to the words and works of Christ.

Physical Objects.   It is notable that Augustine does not include physical objects in this first division of beliefs, because we are also dependent upon the testimony of others for learning the *present* existence and nature of many of these—all of them that lie beyond our own experience. This dependence, however, is only a *practical* dependence, quite unlike the absolute dependence on testimony that characterizes our beliefs about the past. We can come to see for ourselves many physical things in our present world, which suggests that Augustine did not think of sense objects as *inherently* objects of belief, as he did of historical events.

This suggestion accords, incidentally, with our earlier conclusion that Augustine is not a Platonic rationalist in his theory of sense perception. We can aspire to see, and therefore to know, as much of the present physical world around us (people, places, and things) as we like, and thereby transform the testimony of others about these objects into personal acquaintance with them. The limitations on our aspirations are only the practical ones of our health, wealth, and other like limitations of our earthly existence. Of course, we cannot be in two places at once, and that is not just a practical limitation; but this is beside the present point. It does not explain why Augustine never managed to get to Alexandria, or why few Americans manage to get to Rome. No one, however, can aspire to visit the past—except on the testimony of others who were there. Historical events are indeed in a class by themselves as objects of belief.

Correlation of "Objects of Belief" with "Levels of Vision."   Having said all this, however, it still does make sense, from another point of view, to place events in the historical past *and* physical objects *together* in a division of their own. This point of view is the temporal priority of knowledge to belief. For both present physical objects and past events, someone somewhere must *know* them at a time prior to their ever being testified of to others (who then have to begin with belief about them and, in the case of past events, end with it). Augustine, however, takes no special notice of this temporal priority of knowledge to belief, obvious though it is.

His formula, of course, makes the *believer's believing* temporally prior to his or her *knowing*—I believe *in order to* know; and he duly notes *that* priority, as we have seen. But it is also the case that someone *else* must first have known what a believer believes, before the believer can believe on the testimony of someone else that there even is something one might seek to know—with the exception, of course, of historical events. And in this sense, the believer's *belief* is temporally *posterior* to someone else's *knowledge*. If no one had ever known

Cicero by sight and testified about him, Augustine living many years later would have had no testimony about Cicero to believe. Likewise, in his own time, unless someone else had seen Alexandria and testified about it, Augustine would have had no report about that city to believe, which might have interested him in seeing the city for himself. So belief precedes knowledge (in the *believer*, who believes in order to understand), but knowledge (in *someone else*, who testifies of what he or she knows) also precedes the believer's belief based on the testimony of the one who knows.

The Logical Priority of Knowledge to Belief

Which, then, comes first? Are belief and knowledge sometimes like the chicken and the egg? Yes, although their relationship is still more complex than that. Before discussing the other two classifications of belief, we should pause to explore this complexity; it will apply as well to those classifications when we come to them. We are now correlating historical events and corporeal objects outside the believer's present experience, remember, from the point of view that the believer's belief about either of these presupposes the temporally prior knowledge of someone else who testifies to them. But this priority, we should now observe, is a logical one as well. Augustine's belief on testimony about Cicero or Alexandria is logically impossible without someone else's knowledge of these. No one can believe on testimony what no one else has ever known.

Augustine appears, however, to hold an even stronger thesis, namely, that one cannot believe on testimony what *one oneself* has not first known. We may distinguish two stages in his argument for this thesis. He argues first that we cannot believe the testimony of someone else unless we first of all know the *meaning of the words* in which that testimony is expressed. It is a point he grants a hypothetical opponent who disputes the priority of faith: "My opponent too . . . has something when he says: 'I would understand in order that I may believe.' Certainly what I am now saying, I say with the object that those may believe who do not yet believe. Nevertheless, unless they understand what I am saying, they cannot believe" (*Sermon 43*). The point is obvious, and hardly needs to be argued; Augustine cannot believe a report about Alexandria unless he first knows the meaning of *Alexandria* as the proper name of a city, of *city* as the general name for the kind of thing Alexandria is, and of many other words as well. How did he come to know the meaning of all these words?

Augustine's answer to this new question brings us to the second stage of his argument for the priority of knowledge to belief. He presents this argument in *The Teacher*, a dialogue that Augustine purportedly conducts with Adeodatus, his philosophical teenage son. The main question of the dialogue is slightly different: What is the function of language in learning and teaching? Augustine's answer to that question, however, implies an answer to the present question, How do we learn the meaning of words? Let us see how this works out. How do words function in learning and teaching? In short, says Augustine, they are meaningless sounds that become meaningful (i.e., they become *words*) when these sounds are transformed into *signs* of the objects before us. In "St. Augustine on Signs" R. A. Markus observes that this thesis—that language functions as a sign to our minds of the reality it knows—is original with Augustine:

> For no [earlier] writer is the theory of signs primarily a theory of language, nor is reflection on language carried on in terms of 'signs'. . . . Words are for Augustine, signs *par excellence*, and his theory of signs is meant to be, from the start, a theory of language as well as of other types of signs. In this consists the originality of his reflection on meaning, and its ability to focus so many of his interests. (66)

But seeing words as signs of things is misleading in an important way, as we shall discover presently; so that Markus's observation about Augustine's originality is of more than historical interest.

For it turns out that, according to Augustine, vocal sounds cannot even function as signs of objects unless we know those objects first. Augustine illustrates this claim with an example (of a corporeal object) from the Bible. Suppose I read, "Their *saraballae* were not changed" (Dan. 3:27). If my teacher tries to explain the strange word *saraballae* to me by defining it as a head covering, I still will not know what it is unless I know what a head and a covering are. And how do I come to know these objects? Says Augustine:

> Knowledge of such things comes to me not when they are named by others but when I actually see them. When these two syllables first struck my ear, *ca-put*, I was as ignorant of what they meant as I was of the meaning of *saraballae* when I first heard or read it. But when the word, *caput*, was frequently repeated, observing when it was said, I discovered it was the name of a thing well known to me from my having seen it. Before I made that discovery the word was merely a sound to me. It became a sign when I had learned the thing of which it

was the sign. And this I had learned not from signs but from seeing the actual object. So the sign is learned from knowing the thing, rather than vice versa. (x, 33)

So we must first "see an actual object," which is the same as "knowing the thing," *before* we know the word (i.e., know a sound as a sign) that others teach us.

What we come to know, then, is the *language*, not the *objects* of which it provides signs; those objects I "learned not from signs but from seeing the actual object. So the sign is learned from knowing the thing, rather than vice versa." In other words, my original knowledge of physical objects (and temporal events) around me "comes to me not when they are named by others but when I actually see them." Now to take the vocal sounds of other people as the signs of the objects I already know is to trust these people; and that is faith! What Augustine says here, thus, amounts to the claim that knowledge is logically prior to faith. We cannot believe on the testimony of others that some vocal sound is a sign of some physical object unless we know that object first. (Note that the issue is not whether a certain vocal sound is the correct word for an object, but whether some vocal sound must be heard for the object to be known.)

The Origin of Knowledge. But, is Augustine correct in this account? Does anyone really see an object, in the sense of know it, prior to or apart from having learned some *name* for it from others whom one trusts? It would hardly seem so. A year and one-half old child sees many objects in some weak sense of the term *see*, but we only give the child credit for *knowing* them when it can either say the names it has learned for each one or point to them when it hears the names spoken by someone else. The study of feral children, beginning with J. Itard's *The Wild Boy of Aveyron*, also counts against Augustine's view. So, too, for adults; it is hard to see that even they really know what some strange new object is until they have given a name to it (or learned its name from others) that classifies it with other objects like it. Hence it seems more likely that our original knowledge of physical objects depends as much on our hearing (i.e., on our believing) the language that others use for those objects (and that we then come to use ourselves) as it does on our directing our visual attention to those objects; and thus that our knowledge of objects is not prior (temporally or causally) to our believing what we hear others say, but that such knowledge is instead the mysterious product of our simultaneously hearing what other human beings say and attending to an object in our visual field.

Asking whether original knowledge precedes faith or faith knowledge, then, is like asking whether the chicken or the egg came first. But perhaps it is even worse, for the relationship is not one of temporal or causal priority but one of causal interdependence. For it seems just as plausible to claim that our knowing (or coming to know) physical objects depends on our believing others who teach us the language, as that our believing others who teach us the language depends on our coming to know the physical objects in our presence. The two processes are not only simultaneous but also necessary conditions for each other. In response, Augustine might insist that the *intelligibilty* of the content of this original believing depends just as much on our taking the vocal sounds of our parents and teachers as *words*, that is, as signs of the objects we *see*, as our knowing these objects depends on our faith in those sounds of our parents and teachers. Fair enough, but then the knowledge of objects implied by this intelligibility of language depends on our faith in other human beings for the necessary words as much as it does on our own seeing those objects; and thus the relationship between faith and reason in our originally coming to know objects is more complex than Augustine's account suggests.

How did Augustine come to overlook this complexity? By confusing, it seems, the *origin* of knowledge with later *additions* to it. He says: "The utmost value I can attribute to words is this. They bid us look for things, but they do not show them to us so that we may know them. He alone teaches me anything who sets before my eyes, or one of the other senses, or my mind, the things which I desire to know" (xi, 36). The subordination of the importance of words to knowledge implied here presupposes that the believer who desires to know *already* knows some things and *already* understands the function of language as a sign of those objects in reality that he or she does not yet know but desires to know. That is why those words can "only bid him look for things" but "not show them to him so that he may know them." Hence one must, by some further effort, turn one's faith in the testimony of others expressed in these words into one's own knowledge, to express which, of course, one needs to use the same or similar words (another point that Augustine ignores). But Augustine goes on to say that his effort will be assisted by the teacher, "who sets before my eyes, or one of the other senses, or my mind, the things which I desire to know." This effort of our teachers is necessary, however, only when we are *first* learning the language, when we are *first* coming to acquire our knowledge of objects. Subsequently, we can make the effort in question ourselves; Augustine can *himself* go to Alexandria and "set it before" his eyes, because the word

Alexandria used by others now (at this later time in Augustine's life), indeed, does no more than "bid him look for" something without "showing it to him so that he may know it."

Perhaps the theory itself of words as *signs* of things misled Augustine. Markus points out that, prior to Augustine's taking words as signs, the theory of signs in antiquity was always a theory of inference (p. 66); for example, when we say that smoke is a sign of fire, we imply that we may infer fire from smoke. Can we then infer objects from words conceived of as signs of these objects? It seems that we can, for when we hear reports of Rome or Alexandria, we may infer from these reports that these cities exist. We can also infer words from an object; that is, if we do not know its name, we can infer from seeing it that it probably has a name. But it is not nearly so clear that such an inference occurs when we first come, as children, to know what objects are from hearing our parents use the names for those objects; for there does not seem to be a causal relationship between the objects and their names, such as that which underlies our inferring fire from smoke.

We can ignore here, however, the question of the final validity of the theory of language as a sign of things. All we need to note is that the theory tends to subordinate signs (the words) to what they signify (objects) as effects are subordinated to their causes. Whatever is a sign of something else leads us to think of that something else as the more important thing, for it is the cause; and the sign of it is only a sign, an indicator, a clue. To paraphrase Augustine: "The utmost value I can attribute to smoke is this. It bids us look for fire, but does not show fire to us so that we may know it. He alone teaches me fire who sets it before my eyes, or one of my other senses, or my mind, for that is what I desire to know—not the smoke." Possibly, then, this *picture* of words as signs, as mere indicators of something else, that is, of the real objects that we know or want to know, leads Augustine to subordinate the role of words to things in explaining the origin of knowledge.

Degrees of Completeness and Clarity. While we are correlating events in the past with physical objects, we should note one more important feature of anyone's original knowledge of these: that such knowledge will vary considerably in both clarity and extent from individual to individual, and even within an individual from time to time. The variation will occur whether we speak of knowing, understanding, or comprehending such events and objects. Thus the person who has taken the way to Larissa only once, and some time ago, may still know the way, but not nearly as well—that is, as clearly or completely—as the one who has taken it many times, including just yesterday. So, too, with other physical objects and events; we all know many of these, that they exist or occur, and we understand what they are like—with more or less clarity and completeness, but the trained and careful observer, say the detective, the scientist, or poet, each in his or her own way, knows—or comprehends—them more clearly and completely than the rest of us. Now because the believer's belief on testimony presupposes the knowledge of someone else, the clarity and completeness of that person's belief, it would seem, can be no better than the clarity and completeness of the knowledge of the one on whose testimony that belief depends. This restriction will not hold, of course, for the import or significance of the belief itself. For example, Miss Marple, the detective, may see the implication of a certain fact she believes for solving a murder that quite escapes the maid who saw and reported it.

We can now conclude our discussion of Augustine's first kind of object of belief by summarizing what we have found to be two important features of anyone's belief about the past (or about distant sense objects in the present) that is based on testimony. First, such belief depends on the knowledge of those events or objects possessed by someone else; and second, such belief will be no clearer or more extensive than this knowledge on which it depends. These two features will apply as well to the second and third divisions of belief. We turn now to the second.

"Objects Which, as Soon as They Are Believed, Are Understood"

Incorporeal Objects.   What does it mean for faith (belief) to seek understanding (knowledge) of incorporeal objects? Take, for example, the objects of mathematics. I once heard my parents or teachers say that twice 2 is 4; and as soon as I *believed* them, or more precisely, the proposition expressed by their sentences, I came to see, to know, the relationship between these numbers which that proposition represents. But I would not have been able to see that reality unless I had *understood* what my teachers said, and how could I do that without directing my attention to the objects themselves? But still, Augustine suggests, my mental state of belief gets transformed into that of knowledge *as soon as* I understand the words that express the proposition; and I understood those words as soon as I saw the objects that they signify, viz., the numbers and their relationship. As it is for numbers, so—according to Augustine—it is also for the objects of moral knowledge, for example, the virtues of love and justice, and for the objects of metaphysical inquiry, such as existence, essences, and properties (*Confessions* IV, 16; X, 9, 10).

Corporeal Objects, Incorporeal Objects, and the Mind.   But, it may be asked, how does this description of our coming to know incorporeal objects by believing the words for them uttered by others differ from the description we developed earlier of our coming to know corporeal objects on believing the words we hear others utter for them? The answer is, there is no essential difference. Both our coming to know sense objects and our coming to know numbers are the products of faith in the language of our elders combined in a mysterious way with the attention of our mind to the object in question. The only difference is the relatively incidental one that in the case of sense objects our sense organs are involved, whereas in the case of incorporeal objects they are not. Thus Augustine's description of the second class of objects of belief as those that we understand as soon as they are believed does not *by itself* pick out these objects from sense objects. It does, of course, pick out both of these from historical events, which can only be believed and never known. But clearly Augustine's way of classifying objects of belief breaks down.

The key difference between sense objects and incorporeal objects as objects of belief is rather that the beliefs we have about them are derived from different ways of knowing, the former by the senses, the latter without them. Like Plato before him, Augustine regards human reason as fitted for *seeing* incorporeal objects, just as our senses are fitted for *seeing* physical objects. He also believes that reason is, ultimately, the *only* faculty of knowing, so that, even for sense objects, it is not strictly speaking the senses that know these objects, but reason *by way of* the senses. This view leads Augustine on occasion to say, as we have seen, that images intervene between the mind and the physical object it sees. By contrast, he says, no images come between the mind and its incorporeal objects. In his famous inventory of the mind in Book X of the *Confessions*, for example, Augustine says of these incorporeal entities: "Of these things it is not images that I carry about, but the things themselves. . . . I have not retained the image while leaving the reality outside" (X, ix, 16). In some way, then, suggests Augustine, incorporeal objects can themselves be in the mind, whereas corporeal ones cannot.

This way of understanding reason's knowledge or vision of the objects of the incorporeal world reflects Plato's *Republic* approach, the essence of which is the immediacy of the contact between mind and object. Physical objects do not literally *enter* our reason when it knows them, for they are material in nature and reason is not. On the other hand, it seems plausible that incorporeal objects might do just that—literally enter our reason, when they are known by it; for reason, like these objects, is also an incorporeal thing. We can put stones into a bag, but not into the mind; we can have only the images of both stones and bag in our mind. But perhaps we *can* put numbers and virtues into our minds, so that when we do, "it is not the images that I carry about, but the things themselves." Here, then, is the critical difference between sensible and nonsensible objects. The latter seem to have the same kind of incorporeal nature as the mind itself.

Illumination vs. Recollection.   This model provokes the question, Where are these entities of the incorporeal world before we come to know them? This is a difficult question, for as incorporeal objects, these objects are not anywhere in particular; this is what is meant by calling them *universals* (as do the medievals, whose disputes over them are well known). Either they are in the mind before they are known or they are not. If they are in the mind, why do we not just see them immediately, quickly, and with no effort at all? If, on the other hand, they are not in the mind, how does the mind become acquainted with them, which is what *knowledge* of them is, for both Plato and Augustine?

Plato resolved the dilemma in favor of the former alternative. Universals have always been in our minds, but we are initially ignorant of them because the mind forgot them when the soul was plunged into the body at birth. Learning them, or *coming* to know them, is a process of recollection (*Phaedo* 76). Augustine, however, rejects the previous existence of the soul implied by this doctrine. Still, in his theory of divine illumination he too seems to hold that universals are in the mind. In this theory, learning can still be seen as recollection, but, as Ronald Nash states it, in *The Light of the Mind: St. Augustine's Theory of Knowledge*, such learning is "a remembering of the *present*" (83). This is what Augustine suggests in his *Retractation* to the *Soliloquies*:

> When even untrained persons, suitably questioned, are able to return correct answers about some of the arts, a more credible reason is that they have according to their natural capacity the presence of the light of eternal reason. Hence they catch a glimpse of immutable truth. The reason is not that they once knew it and have forgotten, as Plato and others like him have thought. (I, 4; cited by Nash, 83–84)

In this model, when we come to know universals, we do so in virtue of the divine light that shines on them in our minds, which is "where" they are, because they truly are everywhere.

Augustine has another model for explaining our knowledge of incorporeal objects, which is that of the "inner teacher," who is Christ himself, the *logos* of God. He introduces both models side by side in

The Teacher, following his explanation of how language functions in our coming to know physical objects, which we discussed earlier:

> Concerning universals of which we can have knowledge, we do not listen to anyone speaking and making sounds outside ourselves. We listen to Truth which presides over our minds within us, though of course we may be bidden to listen by someone using words. *Our real Teacher* is he who is so listened to, who is said to dwell in the inner man, namely *Christ,* that is, the unchangeable power and eternal wisdom of God. (xi, 38 [emphasis added])

> But when we have to do with things which we behold with the mind, that is, with the intelligence and with reason, we speak of things which we look upon directly in *the inner light of truth which illumines* the inner man and is inwardly enjoyed. There again if my hearer sees these things himself with his inward eye, he comes to know what I say, not as a result of my words, but as a result of his own contemplation. Even when I speak what is true and he sees what is true, it is not I who teach him. He is taught not by my words but by the things themselves *which inwardly God has made manifest* to him. (xii, 40 [emphasis added]; see also *On the Trinity* XII, 15)

Here again, it is important to note, Augustine minimizes the role of language in our coming to know the objects of the incorporeal world. "We do not listen to anyone speaking and making sounds outside ourselves." He confuses the valid point that teachers cannot become acquainted with these objects *for us* (we must do that ourselves in virtue of the divine light, the inner teacher) with the dubious suggestion that hearing the human words for these incorporeal realities plays no necessary role in our coming to know them.

Thus Augustine rejects a Platonic theory of knowledge in favor of a theological theory. That fact, however, may obscure a more fundamental question. The heart of Augustine's view, as it is of Plato's, is that, for incorporeal objects, "it is not the images that I carry about, but the things themselves." But knowledge of such objects cannot be as simple as Augustine here suggests it is. The mistake he makes is the same as Plato's. Plato, we saw, fails to distinguish the *Forms* from our *knowledge* of the Forms, which requires the mind's formulation of their nature and relationships in *propositions,* for itself as well as for other minds to whom it wishes to communicate what it knows. Similarly, Augustine here fails to distinguish the "things themselves" that the mind knows from the *concepts* that the mind must form of these things when it comes to know them. Just as I cannot know that something is a head unless I know the name for it and form a concept for it, so I cannot know the number 2 or the virtue justice unless I know their names and form concepts of them in my mind. If knowledge of either of these incorporeal realities were in fact nothing more than *their being in* the mind, the *difference* between the mind, which has the power to know, and these realities, which are not powers to know, would entirely collapse in the mental state called *knowledge*. So would the Platonic and Augustinian realism, on which the *truth* of what is known is determined by the object known rather than by the knowing activity of the mind. Knowledge is a *mental state;* justice and the number 2 are not. But Augustine fails to explore the nature of such *knowledge* of incorporeal objects as a *mental state* to be distinguished from those objects themselves.

The Role of Teachers. We should not jump to certain false conclusions from the rapidity with which we come to know the simple objects of intellectual vision upon believing what our teachers say about them. In *The Teacher* Augustine is quite explicit about one of these conclusions. We should not conclude, he says, that our teachers give *their knowledge* to their students "in an external fashion" just because "very often there is no interval between the moment of speaking [by the teachers] and knowing [by the students]" (xiv, 45). Here Augustine comes very close to recognizing that the priority of believing to knowing is not really a temporal priority at all (as I argued earlier). Still, the prevailing picture Augustine gives us is one of temporal priority; students will "take thought within themselves whether what they have been told is true, looking to the inward truth, that is to say, so far as they are able" (xiv, 45). Augustine's main point, of course, is that the students will not *know* what their teachers teach them by merely *accepting* what they say as true; they must acquire this knowledge for themselves, because the teachers cannot give *their knowledge* to them.

Simple vs. Complex Objects. The second false conclusion to avoid is that all incorporeal objects will become known as quickly as the more familiar ones; some of these objects may well be *beyond* our ability to understand them "as soon as," and even though, we believe the testimony of those who know them. Although Augustine is less explicit on this point, he hints at it with his phrase, "so far as they are able." But notice that he has also shifted from our *original* knowledge of the simple entities of mathematics, which comes *as soon as* we believe (and, as I have argued, is a product of our hearing the language combined in a mysterious way with our mental attention to the object) to a *later time* when we are able to believe many things intelligibly *without* knowing them (when the words truly bid us to understand the objects for which they stand). At this later stage, the knowledge of our teachers temporally precedes our belief, and our belief temporally precedes our coming to know what we believe. Most of us will have to trust the testimony of experts in mathematics for most of what can be known in the field of numbers; likewise, the young must trust their elders for some complexities about right and wrong until they are able to see these for themselves.

Thus, although at the simplest level seeing numbers and moral obligations can happen with no perceived interval following our believing them, and hence involve no faith *experienced* as *seeking* understanding, at a more complex level and having gained some maturity, we *can* experience the search to understand more objects in the mathematical world and in the moral world than we do already. Thus originally coming to know the simplest incorporeal objects is not the proper model by which to understand our coming to know the more complex. The extent to which we add the latter to the former will be the result of our conscious seeking, and this in turn will be a function of our motivation, our intellectual ability and training, and our opportunity.

Augustine certainly does not mean to deny that even well-educated people need to accept a great many difficult propositions about the incorporeal realm on the testimony of others who, in virtue of their gifts and training, may have come to know by their own understanding the realities to which they testify. As with corporeal objects, everyone can, abstractly considered, increase their own knowledge of incorporeal objects indefinitely. Everyone can learn more for themselves of numbers, geometric shapes, virtues, essences, properties, and one way to begin is to take on faith what others have found out for themselves. No one is prevented from seeking such knowledge in the way that everyone is prevented from seeking an acquaintance with events in the past, for the knowledge of which no one can get beyond faith in the testimony of others.

Degrees of Comprehension. The third false conclusion to avoid is that, just because our belief in simple incorporeal objects is quickly transformed into knowledge, we immediately comprehend these objects or the relationships between them with clarity and depth. For example, we all came in a mysterious way to our original knowledge of justice on hearing the term used for it when we were young, and we all have come by experience and reflection to learn what it is with greater clarity and depth than we knew of it on our first acquaintance with it. But how many of us know very thoroughly what it is, let alone its proper relationship to the other virtues—for example, to agapic love? To deepen such knowledge and understanding is one of the aims of philosophy, as noted earlier. It is Plato's aim in the *Republic*, Augustine's in the *City of God*. We study Plato or Augustine not to *discover* justice; it exists, like its opposite, injustice, for all to see, any day of our lives, both in itself and in its exemplifications. So we do not need the testimony of Plato or Augustine or of our parents and teachers to its *existence;* what we need is their help in *understanding* it, in the sense of seeing more clearly and completely what it is. The same goes for geometry; we study Euclid—and Riemann and Lobachevsky—not only to discover entities, properties, and relationships in the mathematical world we may have never seen but also to comprehend more fully (to see more clearly) those we already do see—and to *question* some we think we have seen but may not have, such as the relationship between parallel lines.

Of course, we should not conclude either, contrapositively, that, because we have only a dim or confused view of things mathematical or moral or because people's claims about these objects are often in conflict, these objects cannot be known or that they do not even exist. These are inferences that skeptics and relativists (respectively) are apt to make, but ones that Augustine would reject.

Understanding in the sense of comprehension, then, is a goal that we attain only in degrees. Just as we can seek to know more than we do at the moment about objects in the physical world, so we can seek to know more about objects in the incorporeal world. In both cases, we seek to know not only what exists, but the nature of what exists. We know the existence of some objects, and something of their nature, by seeing them, either by means of the senses or by means of reason alone. In order to *know them better*, for example, triangles or justice, we either go to authorities in mathematics or ethics, or try to ask and answer our own questions about these objects, or, what is more likely, a combination of both. In order either to acquire such knowledge by acquaintance in the first place or to extend it, however, we cannot just believe the authorities; we must come to see for ourselves that what they say (and what we believe on their testimony) is true. This means we must *look at* these incorporeal realities more carefully *ourselves*. What the authorities do for us as our teachers, says Augustine, is to express what they know or believe in words; and these words, as *signs*, indicate what realities we should look for ourselves, so that we also may come to know more about triangles or justice than we knew before.

In all of this, however, Augustine, like Plato, tends to minimize the value of believing on testimony in favor of knowing for oneself, except for his all-important claim that the former is the necessary starting point for seeking the latter. "Unless you believe, you will not understand." Still, he does not compromise his principle that knowing by acquaintance is more desirable than accepting on testimony; and he never even considers that belief on testimony itself can itself be knowledge in the more comprehensive framework offered by a justified true belief approach.

Reason. It is fascinating that we can conduct an inquiry into the nature of reason itself, the very capacity we have for inquiring into all those incorporeal realities other than itself. For reason is itself one of the incorporeal realities. Before leaving the second division of "objects of belief," therefore, we should discuss Augustine's view of it. Reason, for Augustine, is (among other things) the faculty human beings possess by which they are capable of seeing, that is, knowing, a world of incorporeal realities—a world that includes, therefore, God himself. Augustine explicitly adopts the classical Greek and Roman definition of a human being. Having distinguished authority and reason as the two ways to knowledge in the passage cited earlier from *Divine Providence and the Problem of Evil*, Augustine goes on to define man in terms of the latter: "Of particular interest to us ought to be the fact that man has been defined thus by the ancient philosophers: *Man is an animal, rational and mortal*" (II, 11, 31).

Augustine thus appeals for his view of human nature to the authority of the the ancient pagan philosophers, thereby exhibiting in practice his own "twofold way." He begins with authority; still, it is not what such authority *says*, but what it *sees*, that is important. What the ancients saw by reason, Augustine thinks, we, too, can see, viz., that "by the one term, *rational*, man is distinguished from brute animals; by the other term, *mortal*, he is distinguished from God" (II, 11, 31). Moreover, we can see that being rational *manifests itself* in "reasonable things," which are of two kinds: "the works of man which are seen and his words which are heard" (II, 11, 31–34). The works and the speech of human beings exhibit an order and design that is both useful and enjoyable in human life. Such reasonable expressions of human beings form a bond between human beings, which is, indeed, a necessary condition of human society, "since men could not be most firmly associated unless they conversed and thus poured, so to speak, their minds and thoughts back and forth to one another" (II, 12, 35).

It is worth noting here that Augustine takes the ancient philosophers to have discovered all these things about human nature without the help of revelation. To accept the authority of the ancients on human nature is one thing, and precedes our own understanding it; but such understanding is itself a function of reason, and it is possible without divine authority. Reason increasingly dispenses with the human authority that it initially accepts on faith, as it comes to see for itself what human beings are and what reason itself is: "By some kind of inner and hidden activity of mine, I am able to analyze and synthesize the things that ought to be learned; and this faculty of mine is called reason" (II, 18, 48). Such self-knowledge distinguishes us especially from the beasts, some of which, like human beings, possess great skill in their works—for example, the swallow making its nest, the bee its honeycomb: "Therefore, it is not by making well-measured things, but by grasping the nature of numbers, that I am more excellent. . . . Why is man superior to brute animals, and why is he to be ranked above them? Because he understands what he does" (II, 19, 49). Such "understanding" of our own nature and abilities, what is it? It is to know by acquaintance, that is, to *see* something of *what we are*, as opposed to just believing it on the testimony of others. Reason is an interior eye that can see not only eternal, invisible things that exist independently of itself; it can also see itself and something of what it is as a human capacity or power. For example, as Augustine says in his *Letter to Paulina*, reason itself sees even the difference between seeing by itself and seeing by the senses: "Although we see some things with the body, others with the mind, the distinction between these two sorts of sight is seen by the mind, not the body" (*Letter 147*, Ch. 38).

Thus Augustine's claims for reason are impressive, and they originate with human authority, not divine revelation. Still, his admiration of reason is inseparable from his worship of God its creator. Indeed, this coupling of what Augustine knows by reason itself about reason with his praise of God its creator is strewn throughout his writings. In the *Letter to Consentius* we read: "God forbid that He should hate in us that faculty whereby he made us superior to all other living beings" (*Letter 120*). In *On Free Will:* "Can you, I pray, find anything in human nature higher than reason?" (II, vi, 13) In *Sermon 43:* "It is in this that we are made in the likeness of God." In *Of True Religion:* "No human authority is set over the reason of a purified soul, for it is able to arrive at clear truth"; it is subject only to God, the source of truth (xxv, 47; xxx, 56; xxxi, 57). In *Divine Providence and the Problem of Evil:* Reason is that "in which all things are, or rather, which is itself the sum total of all things" (II, 9, 26; the sentiment goes back to Aristotle [*On the Soul* 430a 14, 15]; I have not found it in Plato.)

Human beings, of course, are more than rational souls; they also have emotions and the power to choose, as both the Greeks and

Augustine acknowledge. Still, their reason, their ability to believe and to know, marks their essence in a conspicuous way. As Augustine reminds us in his *Retractations*, he once conducted an entire dialogue with his own reason "as if there were two of us present, though I was actually alone. To this work I gave the name *Soliloquies*" (I, iv; the word is original with Augustine). A study of this dialogue in the next chapter will open up what "faith seeking understanding" means for the highest knowledge of all, the knowledge of God. But first we must introduce the third classification in Augustine's outline of the kinds of objects of belief, the one to which God belongs.

"Objects That Are First Believed and Later on Understood"

God is incorporeal, like all the objects of belief in the second division. It is not this similarity between God and those objects, however, that impresses Augustine, for he places God, as an object of belief, in a division all by himself. This third division, he says, contains "those objects that are first believed and later on understood: such are those items that cannot be understood about divine matters except by the clean of heart, a condition achieved by obeying the commandments which have to do with proper living" (*Eighty-Three Different Questions*, Q. 48). The differences between "divine matters" and all other incorporeal objects that warrant such special treatment are two. First, these divine matters are not typically known "as soon as they are believed," by which he refers to the other, simpler objects in the incorporeal world, but only "later understood." Second, these divine matters are not known except by the "clean of heart," a moral restriction that Augustine does not place on our knowledge of those other objects in the incorporeal world. A consideration of these two characteristics of divine matters will lead us directly into the most important application of the formula, faith seeking understanding, as Augustine moves from nonreligious to religious belief and, specifically, to the Christian faith.

What, more exactly, are the "divine matters" to which Augustine here refers? Some Christian teachings we can only believe in this life, and neither know nor understand until the next life. For example, we can only believe on testimony, not know (i.e., see for ourselves), that we shall live again after death by way of a resurrection. Again, we can only believe, not know, that then we shall be free from sin as well as from the sufferings of the present life. We shall be able to know these things, and others like them, only by *leaving* this life and *entering* the one that God promises. We can, during this life, no more transform our belief in these future things into knowledge than we can our belief in the events of past history. In his *Letter to Consentius* Augustine even couples these two cases together:

> As a matter of fact, we hold things visible but past by faith alone, since there is no hope of seeing again what has slipped away with time.... The things which are not yet in existence but are to come, such as the resurrection of our spiritual bodies, are believed in such wise that we hope to see them, but they cannot be experienced now. (*Letter 120*)

It may be doubted, however, whether beliefs like the resurrection constitute in a central way the "divine matters" that Augustine has chiefly in mind here, because strictly speaking these beliefs refer not to "divine matters" but to human matters—to the life and experience of human beings. Still, this third division is where such beliefs belong, for it is the one that includes those objects of belief that cannot be understood at all (i.e., known by acquaintance) until "later," in the significant sense of "in the next life," and for the attainment of which Christian faith in this life is a necessary condition.

But is it the case that, like our own resurrection, we can also know God only in the next life? If so, then all we can have in this life is belief on testimony (or possibly rational proof) that he exists. Then, too, it will be a distinguishing mark of *every* object of belief in this third division that it *cannot* be known in this life. I will argue that this is not the way to take Augustine's teaching on our knowledge and understanding of God. Even though much, and probably most, of our knowledge of God must await the life to come, something of what faith is to *seek* in this life, it can also *find* in this life. How this is possible is the topic we will explore next.

4 Augustine: Vision or Proof?

Can we know God in this life? That is, can we know that he exists and something of what he is, given the conditions and limitations of our finite and morally corrupted existence? Augustine's answer to these questions is, Yes; but he develops this answer along two quite different lines. One line is that of inference and proof; the other, of vision. The former is to be found in *On Free Will*; the latter, in the *Soliloquies* and the *Confessions*. I take *vision* to be Augustine's characteristic term for knowledge by acquaintance or experience, as it is for Plato. In this chapter I argue that the way of vision, not the way of proof, is the authentic Augustinian way to interpret the formula, faith seeking to understand, as applied to the knowledge of God.

Faith Seeking Understanding Considered as Proof

Prologue to the Proof. Augustine's proof for the existence of God is to be found in Book II of *On Free Will*. Augustine elaborates on the proof over many pages, but his aim, briefly stated, is to reach the existence of God from the existence of truth. It is interesting that Augustine provides the essential ideas for his argument already in the *Soliloquies* (I, 15; II, 14–20), the very work to which I will appeal later for his alternative to proving the existence of God. The argument from truth to the existence of God is intriguing, but philosophers have generally neglected it by comparison with the others, for which they have produced an extensive literature. I am not concerned here to make up that regrettable neglect, however, but to expose the difficulties in Augustine's own conception of the proof. I begin with those difficulties he fails to recognize, but which fairly leap out from the prologue he offers before embarking on the proof itself, and I conclude with a difficulty he does recognize when he has completed it.

Now the project of proving the existence of God after believing it on the testimony of others provides a possible interpretation of the formula, faith seeking to understand. And this is precisely how Augustine describes his project before he begins. He says to Evodius, his interlocutor:

We read in Scripture: "The fool hath said in his heart: there is no God" (Ps. 52:18). If such a fool were to say to you there is no God, and would not believe as you do, but wanted to know whether what you believe is true, would you simply go away and leave him, or would you think it your duty somehow to try to persuade him that what you believe is true, especially if he were really eager to know and not merely to argue obstinately? (II, ii, 5)

Evodius agrees that he should do something to help the foolish unbeliever, but reminds Augustine that such an unbeliever ought first, at least, to *believe* "that God exists" on the testimony in Scripture of the "great men" who were eyewitnesses to Jesus Christ. Augustine's response to this is remarkable, as is Evodius' rejoinder:

Aug.   If you think the existence of God is sufficiently proved by the fact that we judge it not to be rash to believe the Scripture-writers, why don't you think we should similarly trust their authority in the matters [e.g., the origin of evil] we have begun to investigate as if they were uncertain or quite beyond our knowledge? So we should be spared much labour in investigation.

Ev.   Yes. But we want to know and to understand what we believe. (II, ii, 5)

Thus Augustine here takes as his starting point the belief that God exists on the testimony of the authors of Scripture, but he also agrees (implicitly) with Evodius, who explains what the proof is to provide: "We want to know and understand what we believe."

Consistent with what we have heard him say so far, then, Augustine here regards belief on the testimony of others as subordinate in cognitive status to the knowledge that it seeks. This inferiority of belief to knowledge, it should be pointed out, does not lie in any uncertainty in the belief, for Evodius has just said, "I firmly believe it." The inferiority must, therefore, lie in something else. What knowledge has, and faith lacks, we have found in our study of Augustine so far, is seeing something for oneself instead of taking it on the word of another. And that, we may recall from Chapter 1, is one of the appealing features of knowledge considered as proof, for a proof is also, like acquaintance with an object, something we can "see for ourselves." So it is no wonder, perhaps, that proof appears to Augustine as a way to know what is first accepted on faith.

Four specific features of the faith-knowledge relationship

emerge in this discussion between Augustine and Evodius. First, faith is taken to be the *necessary starting point* of their search for knowledge. Augustine says to Evodius: "in matters of great importance, pertaining to divinity, we must first believe before we seek to know." He supports this claim with the authority of Scripture, beginning with his favorite passage, "Except ye believe ye shall not understand" (Isa. 7:9 LXX). Augustine goes on to quote sayings of Jesus himself that support the necessity of faith. These sayings also indicate, second, that faith's search for understanding in this life is a *duty*. We are obligated not to be content with belief when knowledge is available. Third, this duty can be fulfilled only by those who meet the *moral condition* of possessing a "superior character." And finally, the knowledge they seek by way of the proof is taken to be *similar to* the understanding that is promised for the next life.

Because these four features are critical to an evaluation of the interpretation of faith seeking understanding as faith seeking proof, the passage in which Augustine states them is worth quoting in full:

> Our Lord himself, both in his words and by his deeds, exhorted those whom he called to salvation first of all to believe [1]. When he afterwards spoke of the gift that was to be given to believers he said, not: "This is life eternal that they may believe"; but: "This is eternal life that they may know thee, the only true God, and Jesus Christ whom thou hast sent" (John 17:3). To those who already believed he said: "Seek and ye shall find" (Matt. 7:7). He cannot be said to have found, who merely believes what he does not know [2]. And no one is fit to find God, who does not first believe what he will afterwards learn to know [1]. Wherefore, in obedience to the precepts of the Lord, let us press on in our inquiry [2]. What we seek at his bidding we shall find, as far as can be done in this life, and by people such as we are. And he will demonstrate it to us. We must believe that these things are perceived and possessed by people of superior character even while they dwell on earth [3], and certainly, more clearly and perfectly, by all the good and pious after this life [4]. (II, ii, 6)

Here, then, is the *account* of faith seeking understanding that Augustine gives *before* embarking on his proof. It claims (1) that belief in the testimony of Scripture to God's existence is the necessary starting point, (2) that the knowledge to be obtained in the forthcoming proof of his existence is sought to fulfil a duty, (3) that moral virtue is a necessary condition for obtaining that knowledge, and (4) that the knowledge obtained in the proof is continuous with, and therefore similar to, that possessed "more clearly and perfectly, by all the good and pious after this life." Augustine's account, however, as applied to his proof, is open to five serious objections:

1. *The Necessity of Faith.*   Why does Augustine hold that a proof must *begin* with the acceptance of its conclusion by faith in the testimony of Scripture? This seems mistaken, for it implies that only Christian believers who accept this testimony are capable of proving the existence of God; but that certainly is not the case. Further, if this is Augustine's meaning, he should have dealt differently with the fool who denies the existence of God; he should have tried first to make him a Christian believer. Actually, the conclusion that the proof offers to prove need not be accepted on any testimony at all, let alone that of the Scripture. The conclusion may be doubted or even denied, as in the case of the biblical fool. It *is* essential, however, to believe the *premises* of the proof, and that the inference drawn from these premises is *valid*.

How, then, should we interpret Augustine's insistence on faith as the first step to understanding? If we interpret faith not as *belief that* God exists but as *trust in* God himself, that he will enable them to succeed in the proof, the problem will be resolved. And there is room for such an interpretation, even in the language near the end of the passage. There Augustine seeks to do God's "bidding," and expresses his *confidence* both "that God himself will demonstrate it to us" and that Evodius and he already possess the requisite "superior character" made possible by Christian faith. But, as I argued in Chapter 2, the trust in God which is an ingredient in that faith presupposes *knowing* God in a way that obviates the need to prove his existence. Therefore, the kind of knowledge or understanding that Augustine really seeks must be different from that which he is about to seek in the forthcoming proof. That this is so we shall discover presently in Augustine's comments after completing the proof.

2. *The Duty to Seek Understanding.*   The duty to seek understanding is imposed on all believers by the commands of Scripture. If this means, however, that all believers ought to engage in proving the existence of God, they will all need the training and opportunity required for doing natural theology. But this is absurd; certainly Jesus does not, in these passages that express his command to seek and find, ask every believer to become a natural theologian. Moreover, Augustine clearly rejects the idea that believers need to be educated in the liberal arts. In his *Retractations* he writes: "I regret that in these books ... I attributed a great deal to the liberal disciplines about which many saintly persons do not know much" (I, 3, 2; he refers to his

Divine Providence and the Problem of Evil [I, 8, 24; II, 5, 15; II, 14, 39]).
His best reminder of the point was the deep love of Monica, his mother, who lacked a formal education (cf. *Divine Providence and the Problem of Evil* I, 11, 32; *The Happy Life* 2, 10). So, if faith is obliged to seek understanding, as seems clear from Scripture, it must be in some way other than requiring all believers to be learned in the liberal arts; and the understanding that faith seeks must be different from that offered in a proof.

3. *The Necessity of Moral Purity.* Augustine's account further suggests that no one can follow his proof without the moral purity made possible by faith. But this is to lay down the wrong requirement for following a proof. What a proof requires is intellectual ability and concentration, not "moral superiority." So again, Augustine really must have some other sense of knowledge in mind, when he touches here on the role of moral virtue. He does, and we must not confuse that sense (*true wisdom*, as he later calls it) with the knowledge he here seeks by means of proof.

4. *Knowing God in This Life and in the Next.* Is proving the existence of God in this life a suitable foretaste of knowing God in the next? If the latter is a "beatific vision of God," the answer to this question must be an obvious No. Yet just the opposite answer follows from what Augustine says here about his project of proving the existence of God. Again, the only way to avoid this further implausible consequence is to find a better interpretation of faith seeking understanding in Augustine's thinking than faith seeking to prove that God exists.

5. *The Authority of Scripture.* Another difficulty, although it is only implicit in Augustine's account, needs to be faced. It is this. If reason can prove the existence of God, then the biblical authority on which the belief in that existence rests is no longer necessary for those who have proved it. But Augustine nowhere, here or elsewhere, ever suggests that anyone in this life can replace the authority of Scripture in any respect. Instead, he always regards Scripture, divine authority, as the supreme authority for Christian faith. So once again, there must be in Augustine a different way of taking the formula, faith seeks understanding, than as belief on testimony seeking to know by inference and proof.

Epilogue to the Proof. These quite specific objections to taking Augustine's proof as the model for interpreting the famous formula

arise out of his own account of what he is about to do, *before* he
embarks with Evodius on the proof itself. Let us turn now to his
account of what Augustine thinks he has come to know *after* completing the proof. There we find him remarkably hesitant about what he
has accomplished. He says: "Hence there should be no further question, but we should accept it [this conclusion] with unshakable faith.
God exists and is the truest and fullest being. This I suppose we hold
with undoubting faith. Now we attain it with a certain if tenuous
form of knowledge" (II, xv, 39). Augustine says they now *know* what
they had earlier only believed. But notice the qualification he adds: it
is a *"tenuous* form of knowledge." Why this qualification, and what
does it mean? Evodius clearly missed it in his initial burst of enthusiasm: "I accept what you have said with incredible and inexpressible
joy, and I declare it to be absolutely certain" (II, xv, 39). But Augustine
proceeds immediately to show Evodius by means of a short syllogism
that he has *not yet found* the knowledge that he thinks he has found.
The syllogism:

> True joy comes only from wisdom;
> You (Evodius) are not yet wise, but only seeking
>   wisdom.
> Therefore, your joy is not true joy.
> Therefore the knowledge you have gained from this proof
>   is not the knowledge you seek, which wisdom requires.
> (II, xv, 40)

So the knowledge they have attained by way of proof is not the
knowledge that faith properly seeks after all!

Wisdom. Why does Augustine hesitate to share Evodius'
enthusiasm? What knowledge is it that Augustine suspects Evodius
has not attained by means of his proof? Augustine's answer is clear
enough. The proof has failed to provide them *wisdom.* Augustine does
not here elaborate on what wisdom is. Elsewhere, however, he makes
it clear. One of his favorite Scripture passages sums it up: "Wisdom is
piety" (Job 28:28; cf. *Confessions* V, 4, 7; VIII, 1, 2; and *On the Trinity*
XII, 14). Thus the knowledge of God which faith seeks, and proof fails
to give, is a knowledge characterized by piety, and the word for such
knowledge is wisdom.

In *On the Trinity* Augustine distinguishes wisdom (*sapientia*) as
the contemplation of eternal things from knowledge (*scientia*) as the
right use of temporal things (XII, 14). Wisdom and knowledge so distinguished represent two directions of just *one* mind: upward to God

(*ratio superior*) and downward to the affairs of this life (*ratio inferior*) (XII, 3). If the mind, which must by its nature look in both directions, is governed by piety, it will be wise in its living of this life, as well as in the worship of God; if it is proud (of which more in a moment), it will not acknowledge its dependence on God for the proper use of temporal things, nor will it love and worship him. Among the ancient philosophers, says Augustine in *The City of God*, Plato alone saw that "the pursuit of wisdom [philosophy] follows two avenues—action and contemplation," and that "it is contemplation especially which claims to reach a vision of the truth" (VIII, 4). The vision is necessary not only for knowing God, but also for living virtuously in this world. Such vision, then, not proof, is the source of wisdom; this is the point implicit in Augustine's remarks to Evodius. Wisdom is a knowledge of God accompanied by love, gratitude, and praise; it is the knowledge of piety, made possible only by faith. This is why Augustine is disappointed with his proof, and why we need to look elsewhere for what he means by faith seeking to understand.

No Proof for the Existence of God. Augustine is not only disappointed with his proof. On two other, quite different though related occasions, he explicitly sidelines the way of proof, and perhaps even rejects it. On the earlier of these occasions, in *Of True Religion* (390), he writes: "Do not go abroad. Return within yourself. In the inward man dwells truth. . . . Make for the place where the light of reason is kindled. What does every good reasoner attain but truth? And yet truth is not reached by reasoning, but is itself the goal of all who reason" (xxxix, 72). And again: "Let our religion bind us to the one omnipotent God, because no creature comes between our minds and him whom we know to be the Father and the Truth, i.e., the inward light whereby we know him" (lv, 113). These passages, it may be noted, recall Plato's dialectic, which subordinates the inferential function of reason to the vision of the Good. On the later occasion (c. 414), in a letter written to Evodius himself, his interlocutor in *On Free Will*, Augustine refers Evodius to *Of True Religion*: "You also have some help in the book on religion; if you would review it and look into it, you would never think that reason can prove the necessity of God's existence, or that by reasoning it can ever be established that God must necessarily exist" (*Letter 162*). This is decisive evidence against taking Augustine's proof in *On Free Will* as the key to interpreting faith seeking understanding.

Sources of Augustine's Thought. Augustine's hesitation over finding God by way of proof should come as no surprise, considering that the main sources of his thought lie in Platonism and Christianity. Each of these in its own way disposed him toward construing our basic knowledge of God on the model of vision, not proof. In *The Christian Philosophy of St. Augustine* Etienne Gilson suggests the same point when he writes: "Analysis of pure thought will show that God exists. Of course this will not be a dialectical demonstration of God's existence by means of abstract concepts; it is rather an experimental verification of it effected by isolating those features of human thought which God alone can account for" (66). Gilson goes on to discuss the two most conspicuous features of Augustine's account of the knowledge of God, the divine illumination and the inner teacher. Both of these features suggest the direct acquaintance with God as a *personal* being who is "experimentally" known, not a possible being whose existence is reached as the conclusion of a logical proof.

Indeed, following Gilson's lead, perhaps the way to interpret Augustine's proof in *On Free Will* is that it is not a proof so much as an "analysis" of the mind's experience of truth that shows that, properly understood, this experience occasions an experience of God. This interpretation would bring Augustine's proof into into line with the many other discussions in which he associates knowing truth with knowing God (cf., e.g., *Confessions* IV, 12; X, 23, 24). Furthermore, there is the fact that Augustine did not retract his proof in *On Free Will* (*Retractations* I, 8), a fact that can then be explained as showing that Augustine himself did not look at what he was doing there so much as proving the existence of God as explicating the experience of truth as an experience of God. There is no need for this strained exegesis, however, for I am arguing only that the way of vision is Augustine's characteristic and authentic approach to God, not that the impulse to prove God's existence is totally absent from his thought.

Pride. As further evidence against taking the way of proof as authentic Augustine, I take his associating it with pride, the cardinal Christian vice that prevents the attainment of wisdom. He confesses his own sin of pride on many occasions. One of these is his discovery, through the reasonings of the Neoplatonists and apart from faith, of the great truth of God's incorporeality. As he tells the story in his *Confessions*, these reasonings, for all of their success in bringing Augustine to the truth about God's nature, not only failed to make him humble, but actually fed his pride: "Now I began to desire to appear wise. Filled up with punishment for my sins, I did not weep over them, but rather I was puffed up with knowledge. Where was that charity which builds upon the foundation of humility, which is Christ Jesus? When would these books teach it to me?" (VII, 20, 26). Such reasonings, he suspects, might even have drawn him *away* from faith, had he come upon them after his conversion:

> It is for this reason, I believe, that you wished me to come upon those books before I read your Scriptures, so that the way I was affected by them might be stamped upon my memory.... If I had first been formed by your Sacred Scriptures and if you had grown sweet to me by my familiar use of them, and I had afterwards happened on those other volumes, they might have drawn me away from the solid foundation of religion. Or else, even if I had persisted in those salutary dispositions which I had drunk in, I might have thought that if a man studied those books alone, he could conceive the same thoughts from them. (VII, 20 26)

Advocates of natural theology can, and typically do, readily grant its moral insufficiency. My point is that Augustine saw in human reasoning not just its moral inadequacy, but also its moral danger, and that this, too, counts against taking his proof for the existence of God in *On Free Will* as the paradigm for for interpreting the formula, faith seeking understanding.

Knowledge as Proof for Existence

I want to mention one final line of evidence against taking Augustine's proof as such a paradigm. When we read his other writings—both the philosophical ones that precede *On Free Will* and the increasingly theological ones that follow it, we find that knowledge of anything conceived of as proof for its existence is conspicuously absent. Instead, the sense of knowledge and understanding that pervades all these writings is vision, direct acquaintance with an object. Recall the passages cited earlier in our explication of the first two kinds of "objects of belief." Not once did we find Augustine trying to prove the existence of either corporeal or incorporeal entities. What he emphasizes is that they are visible to the mind, the former by way of the senses, the latter with no help from the senses at all. His teaching is that we come to know of both kinds of object that they exist simply by seeing them, so that it is not their existence that requires proof but their contrasting natures that requires due recognition. Why should Augustine, then, in the case of God, think he needs a proof? The answer, as we shall soon see, is that he does not really think he does.

Refutation of Skepticism. In this connection, consider also Augustine's refutation of skepticism. The need to overcome the lure

of skepticism loomed large at that stage in his life between his abandoning Manichaean rationalism and his reading the Neoplatonists.
Let us look first at these refutations in *Answer to Skeptics*. This work is
Augustine's first following his conversion. Its most striking feature,
for the purpose of the issue we are discussing, is its shift from the
arguments of Books I and II to its direct appeals to the skeptic's own
rational "vision" in Book III. The arguments in Books I and II are not
metaphysical, but moral and epistemological arguments. In Book I he
argues that it is not sufficient for human happiness only to be seeking
the truth; we must also possess it. Augustine agrees with the skeptic
(*skeptikos:* "inquirer") that we must *search* for the truth, but disagrees
with skeptical claims that the truth cannot be found, and that we
must always, therefore, withhold even our belief (*epoche:* "the suspension of judgment"). In Book II he argues that a moderate skeptic (for
example, Carneades) who holds that we can follow what is likely
(*verisimile*) or probable (*probabile*) must admit that he has a prior
knowledge of the truth itself (*veritas*). To admit that something is like
the truth presupposes knowledge of the truth itself, an argument similar to Plato's argument that even a false belief that might appear true
presupposes knowledge—knowledge of the "true" constituents of the
belief, which are the Forms.

In Book III Augustine abandons the way of argument and
appeals to the rational vision of the skeptic. This appeal is significant
for the issue at hand, namely, whether Augustine's general method is
one of inferential proof. In Book III it certainly is not. There he simply
appeals to the skeptic to consider the clearest possible examples of
truth, for to see them just *is* to know them: the *necessary* propositions
of logic and the *contingent* propositions of sensory appearances. The
former include, for example: "Either there is only one world or there
are more worlds than one" (III, 10, 23); "three times three are nine"
(11, 25); "either there is no supreme good of man—where life's happiness abides—or it is either in the mind or in the body, or in both" (12,
27); and logical rules of inference like "if one or several parts of [a dis-
junction] are removed by negation, there remains something that is
confirmed by that removal" (13, 29). Indeed, "dialectic [logic] is itself
the science of the truth," which presupposes the fundamental contradiction itself between truth and falsehood (13, 29). Contingent propositions that represent the testimony of the senses are also immediately
knowable, even by the skeptic. Even if he has doubts about the *nature*
of physical objects, he can neither doubt the way these objects *appear*
to him nor that there *is* something that appears. Augustine feels no
need to prove the existence of the corporeal world, even if he believes
we should avoid being rash in what we conclude about its nature

from the testimony of the senses (11, 24; 26). As we noted earlier, Augustine is not a self-confessed skeptic with regard to our knowledge either that the external world exists or what it is like, even though his account of sense knowledge is inadequate.

The choice of such clear examples of knowledge suggests that Augustine takes something like the Stoic's cataleptic presentation or Cartesian indubitability as the mark of knowledge. He is not at all explicit about this, however, even though he opens up the question by accepting the definition of knowledge widely held by both skeptics and their "dogmatic" counterparts, the Stoics. This is the definition of Zeno the Stoic (as Augustine formulates it): "Truth can be recognized through those marks which the false cannot have" (II, 5, 11). Although his elaboration of this definition is faulty, as Christopher Kirwan shows in his *Augustine* (Chapter 2), this fact should not obscure the significance of Augustine's method here, which is to appeal directly to the "light of reason" in the skeptic for some things he can know, instead of to discursive proof.

Not that proof is not also, in its way, an appeal to reason, for of course it is. But in his appeal to the skeptic, Augustine reveals his preference for vision over inference. A necessary condition for such vision according to Augustine, as we have seen, is belief. Thus what Augustine appeals to in the first instance is precisely that: he urges the skeptic to *believe* these propositions instead of *suspending* belief. The skeptic who believes these propositions has taken the first great step toward *knowing* the objects they represent, whether in the corporeal or incorporeal world. The formula, faith seeking understanding, is thus not only the proper *way to* the knowledge that Augustine himself sought but did not find as a rationalist, it is also the *way out of* skepticism, in the grips of which he himself was subsequently caught.

Si fallor sum.   There is one famous argument in Augustine that does look like a proof of existence. It is the argument, found in several passages scattered throughout his writings, in which he appears to prove that he himself exists (*On the Happy Life* ii, 7; *Soliloquies* II, 1, 1; *On Free Will* II, iii, 7; *On True Religion* xxxix, 73; *On the Trinity* X, 10; XV, 12). Careful reading will show, however, that in these passages Augustine is offering, not a metaphysical proof (of the proposition "I exist"), but the *immediacy* of still one more kind of knowledge, the knowledge of oneself. The passage containing the most complete version of the "proof" is found in *The City of God*. Immediately preceding the passage, Augustine makes the following claims: "I am certain that I am, that I know that I am, and that I love to be and to know" (XI, 26).

Having made these several claims on the basis that such "inner realities" are directly open to reason (unlike the "external objects" of the physical world of which we can have only images and about which, therefore, we can more easily be mistaken), Augustine imagines that the skeptic will ask, in typical fashion: "What if you are mistaken?" Augustine replies:

> Well, if I am mistaken, I am. For, if one does not exist, he can by no means be mistaken. Therefore, I am, if I am mistaken. Because, therefore, I am, if I am mistaken, how can I be mistaken that I am, since it is certain that I am, if I am mistaken? And because, if I could be mistaken, I would have to be the one who is mistaken, therefore am I most certainly not mistaken in knowing that I am. Nor, as a consequence, am I mistaken in knowing that I know. For just as I know that I am, I also know that I know. And when I love both to be and to know, then I add to the things I know a third and equally important knowledge, the fact that I love . . . [the argument continues, but the argument as cited thus far is sufficient for our purpose]. (XI, 26)

The argument is in two stages, the second one building on the first:

Stage 1:

1. I am mistaken that I exist (skeptic supposition)
2. If I do not exist, I cannot be mistaken
3. Hence, if I can be mistaken that I exist, I exist (from 2)
4. If I am mistaken that I exist, I can be mistaken that I exist (modal principle)
5. Hence, if I am mistaken that I exist, I exist (from 4 and 3)

Stage 2:

6. Hence, I exist (from 5 and 1)
7. Hence, I know that I exist (from 6, as proved)
8. If I know I exist, then I cannot be mistaken that I exist (to know is not to be mistaken)
9. Hence, I cannot be mistaken that I exist (from 8 and 7)
10. If I cannot be mistaken, then I am not mistaken (from 4)
11. Hence, I am not mistaken (from 10 and 9)

Thus if I am mistaken that I exist, as the skeptic supposes I may be, then I am not mistaken, which is contradictory. Hence the original supposition of the skeptic is false, for it involves a contradiction. Hence when I *say* that I exist, I say something that cannot be mistaken; if I then *believe* what I say, I must *know* it as well.

What is the significance of this argument? It is not that Augustine has proved his own existence (step 6), but that he has shown that *knowing* one's own existence is another example of knowledge that the skeptic who carefully considers it will be unable to deny. Three considerations support this conclusion. First, whether Augustine exists was not the issue in the first place, but whether knowledge is possible. In reaching the conclusion of the second stage of the argument, Augustine has shown that knowledge *is* possible in the case of knowing one's own existence, for to suppose one is mistaken about one's own existence is incoherent. Second, if Augustine were interested in proving his existence, he would have drawn that conclusion as an explicit proposition that followed from his premises, and concluded his argument right there. As it is, however, that conclusion, although it is necessary to the proof, is only tacitly implied along the way for the sake of getting on to the antiskeptical conclusion that knowing one's own existence is possible.

Finally, if Augustine's proof were a proof of his existence analogous to his proof for the existence of God in *On Free Will,* he would have to represent himself here as initially *believing* his own existence on the testimony of someone else, as he there represents himself as initially believing God's existence on the testimony of Scripture, and *then* as seeking to replace such belief with a proof. But he does not do this, for it would be absurd. The whole point of his argument is that his own existence is so plainly evident to him that he cannot be mistaken about it; whereas the prospect of having to believe it on the word of someone else is as odd as the idea that he must prove it. Augustine knows he exists *as soon as* he understands the words, *I* and *exist.* In the same way, the skeptic can know that *he* exists. Thus, incidentally, but all-importantly, Augustine adds another incorporeal entity to the second division in his "objects of belief," the self; like numbers, virtues, and so on, the self sees by reason, directly and immediately, that it exists.

Augustine's proof for the existence of God in *On Free Will* is his only straitforward effort to prove the existence of a fundamental kind of being—God. Because he puts forth no similar efforts to prove the existence of the physical world, the self, other minds, or the world of incorporeal objects, I conclude that his proof for the existence of God is not typical of his approach to knowledge of existence. In view of this conclusion, as well as the specific objections I raised earlier against the proof itself, I draw the further conclusion that Augustine's proof for the existence of God is an improper model for interpreting his formula, faith seeking understanding. It should therefore give way to his approach to the knowledge of God as vision, which we are now ready to explore.

Faith Seeking Understanding Considered as Vision

I have said that Augustine's doctrines of divine illumination and the divine teacher contain his authentic approach to the knowledge of God. These doctrines open the way to taking this knowledge as vision, not proof. Augustine best exhibits this approach to the knowledge of God in the comparatively early *Soliloquies* (386–387) and in his great religious autobiography, the *Confessions* (397–400). In the former, Augustine speaks with himself; in the latter, with God. In the former he anticipates descriptively what he personally embodies in the latter; for in the *Confessions* he shows by his own example what he thinks it is to know God. To know God is to acknowledge him with praise, confession, and contemplation and to recognize his presence in one's mind and his providence in one's life. I shall focus here mainly on the *Soliloquies*, however, because it has been overlooked as a key to Augustine's view of the knowledge of God.

The Qualitative Priority of Reason. The *Soliloquies* contains Augustine's first extended discussion of faith and reason following his conversion. In his *Retractations*, he describes his motive in writing this dialogue; it was "zeal and love for searching out, by reason, the truth concerning those matters which I especially desired to know, ... questioning myself and answering myself as if we were two—reason and I—although I was alone" (I, 4, 1). And what are "those matters" that Augustine especially wants to know? Two, as he says in his famous answer, early in the *Soliloquies:* "I desire to know God and the soul" (I, 2, 7). Notice that Augustine says he wants to search out these matters by *reason*. He does not say "by faith." He was, of course, already a believer. Why, then, does he not say he will search out these matters by faith? Because he wants to *see*, to *know*, to *understand*, and these are not the function of faith. As noted earlier, the functions of faith, for Augustine, are to *believe* and to *trust*, that is, to believe the testimony of an authority that it trusts. By contrast, it is the function of reason to see, to know, to understand. If there is something to see, in the incorporeal world, it is for reason to see it—not the senses, and not faith—even though, of course, these, too, depend in their own way upon reason to formulate the propositions that represent what is believed and what is seen by the senses.

We also observed that the project of sorting out these various functions of faith, the senses, and reason's involvement in them is for reason itself to undertake, not for the senses or faith. What knowing and believing are, what are their objects, and what are the faculties with which we do these things is an inquiry of reason. Augustine's name for this inquiry is *dialectics*, which includes much of modern logic and epistemology. In *Divine Providence and the Problem of Evil* he defines the word: "This science teaches both how to teach and how to learn. In it, reason itself exhibits itself, and reveals its own nature, its desires, its powers. It knows what knowledge is; by itself, it not only wishes to make men learned, but also can make them so" (II, 13, 38). Reason alone can discover the truth about such matters, because they, like numbers and justice, are not corporeal but incorporeal things. The *Soliloquies*, then, nicely exhibits what I have called the qualitative priority of reason over faith, on at least three points. First, reason is the faculty of knowing, the faculty by which, therefore, we know God. Second, reason is the faculty that discovers this very ability it possesses. Third, reason is the faculty that discerns the nature of this knowledge, whether, for example, it is originally by vision or proof. Nowhere does Augustine engage in a similar dialogue with faith!

The Temporal Priority of Faith. What does it mean to know God? This question is center stage throughout Book I of the *Soliloquies*. Augustine must begin, says Reason, by searching for God. Augustine, of course, already is a believer, having begun his dialogue with an extended prayer to God, at the behest of Reason. Actually, then, his faith, in so far as it manifests itself in prayer, is still his starting point; but to know God, he must *search*, and that involves the use of reason. His faith seeks understanding, which reason alone can give. About ten years later, Augustine begins his *Confessions* in the same way, by praying to God, asking whether he should *call* on God in order to know him, or *know* him in order to call upon him. Scripture answers: he must call on God in order to know him (I, 1, 1). Faith (trust in what Scripture says) is thus the first step, understanding the reward. Thus far, the *Soliloquies* and the *Confessions* parallel *On Free Will* exactly; the great difference is that Reason says nothing in the *Soliloquies*, nor does Augustine, writing in his own voice in the *Confessions*, about reaching that understanding by proof.

It is important to be clear on this, for at one point in the *Soliloquies* Reason asks, "But first explain how, if God is demonstrated to you, you will be able to say that it is enough" (I, 2, 7). The term *demonstrate* might suggest that Reason will try to prove to Augustine that God exists. It is the same term he uses to describe his proof in *On Free Will* (II, ii, 6). In the *Soliloquies*, however, Reason is not offering to prove the existence of God (no proof is given), but to *show* God to Augustine in a way that assumes that Augustine already knows *that* he exists. As John Burnaby says in *Amor Dei*, "The aim is not to demonstrate theological propositions, but to *show* God, to bring Him into the heart so that he may be felt" (65). The *existence* of God is not the issue at all, but *knowing God* definitely is. What, then, is the difference? How can Reason not need to prove the existence of God, and yet desire to know him?

Analogy with the Sun. The answer to the first part of this twofold question is, Reason does not need to prove that God exists because it already knows that God exists, which it does by having directly seen him with its "interior eye." This is why Reason "pledges to make God known to your mind just as the sun is shown to the eyes" (I, 6, 12). In this analogy,

> the senses of the soul are, as it were, the mind's own eyes. . . . I—Reason—am in minds as the act of looking is in the eyes. To have eyes is not the same as to look, and to look is not the same as to see. Therefore the soul needs three distinct things: that it have eyes which it can properly use, that it look, and that it see. (I, 6, 12)

Thus knowing God is not the result of *reasoning*—the discursive ability associated with inference, demonstration, and proof. Rather it is a matter of directly seeing him with the mind—reason in its intuitive sense. The import of the analogy between God and the sun can be elaborated in three points: first, that knowing God is to see him, just as knowing the sun is to see it; second, that having seen God is to have no need to prove his existence, just as having seen the sun is to have no need to prove its existence; and third, that just as no one *first* comes to know the sun by proof, so no one *first* comes to know God by proof either. This third point is the most important one. The ability to see is the *original* and *sufficient* way to know not only that there is a world of physical objects but also that there is a world of incorporeal objects, the highest of which is God.

Analogy with the Friend. The answer to the second part of the question removes a paradox: How can Reason still desire to know what it already knows because it sees it? To explain this, Reason draws a second analogy, one from the knowledge we have of our friends. Would it satisfy Augustine, Reason asks, if he could "know God just as you know Alypius" (I, 3, 8)? Augustine replies that he would be grateful for such knowledge, but that it would not be enough. It would not be enough "because I do not even know God as I do Alypius, and yet I do not know Alypius enough" (I, 3, 8). This analogy holds the key to the deepest sense of what it means to desire the knowledge of God. Again, as with the sun, it is not a knowledge that proves existence. For once we have come to know our friends, their existence is not even in question (nor was it, really, when we first came to know them). What we still want to know, when we already know our friends, is to *know them better.*

Here, then, is a kind of knowing that we can seek even though we already have it. This is not so paradoxical as it may sound. The point is that this kind of knowing, unlike knowing that something exists, is one that comes in *degrees.* We have seen this sense of knowing before—the clearer and deeper comprehension we seek of mathematical or moral entities the existence of which we already know by seeing them with the mind. Because, unlike those entities, God is a personal being, Augustine illustrates this kind of understanding that faith seeks with the example of the friend. Unless we already know our friend, however slightly, we cannot even desire to know him better. Indeed, we only want to know him better *because,* as Augustine brings out, we *love* him. And we love him because we have found him, and his friendship, to be something good. But, as Augustine discusses at length in *On the Trinity:* "no one can love at all a thing of which he is wholly ignorant" (X, 1). We are not wholly ignorant of our friend, not because we proved his existence after having believed he exists on the testimony of others, but because we have *seen* him and made his *acquaintance.* Having thus known him and found his friendship good, we are also made happy. Our happiness consists not only in knowing him but also in coming to know him better. And we are *able* to know him better because of the depth in the reality of a human being; there is always more to our friend than we already know. There is infinitely more to God, of course, than we already know.

The combined implications of these analogies for what it means to know God are obvious. First, the knowledge of God is by an intellectual vision, which is analogous to the corporeal vision by which we know that there is a sun. We also know by corporeal vision a little of *what* the sun *is,* for example, that it is the brightest object in the sky. So, we can know by an intellectual vision not only that God exists, but a little of *what he is,* for example, that he is the brightest object in the world of incorporeal things. Second, the intellectual vision of God is also like that vision by which we know our friends. Just as the more we know them, the more we want to know them because we love them, so the more we know God, the more we want to know him because knowing him is good and gives us joy.

Here we should recognize the important point John Burnaby makes in *Amor Dei,* viz., that "for this profoundly personal apprehension of God, the term 'vision' is indeed inadequate" (156). Burnaby defends the term by explaining that Augustine is responding to the aesthetic dimension of its Platonic and Neoplatonic connotations: "But to the Greeks and to the Greeks alone had been given that extraordinary combination of visual sensitiveness and intellectual passion which led to the discovery that if truth is to be worshipped, the truth is beauty" (157). But this defense misses the point that the term *vision* fails to capture the intensely *personal* character of the *Christian* Augustine's experience of knowing God. It would be more pertinent to observe that the personal character of Augustine's experience of God just breaks through the restrictive connotations of the term, not only here in the analogy of knowing a friend but also in the *Confessions* and, for that matter, throughout his writings.

It is true, of course, that the knowledge we have of God in this life is only a *partial* knowledge of him, just as the knowledge we have of the sun or of our friends is never exhaustive or complete. And, of course, we cannot know or see very much of the goodness of God without believing what he has revealed himself to be and to have done for us in the incarnation of his son, Jesus Christ. Thus the believer's total knowledge of God will be a fusion of what his Reason sees by the natural divine light and what he believes (and begins to understand) on the divine testimony in his revelation. Faith and reason form an organic epistemic whole.

Faith Cannot Be Left Behind.   Here is the deepest meaning of the Augustinian formula, faith seeking understanding. Faith, by which Christians *trust* God and therefore *believe* many things about him that he reveals to them, some of which they may have even begun to glimpse for themselves, others of which they may not understand very well at all, seeks to know him better for the former, and for the first time for the latter. Thus, too, it becomes evident what Augustine means when he says that Christian believers can never, for all their beginning to know God in this life, leave their faith behind. They must always *trust* the God they have come to *see and know,* for much of what he says about himself they can only believe, because they do not as yet see and know it, or at least do not as yet see and know it very clearly, even though they are acquainted with him. Augustine puts the point nicely in *On the Trinity* as he struggles to know God as three persons in one being:

> For a certain faith is in some way the starting-point of knowledge; but a certain knowledge will not be made perfect, except after this life, when we shall see face to face. Let us therefore be thus minded, so as to know that the disposition to seek the truth

is more safe than that which presumes things unknown to be known. Let us therefore so seek as if we should find, and so find as if we were about to seek. (IX, i)

Knowing God Is Unique.   Reason tells Augustine still more, in the *Soliloquies*, both about God and about itself. First, about God. God is an incorporeal object like numbers, duties, virtues, human minds, and all the other objects in the incorporeal world; but he differs significantly from them all by being the transcendent being who is the source (in a way which is ultimately quite mysterious) of all these things and of their very knowability by us:

> God is, of course, intelligible [incorporeal], as those principles of the sciences also are intelligible, yet there is a great difference between them. The earth is visible and light is visible, but the earth cannot be seen unless it is brightened by light. So, likewise, for those things which are taught in the sciences and which everyone understands and acknowledges, without any cavil, to be most true—one must believe that they cannot be understood unless they are illumined by something else as by their own sun. Therefore, just as in this sun one may remark three certain things, namely, that it is, that it shines, and that it illumines, so also in that most hidden God whom you wish to know there are three things, namely, that He is, that He is known, and that He makes other things to be known. (I, 8, 15)

Thus God is in a class entirely by himself. The passage recalls Plato's description of our approach to the Good (*Republic* 506–508). It also anticipates St. Anselm's conception of God as that which none greater can be thought. Elsewhere Augustine defines God as "the supreme and best good" (*Confessions* VII 4, 6) and as a being "than which there is nothing better or more sublime" (*City of God* I, 7, 7). In *St. Augustine and the Augustinian Tradition* J. F. Callahan shows in detail how these passages anticipate Anselm's ontological proof (1–47).

Weaknesses of Reason.   Second, the *Soliloquies* suggests frequently that reason is limited in two important ways, by its finitude and the effects of sin. Augustine articulates the finitude of reason more eloquently, however, elsewhere. For example, in the *Literal Commentary on Genesis* he writes:

> But distinct from these objects is the light by which the soul is illumined, in order that it may see and truly understand every-

thing, either in itself or in the light. For the light is God himself, whereas the soul is a creature; yet, since it is rational and intellectual, it is made in his image. And when it tries to behold the Light, it trembles in its weakness and finds itself unable to do so. (II, 31, 59)

Thus it is not only God's surpassing greatness but also reason's weakness as a "creature" that qualifies its vision of God in this life. Reason can have only a dim, partial knowledge of God in this life because of God's overwhelming radiance. Again, Augustine's language is reminiscent of Plato, who expresses great reserve about the possibility of defining the Good (*Republic* 505–506), as it is of Plotinus, who expresses the same reserve with respect to the One (*Enneads* VI, 9, 1). The Platonic response to transcendence is not alien to Augustine's Christian sensibility, for Scripture, too, declares that God "alone has immortality and dwells in unapproachable light, whom no man has ever seen or can see" (1 Tim. 6:16; see also Psalms, 36:9; 43:3; John 1:4). No wonder Augustine exclaims at the outset of his *Confessions:* "What does any man say when he speaks of you? Yet woe to those who keep silent concerning you, since even those who speak much are as the dumb" (I, 4, 4).

But reason is weak also because it has been vitiated by sin. What reason most needs for its knowledge of God is the purging of a rebellious will that has turned it away from loving God to loving the lower goods of his creation. And it is just at this point that faith is necessary for the healing reason needs. Augustine distinguishes that faith from all other faith. The faith that heals, of course, is the *Christian* faith. Like all faith, it requires trust; but the *object* of its trust is the God who reveals himself in the Bible and in Jesus Christ, and the *testimony* it believes is, therefore, the testimony of God himself about himself and about his incarnation. The faith that so trusts and so believes purifies reason for the seeing of God. Augustine is quite clear in his soliloquy with Reason that it depends on such faith for the moral cleansing it needs for the pious vision of God it lost in the fall: "The mind is like healthy eyes when it is cleansed of every taint of the body, that is, detached and purged of the desires of earthly things—which cleansing it obtains, at first, only by *Faith*." (I, 6, 12). Such faith, of course, goes quite beyond the ordinary sense of faith. It will be recalled that, for the first two divisions of the objects of belief, Augustine does not associate the faith required with moral purification. Nor does he there connect faith with hope and love, as he does Christian faith here. "It follows, then," concludes Reason, "that without these three no soul can be healed so that it can see—that is, know—its God" (I, 6, 12).

Christian Faith a Virtue. In short, the Christian faith that emerges here in Augustine is *divine* faith; it is dramatically different from every-day human faith. It is a *virtue*, with God as its special object of trust and the moral purification of the soul by God as its special consequence. When such faith seeks understanding, we see Augustine's formula at work in its most important sense—faith seeking true wisdom, the pious knowledge of God. No wonder, then, that Augustine classifies the belief that has "divine matters" as its object in a division by itself.

Early in our study of Augustine we noted his tendency to emphasize the intellectual aspect of faith—*what* it is we believe. We see now, however, that when faith is *divine* faith its intellectual aspect is embedded in a moral framework that requires trust in God himself. Trust, in turn, involves the will. Accordingly, Reason's final admonition, at the close of Book I of the *Soliloquies*, sounds like a scriptural command from God himself, requiring this element of trust in faith:

> Believe steadfastly in God and, as far as you can, entrust your-self wholly to Him. Do not choose to be, so to speak, your own master and under your own dominion, but proclaim yourself the servant of Him who is our kindest and most helpful Lord. For, if you do this, He will not cease to lift you up to Himself, and He will allow nothing to happen to you which is not for your good, even though you do not know it. (I, 15, 30)

Augustine's response to the admonition reflects the full complexity of biblical faith. Such faith, as we saw in Chapter 2, includes not only belief and trust but also obedience: "I hear, I believe, and, as far as I am able, I obey; I pray very much to God Himself in order that I may accomplish much. Or do you want anything further of me?" (I, 15, 30). Reason replies: "It is well enough for the time being. Later on, when you have beheld Him, you will do whatsoever He commands" (I, 15, 30).

Augustine writes here as a new convert, at the threshold of a Christian life of faith seeking understanding. There is no suggestion yet that such understanding consists in finding a proof for the exis-tence of a God in whom Augustine believes on the testimony of oth-ers; instead, Augustine has set himself to see God—whom he already sees—more clearly and deeply in a continuing life of faith, confession, love, obedience, and prayer. Of course, he has heard about God in the testimony of the Church and Scripture, but now he has also begun to see God, that is, to know and experience God for himself. He has a faith that not only seeks, but also has begun to find, in a vision of heart and mind, what it seeks.

This interpretation of Augustine gives rise to some important questions. In the next chapter I try to answer these questions to gain thereby a still more accurate, consistent, and complete picture of the religious meaning of the Augustinian formula, faith seeking to understand.

5 *Faith Seeking Understanding: Conclusion*

Several problems arise from the foregoing account of Augustine's views on faith seeking understanding. In this chapter, I propose to resolve these problems either by further clarifying the ambiguities of the terms of the formula or by extending some of Augustine's own ideas toward answering questions that he did not explicitly raise and discuss.

The Vision of God

I have advanced the thesis that the knowledge of God that faith seeks is to be interpreted, in Augustine, in the model of vision, not proof. I have supported the thesis by taking the *Soliloquies* and the *Confessions* as more characteristic of his teaching than *On Free Will*. Augustine teaches, however, that we cannot enjoy the vision of God until the next life, which seems to contradict the thesis I have been trying to establish. If Augustine really does rule out seeing God in this life, then clearly, when he describes "divine matters" as those that are "first believed and later on understood," he must mean by "later" that God can be known only "in the next life." It would follow that the only access we have to "divine matters" in this life is the testimony of other human beings or the "tenuous knowledge" reached by way of proof. With respect to testimony, God would be like objects and events in the past that are "always believed and never understood"—except for the critical difference that, for the latter, belief in these objects and events is anchored in the knowledge of those who originally were acquainted with these objects and events, whereas belief in God would be anchored in no earlier knowledge possessed by any human beings at all.

Beatific Vision. Augustine clearly holds that the "beatific vision" of God is reserved for the future life, and that it is reserved only for those who have been purified in this life by the Christian faith. Several of his *Letters* are devoted to this topic, notably *Letter 147*, addressed to "the noble lady, Paulina," and entitled *The Book on the Vision of God.* It is one of just a very few of Augustine's *Letters* to which he gave a title and on which he commented in his *Retractations* (II, 67). Near the beginning of the letter Augustine writes:

> Since, therefore, we do not see God in this life either with bodily eyes, as we see heavenly or earthly bodies, or with the gaze of the mind, as we see some of those things which I have mentioned, and which you most certainly behold within yourself [that you are living, that you wish to see God, that you seek this, etc.], why do we believe that He is seen, except that we rest our faith upon the Scripture, where we read: "Blessed are the clean of heart, for they shall see God"? (Ch. 3)

He reiterates this theme frequently in the *Letter* (Chs. 3, 13, 24, 27, 32, 35, 37, 46), assuring Paulina that this vision of God will be enjoyed by believers in the next life. Much of his discussion is taken up with the question how the special cases of seeing God in this life described in Scripture are to be squared with 1 John 1:18, which says: "No one has seen God at any time." He also discusses the question whether God will be seen in the next life with the eyes of the resurrected, spiritual body (Chs. 49–51), a question he also discusses in *The City of God* (XXII, 29).

Special Cases.   What Augustine does not do here is to explain how *all* believers may at least begin to see God in this life. When he writes, immediately preceding the passage just quoted, "We believe that God is seen in the present life," he most likely refers only to certain special cases described in Scripture (Abraham, Moses, Isaiah, Job., etc.), for these occupy the greater part of his discussion. His explanation of most of these is that God appeared to Moses, for example, "under that aspect in which He willed, but not in His own nature which Moses longed to see, inasmuch as that is promised to the saints in another life" (Ch. 20). A conspicuous exception is the vision of St. Paul (2 Corinthians 12: 2–4), which was a vision of "the very substance of God." But such a vision, resembling as it does the beatific vision, is to be explained as a special way of leaving this life without dying, for "the mind must necessarily be withdrawn from this life when it is caught up to the ineffable reality of that vision, and it is also not beyond belief that the perfection of that revelation was granted to certain saints, who were not yet near enough to death that their bodies were ready for burial" (Ch. 31). St. Paul's vision, then, was like the vision of all the saints in the next life, by which they "see him as he is," in the language of 1 John 3:2, a text Augustine frequently cites.

Ordinary Vision of God. But does Augustine then leave no room for ordinary Christian believers in this life to see God? I believe he does leave room, but the occurrence and nature of such vision must be inferred from several different ingredients in Augustine's discussion in the *Letter.* The first of these ingredients is his focus on the utter perfection of the vision of God in the next life. His point is that the *perfect* vision of God is impossible under the conditions of this life. Such vision presupposes the perfected holiness of those who enjoy it, a holiness that no one attains in this life. To see God "as he is" requires that those who see him become "like him," as St. John says, and that condition also governs how Augustine interprets the beatitude, "Blessed are the clean of heart, for they shall see God" (Matthew 5:8, Ch. 46 et passim).

But from the perfection of the beatific vision and the perfect righteousness of those who possess it in the next life it does not follow that there is no vision of God at all in this life. That there is in this life some anticipation of the beatific vision can be supported by the principle we have already employed, namely, that seeing something is characterized by a greater or lesser degree of depth and clarity. Augustine himself explicitly makes this very point in the middle of his discussion, in the *Letter to Paulina:* "It is one thing to see; it is something else to grasp the whole of something by seeing, since, indeed, a thing is seen when it is perceived as present in any way whatsoever, but the whole is grasped by seeing, when it is seen, so that no part of it escapes the notice" (Ch. 21). Now God, of course, is present everywhere—also, as we have seen, in the minds of human beings in this life. Whether, and how clearly and deeply, we see God depends on how enlightened we are, which in turn depends on how morally pure we are, which depends, finally, on whether we have the special divine faith that saves and purifies our souls.

Augustine's language clearly implies that such illumination and purity *begin* in this life and are the subjects of *progress;* this progress, too, of course, is a matter of degree:

> Since, then, we have chosen that light [of God which shines for "the eyes of the heart"] in preference to any corporeal light, not only by the judgment of our reason, but also by the longing of our love, we shall make better progress in that love the stronger we become in it, until all the infirmities of our soul shall be healed by Him who becomes merciful toward our iniquities. Having become spiritual men in this life, we shall be able to judge all things, but ourselves be judged by no man. (Ch. 44; see also Ch. 46)

Or, as he puts it in his earlier *Letter to Italica* (a brief letter whose topic anticipates that of the *Letter to Paulina*): "And the more we become like Him, the more we advance in the knowledge and love of Him, because, 'though our outward man is corrupted, yet the inward man is renewed day by day' [2 Corinthians 4:16]" (*Letter 92*). Augustine uses similar "progress" language elsewhere. In *The Usefulness of Belief* he writes: "The more pure a man is from... uncleanness the more easily does he behold the truth" (xvi, 34); and in *On Free Will:* "If ignorance and moral difficulty are natural to man, it is from that condition that the soul begins to progress and to advance towards knowledge and tranquillity until it reaches the perfection of the happy life" (III, xxii, 64).

Again, in the earlier *Letter to Italica*, commenting on one of the texts most relevant to the issue, 1 Corinthians 13:12, Augustine brings out the *continuity* between our knowledge of God in this life and in the next:

> When you read: "We see now through a glass in a dark manner, but then face to face," understand that we shall then see face to face *in the same way* as we now see through a glass in a dark manner. Both of these are attributes of the inward man, whether he walks by faith in that journey in which he uses a glass in a dark manner, or whether, in his true country, he beholds Him in a vision, and this manner of seeing is called face to face. (*Letter 92;* emphasis added)

1 Corinthians 13:12 is one of Augustine's favorite texts. This text implies a great difference between the knowledge of God in this life and in the next; but it also implies a similarity, as Augustine indicates with his phrase "in the same way." Elsewhere Augustine comments on these verses to the same effect. For example, in the *City of God*, another important source for Augustine's teaching on the beatific vision, he writes:

> Men on earth, whatever the perfection of understanding they may reach, understand far less than the angels. For we must remember that not even St. Paul, for all his greatness, could say more than this: "We know in part and we prophesy in part; until that which is perfect is come.... We see now through a mirror in an obscure manner, but then face to face." (XXII, 29; cf. also *On the Trinity*, XV, 8–11, 23, 27)

Notice that Augustine does not say that believers on earth understand nothing, know nothing, or see nothing of God, only that they see "far less than the angels."

In the *Retractation* to *The Usefulness of Belief* (cited in Chapter 3) we also found Augustine commenting on the Corinthians text, with the very purpose of clarifying the difference between the seeking of faith and the finding of knowledge and understanding. Although his main point is to contrast the great difference between the happiness of seeking in this life and that of finding in the next, he nevertheless denies that living by faith in this life is to live without knowledge and understanding:

> For they who are now in that place where we desire to arrive by seeking and believing, that is, by holding fast to the way of faith, are to be judged to have found what is to be sought. If, however, they are considered entirely happy in this life, either now or in the past, I do not think this is true, *not because in this life no truth at all can be found that can be discerned by the mind and not believed by faith, but because it is so limited, whatever it is, that it does not make men entirely happy....*
>
> For in this life, knowledge, however extensive, does not constitute complete happiness, because that part of it which is unknown is by far incomparably greater. (I, 13; emphasis added)

Thus, for all of Augustine's frequent preoccupations with the "incomparably greater" knowledge of the beatific vision, he still implies that such knowledge is greater than a knowledge of God that *begins already in this life.* To be sure, the knowledge that begins in this life depends on a continuing presence of faith, which further differentiates it from the vision of God in the next life. This continuing need for faith raises another issue we must consider: how knowing can depend on believing and not replace it, which is opposed to the way we have interpreted his formula to this point. Still, it is *knowledge* of God that faith makes possible already in this life; and this knowledge, for Augustine, is fundamentally different from faith.

Ontologism. Before turning to that issue, however, I should indicate briefly the bearing of my interpretation of Augustine's view of knowing God in this life on the disputed issue of "ontologism" in Augustine. That issue is posed by the question, do human beings, when in this life they see the truth, which originates in God's mind, thereby also see God's mind and thus see God himself in this life? The ontologist answer is Yes, the antiontologist answer is No. As Ronald Nash points out in *The Light of the Mind,* Augustine can be quoted in support of both answers (7). For example, against the ontologist answer, Augustine sometimes restricts our knowing the truth to knowing truth only as God has imprinted it on our minds, as the following passage from *On the Trinity* states: "Whence [from God's mind] every just law is copied, brought over, and imprinted in the heart of man, just as the image from a ring passes into the wax and yet does not leave the ring" (XIV, 5). Supporting the ontologist answer, however, is the following passage, also from *On the Trinity*:

> The more ardently we love God, the more certainly and the more calmly do we see Him, because we behold in God the unchangeable form of righteousness, according to which we judge that man ought to live. Therefore faith avails to the knowledge and to the love of God, not as though of one altogether unknown, or altogether not loved, but so that thereby He may be known more clearly, and loved more steadfastly. (VIII, 9; cf. also IX, 7; *Confessions* XII, 25, 35)

Here Augustine clearly says that seeing God, knowing him, is possible in this life. In Nash's words: "The vision of God is qualitatively and quantitatively different from the beatific vision, but it is nonetheless a vision of God" (121). That is also the way I interpret Augustine.

Still, there is a tension in Augustine's thinking because he accepts the biblical teaching that God transcends everything he has created, including the human mind. Augustine expresses this tension nicely in the *Confessions*. Frederick Crosson suggested to me this way of reading Augustine here, which he develops in "Structure and Meaning in St. Augustine's *Confessions*." My interpretation of Augustine in what follows is probably more Platonic than his, because he holds that "the Platonic model breaks down" (7). I agree with Crosson that the Platonic model of reminiscence must give way to the biblical model of illumination; Augustine himself is explicit about this (*On The Trinty*, XII, 15; *Retractations* I, 4,4). Still, the Platonic model is helpful for interpreting Augustine's claim that the mind which *searches* for God finds him in some way already *present to the mind* by the divine illumination.

Earlier we observed how, for Augustine, the mind sees incorporeal objects because they, unlike material objects, in some sense, can be *in the mind* itself and thereby present to it. As a Christian, however, Augustine recognizes that God is the transcendent creator of the mind; accordingly, he asks at the outset of his *Confessions*: "How shall I call upon my God, my God and my Lord, since, in truth, when I call upon him, I call him into myself? What place is there within me where my God can come? How can God come into me, God who made heaven and earth?" (I, 2, 2). Later on he contemplates the paradoxical implication of this transcendence for knowing God:

Therefore I will pass beyond even memory, so that I may attain to him who has set me apart from four-footed animals and made me wiser than the birds of the air. Even beyond memory will I pass, so that I may find you—where? . . . If I find you apart from memory, I am unmindful of you. How then shall I find you, if I do not remember you? (X, 17, 26)

Thus he must go *outside* his mind to know God, even though to know something incorporeal is to have it in his mind.

Augustine resolves his perplexity in a Platonic-like embrace of the paradox. On the one hand, God is *in* our minds and thereby present to them; for if he were not, we would not be able to seek him nor judge of anything else that it is *not* God (X, 6): "Behold, how far within my memory have I traveled in search of you, Lord, and beyond it I have not found you. . . . Wheresoever I found truth, there I found my God, truth itself" (X, 24, 36). On the other hand, God is *beyond* our minds, as their transcendent creator:

But where within my memory do you abide, Lord, where do you abide? . . . I did not find you there amid images of bodily things. . . . Nor are you the mind itself, because you are the Lord of the mind. . . . And [yet] you have deigned to dwell in my memory, whence I have learned of you. (X, 25, 37)

Where then have I found you, if not in yourself and above me? (X, 26, 37)

He concludes his struggle to understand the mystery with these famous words: "Behold, you were within me while I was outside: it was there I sought you, and, a deformed creature, rushed headlong upon these things of beauty which you have made. You were with me, but I was not with you" (X, 27, 38).

Even though Augustine thus recognizes a special problem in describing our knowledge of God, he affirms such knowledge and interprets it as a mental vision that begins and grows in this life, however dim and partial it remains. It is a knowledge that, as we have seen earlier in some of the passages cited, seems to presuppose the presence of biblical faith. Whether it does or not requires a closer look at Augustine's claim that such faith is the necessary first step toward the knowledge of God we can already attain in this life. We turn now to this question.

The Indispensability of Faith

It is almost axiomatic with Augustine, as it was with Plato in his *Republic* approach, that believing and knowing are different things, and in such a way that they are contrary states of mind. This view has the implication that if a proposition that has been taken on faith is verified by one's own observation or reason, it no longer needs to be believed; indeed, it cannot be believed. Once one knows the way to Larissa by one's own experience, one no longer has the belief that one had earlier by trusting the testimony of whoever told one the way; one now has knowledge instead.

But religious faith as Augustine generally refers to it is not thus dispensable in this life when a believer acquires knowledge and understanding of God. This is the case whether that knowledge is taken as proof as in *On Free Will* or as vision in the *Soliloquies* and *Confessions*. In the course of Augustine's development of his proof in *On Free Will*, Evodius reflects on the nature of their mutual search. Its goal is "not to state what we merely believe but what we clearly understand." He says he cannot answer a question that Augustine has just asked him about wisdom "unless in addition to believing I also know by contemplation and reason what wisdom is" (II, ix, 25). It is remarkable that Evodius here regards the understanding he seeks as something *"in addition to* believing," not *in place of* it. Moreover, after they reach the conclusion of the proof that God exists, Augustine observes, as we saw earlier: "Hence there should be no further question, but we should accept it with unshakeable faith. God exists and is the truest and fullest being. This I suppose we hold with undoubting faith. Now we attain it with a certain if tenuous form of knowledge" (II, xv, 39). Neither Evodius nor Augustine suggests that his faith is to be *replaced* by the knowledge he has attained, nor does either of them suggest anything like this in the ensuing discussion. Now the same ongoing indispensability of faith is found in both the *Soliloquies* and the *Confessions*. For all the knowledge of God by way of direct vision that Augustine reaches in this life, though it is dim and partial in comparison to the beatific vision of the next life, he nowhere suggests in those writings that such knowledge replaces his faith. How can this be?

Christian Faith. The answer to this question can be found only by returning to the differences between Christian (divine) faith and human faith, and then by deriving from these differences an account of what Augustine holds on the matter. The main differences between Christian faith and human faith, it will be recalled, are two: first, the object of Christian faith is God, not man; and second, the most significant effect of such faith is the beginning of moral purification—salvation. The first point implies that the God who is believed is *already known;* it is *his* word in Scripture that the believer identifies and believes but does not yet understand. The second point implies that the purification of the soul from sin is *only begun* in this life, so that for its completion in the next life the believer must continue to trust God and believe what he says (in a word, to have faith). Let us look at each of these implications.

Understanding as Interpretation of What Is Believed. As we have seen, half of faith is *trust* in an authority who reveals to us what we have not found out or cannot find out for ourselves. Now God is precisely such an authority, one whom we must trust; for he has revealed to us what we had not found out for ourselves but need to believe to be saved from our sin and come to know God properly again. What we must *believe*—the other half of faith—includes a great many things that are not only not discoverable apart from God's revealing them but also not immediately perspicuous to our minds. They are the *mysteries* of faith, such as that God has created all things from nothing, including human beings in his own image; that human beings fell from this created state of innocence by willful disobedience; that God is triune; that he is incarnate in Jesus Christ and redeems human beings by grace; and that human beings will be raised from the dead.

Now none of these beliefs can be demonstrated by argument, nor can any of them be easily understood by conceptual analysis. Instead, the believer must trust God for what he says about himself, the world, and human beings on all these matters. And because the believer never comes to know these things in this life independently of God's revealing them and reminding him or her of them on occasions when he or she might doubt or forget them, there is no way the believer can replace faith in God. What one can do, and what Augustine's formula of faith seeking understanding imposes as a duty on one, is to try to make these beliefs as clear, correct, and intelligible as possible. This effort requires, among other things, *studying* the revelation, and this study, in turn, requires the use of reason. Hence Augustine delivers many exhortations along this line. For example, in *Of True Religion* he writes: "Let us by the diligent study of the divine Scriptures find food and drink for our minds" (li, 100). Augustine is ever conscious that God alone is our teacher, which implies both faith in him and exercise of reason, his gift, working hand in hand. The believer must take God at his word for what he says but also analyze it carefully to grasp it as clearly, correctly, and completely as possible.

What emerges here is another important sense of the formula, faith seeking understanding, viz., the pious and diligent interpretation of Scripture. So understanding as *interpretation* must now be added to understanding as *proof* and as *vision*, which have occupied us thus far. The general purpose of interpretation is to clarify and comprehend what is believed. Augustine gives a good example in the later discussions of *On Free Will*. After Augustine and Evodius conclude their proof for the existence of God, they must still consider whether all good things come from him and whether the created will is a good thing, given that it is the origin of evil. But this discussion looks much more like trying to understand the *implications* of what is *believed* on the basis of God's revealing it than like *proving* anything to be the case. For it is only by faith that Augustine and Evodius hold that God created all things and that all things are therefore good; and that evil cannot originate in God because he is immutably good. These beliefs imply that the created will is good, because it is created by God, but also that it can be the source of evil, because it is created mutable.

By the time Augustine comes to the problem of foreknowledge and free will in Book III, the project of interpretation has moved on still further to being one of *reconciling apparent contradictions* that seem to be implied by what they believe. Says Augustine to Evodius: "Your trouble is this. You wonder how it can be that these two propositions are not contradictory and incompatible, namely that God has foreknowledge of all future events and that we sin voluntarily and not by necessity" (III, iii, 6). So reason must now remove the apparent contradiction between propositions implied by those they accept on faith. In addition, reason must take care to avoid false opinions about issues left unanswered by God's revelation, such as the origin of the soul. Here it must draw the line correctly between what God does and does not reveal. All these exercises of reason are in the service of faith: "God give us a true faith that will hold no false or unworthy opinion concerning the substance of the Creator" (III, xxi, 59).

Thus Augustine distinguishes three aspects of understanding as interpretation: the *correct* formulation of what is believed, the *consistent* formulation of it, and the *avoidance* of false beliefs. Why are these rational endeavors so important? Precisely because, says Augustine near the end of *On Free Will*, "by the path of piety we are wending our way towards [God]. If we hold any other opinion concerning him than the true one, our zeal will drive us not to beatitude but to vanity" (III, xxi, 59). Recall what we found Augustine saying in Chapter 3 on the danger of "holding opinions," that is, of thinking we *know* what we do not know; here he focuses on the related danger that we may *believe* something true that is actually false. Both could be signs of vanity and pride.

Of course, Augustine engages in the project of interpretation in many other writings besides *On Free Will*, notably in *Confessions* (XI–XIII), the *Literal Commentary on Genesis*, *Expositions on the Book of Psalms*, *On the Trinity*, *The City of God*, and in his *Sermons* and *Letters*. In none of these does he try to prove on independent grounds that such doctrines as creation, trinity, or incarnation are true; he begins with their truth because they have been revealed by God himself. The basic connection between revelation and reason, for him, is twofold: reason *believes* revelation (to be true) and *studies* it (to understand it). Not only, therefore, does faith continue to be necessary, so does reason. The two are continuously interdependent in the mind of the believer. The goal of both working together is understanding; about to interpret Genesis 1, he prays (in the *Confessions*): "Let me hear [believe] and understand how 'in the beginning' you 'made heaven and earth'"(XI, 3, 5). Faith thus *believes* what God says and then seeks to understand it; for its duty, its goal, and its reward is to know the God who thus reveals himself.

Moral Purification.   The second difference between human and divine faith is that divine faith begins to purify the mind. For this reason, too, such faith continues to be necessary in this life, because that purification is not completed until the next life. The essence of such purification is love, love of God and neighbor, topics that Augustine frequently explores. Such love is necessary, in turn, for the proper knowledge of God. For, as we saw earlier, the difficulty of knowing God arises not only from God's ineffability but also from human unrighteousness, as Augustine says at the outset of *On the Trinity:*

> It is difficult to contemplate and fully know the substance of God. . . . And it is necessary, therefore, to purge our minds, in order to be able to see ineffably that which is ineffable; whereto not having yet attained, we are to be nourished by faith, and led by such ways as are more suited to our capacity, that we may be rendered apt and able to comprehend it. (I, 1)

> The eye of the human mind, being weak, is dazzled in that so transcendent light, unless it be invigorated by the nourishment of the righteousness of faith. (I, 2)

The loving knowledge of God will be enjoyed in its perfection only in the next life; nevertheless, it begins in this life. Since it begins in this life, it must be the believer's natural knowledge of God renewed and enriched by what the believer can come to understand of what he believes. That there is such a natural knowledge of God apart from Christian faith and revelation is the topic of the next section.

   The Indispensability of Faith in the Natural Theology Tradition. The foregoing account of the ongoing necessity of faith in Augustine differs significantly from accounts that reflect the natural theology tradition. In "Faith Seeks, Understanding Finds: Augustine's Charter for Christian Philosophy," Norman Kretzmann offers such an account. Kretzmann discusses the problem of the ongoing indispensability of faith in Augustine as the problem of "the combination of faith and reason" (10). He also considers two other problems, problems we have already discussed. One of these Kretzman calls problem of "the essential precedence of faith" (11); the other, the problem of faith "characterized as seeking" (13). Kretzmann proposes to solve these problems by introducing two distinctions: one between "propositional belief" and the "way of faith"; the other between "propositional understanding" and "supernatural understanding." Propositional belief is "assent to a proposition in virtue of its having been put forward by an authority one has accepted on rational grounds" (6); the way of faith is "professing Christian doctrine and trying to live in accordance with it, faith as a way of life" (14). Propositional understanding is "assent to a proposition in virtue of its having been clarified and certified by one's reason on the basis of analysis and argument" (6); supernatural understanding is the "beatific vision" referred to in 1 Cor. 13:12 (14).

   With these distinctions in hand, Kretzmann resolves the problem of the combination of faith and reason as follows. Designating the way of faith and supernatural understanding as the "religious side" of Augustine's thought, he observes that when the formula refers to such faith and such understanding, the problem of *their* combination "does not arise because no one could be both on the way of faith and enjoying the beatific vision at once" (14), for the former characterizes this life exclusively and the latter, the next life in the same way. The main connections between the two sets of distinctions are two. First, "propositional faith is an essential ingredient in the way of faith" (15); and second, "the propositional understanding attained on the basis of reasoning in this life [is] a foretaste of the full understanding conferred directly in the beatific vision" (16). The *way of faith,* however, not the propositional faith that the way of faith includes, both seeks and is the necessary precondition for the propositional understanding (19–23). And *propositional understanding* consists of the analysis and argument typified by Augustine's proof for the existence of God in *On Free Will* (8–9). How, then, can there be both faith and understanding as compatible states of mind? As follows:

The authority-based faith that God exists, which is incorporated into the way of faith, is indeed supplanted by the acquisition of understanding on the basis of a proof that God exists. What [such] propositional understanding merely supplements is not propositional faith regarding some proposition in particular but the way of faith as a whole. (18)

Thus Kretzmann retains both points: first, that faith (as belief) is contrary to knowledge as a state of mind; and second, that such knowledge is compatible with faith (as a way of life including both the profession of other beliefs not known because not proved and the practice of Christian moral virtues).

So Kretzmann's account achieves the compatibility of Christian faith with the knowledge attained by the inferences of natural theology. But it does so at serious cost. First, only those Christians will be able to seek (and attain) such knowledge who have the ability and opportunity to do natural theology; all others must be content with propositional faith, which is the inferior state of mind. Moreover, these others can have no *duty* to seek the knowledge that natural theology finds (because ought implies can); they will need to interpret Christ's command, "Seek and you will find," in some other way. Second, only those Christians who can do natural theology are able to enjoy the foretaste of the supernatural understanding that it (alone, apparently) provides. Kretzmann's account has these unhappy consequences because it identifies the knowledge and understanding of religious beliefs available in this life with the kind of knowledge offered by natural theology. In other words, Christian *philosophers* are the only Christians who can have knowledge of God in this life and the foretaste of the beatific vision it gives.

Another unhappy consequence of Kretzmann's account is that non-Christians who are good philosophers (and who therefore presumably accept the conclusions of natural theology) can share with Christian philosophers this knowledge of "propositional understanding" and the foretaste it offers of supernatural understanding, both of which are denied to all the nonphilosophical Christians. Says Kretzmann: "Obviously a person who is not living the Christian life of faith may have propositional faith regarding some theological proposition: "God exists," for example. So some propositional faith occurs outside the way of faith, and it may raise particular problems of its own" (16). The problem I raise must be one of these, I think; but Kretzmann does not discuss it. Still, it seems clear from Kretzmann's account that that a non-Christian philosopher should be able to *supplant* propositional faith with propositional understanding by doing natural theology, just as the Christian philosopher can. For despite perhaps not having the motive for such an effort provided by the Christian way of faith, the non-Christian may have some other motive; in any case, all one requires besides a motive is the intellectual ability, training, and opportunity for doing natural theology. If one succeeds in attaining propositional understanding of the propositions supported by natural theology, it would seem to follow that one thereby also has a foretaste of the supernatural understanding that the same attainment offers the Christian philosopher. But it seems incredible that the non-Christian should achieve by doing natural theology the foretaste of heaven that most other Christians are denied because they are not natural theologians.

Two Views of Christian Philosophy. These unhappy consequences arise from Kretzmann's account because he is looking to the Augustinian formula as the "charter for Christian philosophy." But it is clear that he defines Christian philosophy in a non-Augustinian way. Kretzmann defines Christian philosophy as "the enterprise of supporting and clarifying of propositions of Christian doctrine by means of analysis and argument, building on the classical metaphysics around which Christian doctrine developed, beginning with the most fundamental propositions and proceeding in some approximation of logical order" (1). Even though his article purports to find the charter for Christian philosophy in Augustine, it is St. Thomas Aquinas's two *Summas* that he says "ought to be everyone's paradigms of attempts at doing philosophy in this way" (1).

This conception of Christian philosophy is one in which faith and reason lack, in some respects, an organic relationship within Christian thinking as such. Specifically, the faith of the few Christians who are philosophers will seek a knowledge "by analysis and argument"; but this knowledge will have no intrinsic relationship to that faith. The model for such knowledge is St. Thomas's proofs for the existence of God in the "Five Ways." The knowledge attained in these proofs by the Christian philosopher is no different essentially from the knowledge available to philosophers who philosophize without Christian faith (e.g., Aristotle, Maimonides, Averroes). Most Christians, however, as they are not philosophers, must do without such knowledge and be content with believing (by propositional faith) the propositions in which it is expressed, even the proposition that asserts the existence of God. That faith, recall, is "assent to a proposition in virtue of its having been put forward by an authority one has accepted on rational grounds" (6). Now the only way such faith can be *divine* faith (i.e., assent to a proposition in virtue of its having been put forward to the believer *by God*) is by the believer's first having found rational grounds for God's existence and for his revealing himself. The believer who is a natural theologian has found these grounds, of course; but all other believers must be content with human faith, faith in those human beings they have learned to trust who affirm that God exists and that he has revealed himself.

These unhappy consequences can be avoided in my account of Augustine, for in this account, Augustine teaches that the knowledge faith seeks is the direct knowledge of seeing God that is open to every Christian, unlike the inferential knowledge of natural theology available only to a qualified few. Such direct knowledge is a foretaste of the beatific vision because it is accompanied by the love of God, which is made possible by the "way of faith" that constitutes any person who walks in it a Christian. Insofar as Christians *see* God, it is correct to say that they *know* him; they do not just *believe* that he exists on some human authority, however well-attested that authority may be. Their knowledge, too, "supplants" propositional belief, just as in Kretzmann's account, but it does not depend on the inferences of natural theology. The way of faith, likewise, is still a necessary condition for such knowledge; but such knowledge is the renewal by that faith of a direct knowledge of God already naturally possesssed, not an indirect, inferential knowledge newly discovered by rational demonstration.

Thus I see Augustine's charter for Christian philosophy arising from a more organic connection between faith and reason. Faith purifies the reason's own natural vision of God, joins with that vision what it hears God say in Scripture, and issues in the love of God. "A true philosopher will be a lover of God" (*City of God*, VIII, 1). Faith and reason are interwoven not only in the Christian philosopher but in every Christian, in a way that is blocked by Kretzmann's account. "Faith seeking understanding" is indeed the charter for Christian philosophy. However, Augustine (as I see it), not Aquinas, is its paradigm—not the Augustine of *On Free Will*, Book II, but of the *Soliloquies* and the *Confessions*. In these books, as we saw, Christian philosophy is an enterprise of reason's clarification and deepening of its own natural and direct knowledge of God, renewed and informed by a revelation accepted by faith. What reason does not have to do, which Kretzman's definition requires of it, is to support "by . . . argument" those fundamental propositions of Christian doctrine such as "God exists" itself.

We turn now to another distinct application of Augustine's formula that, though not explicit in his writings, is necessary to complete what I have called his authentic view of their relationship.

The Natural Knowledge of God

How the Question Arises.   One problem we considered earlier in connection with taking knowledge as proof was the the problem of the necessity of faith as a *precondition* for knowing God. This was a problem, we observed, because such a precondition seems to imply that only the Christian believer is capable of knowing God, in which case Augustine and Evodius should have agreed that their first step with the fool who denies the existence of God is not to give him a proof but to make him a Christian believer. Now the different kind of knowledge, the knowledge of vision, that Augustine seeks in the *Soliloquies* might also seem to presuppose Augustine the believer, who begins with with the testimony of Scripture. So again we must face the suggestion that the formula, faith seeks understanding, is meant for Christian believers alone—that they are the only ones capable, in virtue of their faith, of seeking and attaining a knowledge of God. If this suggestion is correct, however, it sheds no light on everything Augustine says, which assumes a *natural* knowledge of God in human beings apart from the Christian faith. Indeed, the suggestion would contradict all that Augustine repeatedly says about such a universal knowledge of God and about a universal *seeking* after such knowledge apart from the aid of Christian faith and revelation.

What is the origin and nature of such knowledge? Clearly, an answer to this question cannot be found by taking the formula, faith seeking understanding, in its specific sense as referring to *Christian* faith. For most human beings do not have such faith, and yet they seek after God. And as they all have some natural knowledge of God, so, presumably, does the Christian believer, both before and after becoming a Christian. If the Augustine of the *Soliloquies* is Augustine the convert, Augustine the convert is first of all Augustine the human being (and Augustine the sinner). For being a Christian *believer* presupposes being a (fallen) *human being*, endowed with reason, who differs from fellow fallen human beings only by having faith of a special kind, the saving faith in the God revealed in Scripture.

Autobiographical Evidence.   The best evidence in Augustine for such a natural knowledge of God is his own intellectual development before his conversion. He describes in his *Confessions* how reading Cicero's *Hortensius* in his nineteenth year set him "on fire" for wisdom, many years before his conversion in his thirty-second year. And he credits the Platonists with helping him find God shortly before his conversion. They knew of God that he exists, is infinite and immutable, and that he is the ultimate origin of all things (*Confessions*

VII, 20, 26). Years later, in *The City of God*, he still praises Plato and his followers because "none of the other philosophers has come so close to us as the Platonists have" (VIII, 5).

Although writing as a convert he acknowledges the leading of God in his intellectual and religious development, he does not attribute his prior knowledge of God to his Christian faith. How could he? Such faith, and the conversion it made possible, was not yet his. In fact, as we saw earlier, he was puffed up by pride, like the Platonists whom he praises so highly for the knowledge they had discovered by reason alone. Indeed, even though he was "most certain" of this knowledge, he sees himself, from the later vantage point of a Christian believer, as having been then "on the road to perdition" (VIII, 20, 26). His prior knowledge of God was of no moral value; what the Platonists (and he with their help) knew of God did not overcome the sin of pride.

Of course, these Platonic teachings contained nothing of the revealed truths of the incarnation, the atonement, and the humility these offer as the antidote for human pride and as the source of the love of God that is necessary to knowing him properly. But there it is, a striking knowledge of God attained by pagans without, apparently, any "faith seeking understanding." The most striking truth about God, for Augustine at least, is his incorporeality. He discovered it, he tells us, with the help of these Platonists while he was still an unbeliever, at a time when he was in the grips of a materialist conception of God (IV, 16, 31; V, 10, 18) and quite unimpressed with the contrary testimony of Scripture on the subject (III, 5; V, 11), but also at a time when he was desperately seeking God, though failing to find him (IV, 15, 26; V, 2, 2).

Extension of the Formula to the Natural Knowledge of God. How then does Augustine account for such a natural knowledge of God? How is such knowledge, and even seeking it, possible without the Christian faith that he otherwise suggests is a necessary condition for seeking and knowing God? To answer this question, it will be helpful to return to what we heard Augustine say earlier about *belief* as a necessary step for *knowledge* of objects in the corporeal and incorporeal worlds. What we must do is to extend that model, in a way that parallels the Christian faith in some ways, toward an Augustinian account of this natural, universal knowledge of God.

We saw earlier in our study of *On the Teacher* that our knowledge of things, for Augustine, is not something taught us by others but something we come to see *for ourselves*. Of course our parents and teachers are necessary occasions for such learning, but ultimately the knowledge that we have by our own acquaintance with things in the world is a knowledge no one else can give us; we must acquire it for ourselves. We also saw that Augustine, like Plato before him, construes this knowledge as vision—corporeal or intellectual. We know what a head is because we have seen one with our own eyes, and what a triangle is because we have seen one with our own reason, with the eye of our mind: "The utmost value I can attribute to words is this. They bid us look for things, but they do not show them to us so that we may know them. He alone teaches me anything who sets before my eyes, or one of the other senses, or my mind, the things which I desire to know" (xi, 36). Further, we saw that all *beliefs* we acquire from the testimony of others about what exists in the world *presuppose* not only someone else's original knowledge of what exists, which is then handed down by testimony, but also our own knowledge of the kind of thing that we are asked to believe. So belief is ultimately parasitic on knowledge. We are now in a position to apply these Augustinian principles to the knowledge of God in so far as that knowledge, like other knowledge, is widely and naturally present in the human race, regardless of the specific religion professed at any given time or place.

Why has there been, and does there continue to be, so general a knowledge of God among human beings—however dim, uncertain and confused, from the earliest Semitic tribes and Greek poets down to the vast millions of people in the modern world? How did the concept of the divine arise? Why should there have become embedded in the languages of all nations, races, and tribes the word *God* or its cognates and equivalents? What is the Augustinian account of this universal natural knowledge of God? Who, to use Augustine's own words, "has set God before the human mind as an object to be believed"?

Augustine's answer to that question, had he faced it, would be in two parts. First, just as human beings from time immemorial have handed down their languages, which contain names for rivers and trees, numbers and geometric shapes, the use of which names are the occasion for other human beings coming to know these objects, so have they done the same thing with the name *God* or its cognates. Second, Augustine would say, this human testimony is the occasion, when it employs these names, for God to set before human minds not only those other realities that they come to know but also *himself*. As he says at the very beginning of the *Confessions*: "You arouse him to take joy in praising you, for you have made us for yourself, and our heart is restless until it rests in you" (I, 1, 1). God himself is the ultimate teacher of truth, the light of the mind:

> He did not make all things and then leave them, but they are from him and in him. Behold where he is: it is wherever truth is

known. He is within our very hearts, but our hearts have strayed far from him. (IV, 12, 18)

Besides you there is no other teacher of truth, no matter at what time or in what place he may have fame. (V, 6, 10)

To be sure, not all human beings follow this natural leading of the light of truth in their minds to God who is its source; however, that is not because he is not there, with them in their minds, but because they are not with him, in his truth. Nor, it may be added, is it because they are not natural theologians—philosophers skilled in disputation and argument; for if God is as present to human beings as truth itself, what they require is not the ability to infer his existence from something else that he is not, but the will to *see* him who is the source of that truth. What hinders them, therefore, is not an intellectual or logical deficiency, but a moral blindness brought on by a perverse will; that is finally what prevents their seeing the God who enlightens their minds and teaches them of himself, as well as of all the other things they know.

Thus, for the knowledge of God, it begins to look as if we need to interpret the formula, faith seeking understanding, on *two* levels in Augustine. We have seen what the formula means on the level of *revelation*. Faith, whose initial object is the testimony of Christian parents and the Church to Scripture, subsequently takes as its object God himself who speaks in Scripture, and then seeks to understand what he says there to know him better. On the level of *nature apart from revelation* also exists a testimony to the existence of God: the testimony of the human race in general, whose language is filled with the ideas of religion and God. The parallel between the two levels is this. Just as there is, for Augustine, a revealed knowledge of God that begins with a supernatural faith in what God reveals in Scripture, so there is a natural knowledge of God that begins by a natural faith in human testimony, which is the beginning of a natural knowledge of God. This human testimony, when believed and understood, becomes the occasion for a natural knowledge of God quite apart from Christian faith and revelation, just as a similar human testimony to rocks and numbers, when believed and understood, becomes the occasion for a knowledge of these objects. In each case, the knowledge includes both *that* those objects exist and something of *what* those objects are like.

Words, Concepts, and Things.   Earlier we criticized Augustine's claim that incorporeal objects are themselves in the mind as inadequate to explain their being *known*, because such knowledge must be formulated in concepts *of* the things. We should note here what doctrine of concepts or ideas, if there is any all, is implicit in Augustine. Ideas in the human mind—whether of God, numbers, or rocks—*originate* from realities presented to the mind on the occasion of hearing and understanding the words that signify both these ideas and the realities from which they are derived. This view of the mind and its natural relation to reality differs sharply from the view prevailing in modern philosophy. Ever since Descartes, and especially since Kant, the problem of knowledge is construed as the problem of proving that there is a real world corresponding to our ideas, which are taken to be the direct object of our knowledge. John Locke, in *Essay Concerning Human Understanding*, states the modern problem succinctly. Having defined an *idea* as "whatsoever is the object of the understanding when it thinks" (Introduction, 8) and *perception* as having ideas (II, 1, 9), he asks, "How shall the mind, when it perceives nothing but its own ideas, know that they agree with things themselves?" (IV, 4, 3) The answer is obvious: the mind cannot know such an agreement, for the simple reason that it has been doomed from the start to know "nothing but its own ideas."

In the ancient, realist alternative that governs Augustine's epistemology, the problem is to explain how the objects in that real world which the mind knows *become known* to the mind. The realist approach is that there is nothing in the mind that is not first in reality, except its unique capacity to become acquainted with that reality through the formulation of concepts and propositions that represent it. The only "creative" function that the mind exhibits is to rearrange the realities it thus represents into unreal, fictitious patterns and relationships. Reality that exists independently of the mind is always the *origin* of what it knows, and also the *primary object* of that knowledge. So, too, for Augustine, "words send us to things," only because the ideas that these words signify themselves originate when those things are presented to our minds in the first place. Of course, this concept of knowledge does not relieve the mind of its obligation to conceive and judge *correctly* what it comes to know and to distinguish carefully between the reality it knows and the fictions it can create from its ideas of that reality. Indeed, this concept of knowledge thereby offers a standard by which the mind can itself judge whether its obligation to conceive and judge correctly is fulfilled.

Effects of the Fall. We have distinguished a natural knowledge of God present in all human beings, which they have by the divine illumination of reason, from those things that God reveals, which only Christians are likely to believe. Actually, according to Augustine, this natural knowledge of God exists in all human beings only under the condition of the fall, a condition that diminishes and distorts the natural knowledge of God, as well as any process of natural faith seeking such knowledge. Apart from Christian faith, this natural seeking after God manifests itself in many ways, from the atheist's explicit denial that God exists at one extreme to the Platonists' discoveries about God at the other. This entire range of natural knowledge of God discloses, according to Augustine, a *seeking* for God. Now by the formula faith seeking understanding, where there is seeking, there is faith as its starting point. Because the universal knowledge of God is a *natural* knowledge, the faith that leads to it must be a *natural faith*. Such natural faith is also qualified by the fall and differs accordingly from Christian faith, both in content (what is believed) and moral attitude. Such faith, Augustine would say, issues in self-love and love of the things of this world; Christian faith, in love of neighbor and love of God. Thus the natural knowledge of God is finally differentiated among human beings by two quite different kinds of faith and love.

In summary, then, the formula of faith seeking understanding should be understood on two levels, that of a natural faith in the testimony of human beings to God, which can become a natural knowledge of God, and that of the Christian faith in God's own testimony, his revelation, which becomes knowledge only in so far as that revelation can be understood. On both levels, of course, reason transforms faith into understanding. Christian faith *converts* the mind from its fallen state. It does this in two ways. First, it purifies the *desire* and *will* of the mind to trust the testimony of authority to the existence and nature of God, whether that authority is human or divine. Second, it purifies the *reason*, motivating it to seek and sort out the truth about God, wherever it is to be found, thus enriching its vision of God.

The Paradox of Seeking

Thus seeking to *understand* what is believed on the testimony of others is seeking to *know better* what is known already. This is the place, perhaps, to discuss the paradox contained in the formula on both levels—whether it applies to the Christian knowledge of God or as we have now applied it to the universal, natural knowledge of God. It may be called the *paradox of seeking*. It was first delineated by Socrates in the *Meno*:

> I know, Meno, what you mean; but just see what a tiresome dispute you are introducing. You argue that a man cannot inquire either about that which he knows, or about that which he does not know; for if he knows, he has no need to inquire; and if not,

he cannot; for he does not know the very subject about which he is to inquire. (81a)

Socrates' resolution of the paradox lies in his theory that inquiry and learning are made possible by *recollection* (seeking what is *in the mind* all along); Augustine's resolution is that inquiry and learning are made possible by *divine illumination*, a natural condition of the mind. This illumination shows the mind what the mind is moved to seek by hearing about it on the testimony of others. Here the parallel between our coming to know the abstract entitities of the incorporeal world and our coming to know God is exact. The mind begins to know (to see) God whenever it thinkingly believes the natural testimony of other human beings. This way of coming to know God directly, not the inferential way of natural theology, is the original way in which all human beings, both those who are and those who are not brought up by Christian parents, come to know God.

Augustine works out the paradox in Book X of the *Confessions*. In short, the paradox is that he who seeks God already has found him. Augustine illustrates it with the biblical parable: "The woman who had lost the drachma and searched for it with a lamp would not have found it unless she had remembered it" (X, 18, 27). The woman would neither have sought the coin nor have been able to identify it when she found it unless she already possessed it as an idea in her memory. But she could not have this idea of it unless she knew the coin from previous experience, knew that it existed and what it was like. Likewise, suggests Augustine, when men hear the word *God*, in so far as they understand the word, they already have the idea, which they could not have unless they were already acquainted with God himself; while in so far as they still seek him, this shows only that they are not yet as well acquainted with him as they want to be.

The parable of the lost coin is perhaps misleading because it is supposed to illustrate the search for an incorporeal reality by the search for a corporeal one. When the coin is lost, the mind is no longer acquainted with it except as a memory; whereas when it is found, the mind is acquainted with it again through the senses. With God, however, the case is different. As an incorporeal being who is everywhere present, God is also always present by his illumination to the mind of human beings, as are numbers and the other abstract objects of the incorporeal world. How can it be then that these minds have *lost* their acquaintance with God? That they are no longer very well acquainted with him, of course, is the natural state of the mind as it has been affected by sin.

These questions are analogous, Augustine suggests, to those that may be raised about the search for happiness. Happiness, like

God, is also something that all human beings seek. This fact implies *both* that they know what it is, so that they must have once experienced it, "either each of us individually, or all of us together in that man who first sinned," *and* that they no longer experience it, or they would not seek it so diligently (X, 20, 29). If we have lost God as we have lost happiness, and are now unable to find him, this is not because he is not "with us," illuminating our minds, but because we are not "with him," as we heard Augustine put it earlier (X, 27, 38). We remember him because the attention of our minds was originally *turned toward* him. Now that we have *turned* our attention *away* from him, we still remember him in the idea of him that we have not lost; and we still seek him, though now in the wrong way and in the wrong places. When we find him, either by natural seeking alone or with the help of Christian faith, we find him, as Augustine did, both before and after his conversion, in the incorporeal world to which the mind has direct access. We find him, that is, where he was all along, in our own minds: "Behold, how far within my memory have I traveled in search of you, Lord, and beyond it I have not found you" (X, 24, 25). And in so far as Christian faith assists us in finding God, we also find the happiness we seek; for then we also find out from his revelation the other things about him, ourselves and the world that such happiness requires us to know, or at least to believe on his word.

Thus the search for God, for happiness, is a universal human search, characterized by a paradoxical combination of having and not having the knowledge that is sought, and significantly differentiated in its manifestations among human beings by whether they search for such knowledge and understanding apart from or under the guidance of Christian faith and revelation.

The Priority of Faith and Authority

We have noticed in Augustine both a priority of faith and a priority of reason. After briefly reviewing each of these, I want to examine first Augustine's arguments for the priority of faith in *religion,* and then his arguments more specifically for the *authority* of the Christian Scriptures. I conclude in each case that these arguments are persuasive, even if they are not conclusive. They are exactly the kind of arguments we would expect, given the role of faith and authority in everyday life.

The Priority of Reason. The priority of reason in Augustine consists in its being the faculty of knowledge. More exactly, its priority consists in having, when it knows, reality as its direct object, by contrast with faith, which, with respect to its belief element, does not. Faith has two objects, corresponding to its two elements, belief and trust. The object of trust is another *person* (who is either directly known by acquaintance to exist or believed on the testimony of another to exist); the object of belief is the proposition testified to by that person (and by any others who have handed it down to that person). Thus "in the order of reality," as Augustine says, reason is first; for when it knows, it is directly acquainted with reality, unlike belief, which is limited to the propositions that are its object.

Reason has the priority over faith also in that faith depends upon the capacities of reason for belief and trust. This dependence of belief on reason is twofold. First, the conceptual components of a belief must be formulated in an intelligible way by reason; that is, believers must know the meanings of the terms that express the proposition they believe or are about to believe, and such knowledge is the province of reason, not of belief or of trust. Second, believers must trust someone as an authority, which they can do only if they recognize someone as such; this recognition, too, is something that requires the exercise of reason. To be sure, the believers' trust in someone also requires the consent of their will, but this does not diminish the function of reason in identifying the authority as someone who is to be heard with confidence.

The Priority of Faith.   On the other hand, there is also a priority of faith. Faith has priority over reason, Augustine says, in "the order of time." Much of what we have come to know, that is, to see for ourselves, we first (in a temporal sense) believed on the testimony of another or others. We first believe the propositions, and later come to know the reality the propositions represent. This priority of faith obtains both at the point of our initial believing and of our subsequent coming to know. Initially we are taught the names of both corporeal and incorporeal objects, properties, and relationships, in a context in which we trust those who teach us these linguistic signs. Many of these objects, properties, and relationships we come to know, slowly or quickly, and then can dispense with our teachers and even our trust in them. But initially, our faith in our parents and teachers is absolutely indispensable for our learning a language and thereby coming to know reality. In whom did our first parents believe in order to know? The answer to that question is shrouded in the same mystery as the answer to the question, how could we even have had *first* parents? Scripture says only that we had them and that they had both language and knowledge of themselves, of the world, and of God.

Subsequent to our faith in our parents and teachers, however, we also acquire numerous other beliefs from many other human beings, some of which we replace with knowledge, others not. With respect to these other beliefs, we must distinguish a practical from an absolute indispensability of faith. Faith is *practically* indispensable for those things with respect to which we rely on the testimony of others because we have not the ability or opportunity to see for ourselves everything in our present world that we need or want to count on for living our lives. Faith is *absolutely* indispensable for all persons for most events in the past, which they can in no way see for themselves. This absolute indispensability of faith differs from that absolute indispensability required by the initial learning of language, for its content is *relative* to all individual persons. Those events that all individual persons must take on faith because they are past for them were contemporaneous with, and thus in principle knowable for, those human beings who lived before them (even if for practical reasons those predecessors were not able to know more than a few of them). But the absolute indispensability of faith for learning a language, which is a necessary condition for knowing reality, is not relative to an individual's time and place, but absolute for all human beings as such, if they are to become rational human beings who know anything at all.

Arguments for Faith in Religion

Suppose that the priority of faith and the priority of reason as thus summarized correctly describe Augustine's view of the human noetic condition. Let us consider, now, the arguments he offers from the priority of faith as it characterizes this *general* state of affairs in support of the priority of *religious* faith. The two main sources for these arguments are the *Confessions* and *The Usefulness of Belief*. In the former, more autobiographical work Augustine describes how he came "to prefer Catholic teaching" after being disillusioned "by rash promises of sure knowledge" at the hands of the Manichaeans (VI, 5, 7). In the latter more systematic account he elaborates the main ideas set forth in the former.

Faith a Golden Mean. Augustine recounts the critical period following his abandonment of Manicheanism at the age of twenty-nine. He remembers his skeptical attitude, on the one hand: "I held back my heart from all assent, fearing to fall headlong, and died all the more from that suspense"; and his rationalistic quest for certainty, on the other, "I wished to be made just as certain of [the spiritual] things I could not see as I was certain that seven and three make ten" (VI, 4, 6).

The first argument he offers in support of faith in religion is that it mediates between the thoroughgoing doubt of such skepticism and the rationalistic pretense of certainty that characterized Manicheanism:

> From that time forward I preferred Catholic teaching. I thought that on its part it was more moderate and not at all deceptive to command men to believe what was not demonstrated, either because it was a matter that could be demonstrated, but perhaps not to everyone, or because it was indemonstrable, than for others to make a mockery of credulity by rash promises of sure knowledge, and then commanding that so many most fabulous and absurd things be accepted on trust because they could not be demonstrated. (VI, 5, 7)

Such moderation, he assumes, is just what recommends faith for other, nonreligious matters of life. Without taking a great many things on faith, we will either have to believe nothing or wait endlessly for the demonstrations of reason. Here he applies that general lesson of life to his own religious experience.

In *The Usefulness of Belief* Augustine adds a third alternative to be avoided, viz., believing just anything, which he designates credulity. To believe nothing is to doubt everything, which prevents one from even getting started on the road to knowledge; whereas credulity is the fault of making no discrimination at all between what is true and what is false: "If the mistrustful man is at fault because he suspects everything he does not know, how much worse is the credulous man? For they differ in this, that the former doubts too much when he hears of things he does not know, while the latter does not doubt at all" (ix, 22). Thus the way of faith mediates also between excessive doubt and excessive belief.

The Inadequacy of Reasoning.   As for the alternate way of proof, Augustine allows for its possibility, both in the *Usefulness of Belief* (xi, 24) and the *Confessions* (VI, 5, 7). Still, he discourages this way in favor of faith. Most people, he says, will not be able to follow the way of reasoning. Even those few who can will harm those who cannot by setting a bad example; they may even harm themselves by coming to think too much of their own abilities (xi, 24). He therefore warns against the way of proof and reasoning as a temptation to pride: "It remains for us to consider why we should not follow men who promise to guide us by reason. . . . If one diligently considers the difference between thinking one knows, and believing upon authority what one knows one does not know, one will avoid the charge of error and boorish pride" (xi, 25). His considered advice, then, is to discourage us from finding out inferentially what needs to be known of God. As he says in the *Confessions*:

> Therefore, since we were too weak to find the truth by pure reason, and for that cause we needed the authority of Holy Writ, I now began to believe that in no wise would you have given such surpassing authority throughout the world to that Scripture, unless you wished that both through it you be believed in and through it you be sought. (VI, 5, 8)

Part of his argument here hinges on the weaknesses of reason, which (as we saw earlier) consist of its finitude and moral corruption. Part of his argument, however, is that God himself wants human beings to *seek* him through *faith* in the authority of Scripture, his Word. As evidence for this, he frequently cites Scripture itself (e.g., Isaiah 7:9; Romans 10:14). This part of his argument presupposes, of course, his more specific arguments for the authority of Scripture, which we will presently discuss. But first we must look at his argument for faith in religion from its necessity.

The Necessity of Faith.   The necessity of faith in everyday life, we saw, is both relative and absolute. It is relative to the practical limitations on our finding things out for ourselves, so that we must often believe the testimony of others. It is absolute with respect to the past, for which we cannot find things out for ourselves but must rely on the word of others. It is also absolute with respect to our original learning of the names for the things we know and thus for that knowledge itself. Now, suggests Augustine, the parallels for all of these in religion recommend the parallel thesis for the necessity of religious faith. Consider Augustine's account in the *Confessions* of why he himself came to believe Scripture:

> I considered how countless were the things that I believed, although I had not seen them nor was I present when they took place. Such were so many events in human history, so many things about my friends, so many things about physicians, so many things about countless other men. Unless we believed these things, nothing at all could be done in this life. Lastly, I thought of how I held with fixed and unassailable faith that I was born of certain parents, and this I could never know unless I believed it by hearing about them. By all this you persuaded me that not those who believe in your books, which you have

established with such mighty authority among almost all nations, but those who do not believe in them are the ones to be blamed. (VI, 5, 8)

Just as faith is so large and complex a necessity in everyday life, it should come as no surprise that it is also a large and complex necessity in religion.

The argument is persuasive, considering the examples from ordinary life Augustine mentions. These include both things we must take on faith because they are historical (past events, our parentage) and those other things in the present we believe only because we have not time or opportunity to get to know them directly (things about our friends, physicians, and "countless other men"). Now the persons and events of which Scripture tells us all belong to the past. Some of these persons and events are essential ingredients in Christian faith, for example, the birth, life, death, and resurrection of Jesus Christ. So the argument is significant and persuasive, especially if a religion, like Christianity, is rooted in historical events.

But, it may be objected, Augustine's argument assumes that God is already known. For the examples of faith he gives from everyday life (friends, physicians, other people who are contemporaneous with us) presuppose that we *already know* the *kinds* of things, new instances of which we believe on the testimony of others. For example, as Augustine himself holds, we know the physical objects and temporal events present to us at the moment as well as those we remember being present to us in the past. We also know a great many incorporeal, timeless objects (like those of mathematics and morality) that we see with an incorporeal vision of our minds. When in ordinary life, then, we believe on the testimony of others things about new persons and places or mathematical and moral entities that we have not yet seen for ourselves, we must first have come to know by our own acquaintance other like things. Therefore, we have no initial reason based on total ignorance to doubt what others tell us about some things of which we have as yet no acquaintance. But if we are totally ignorant of God—the objection continues—how can we believe the testimony of others about him? Without being able to assume any prior, independent knowledge of God, the analogy between faith in daily life and faith in religion collapses at a crucial point; so the argument based on it collapses also. The belief element of faith, Augustine himself insists, presupposes the intelligibility of what is proposed for belief, which in turn presupposes a knowledge of things like those that are unknown but proposed for belief. In other words, belief cannot begin from scratch.

The objection falls away, however, if human beings already possess a natural knowledge of God. Fortunately for his argument, Augustine holds (as I argued in an earlier section) that there is just such a knowledge of God in all human beings. If so, then his argument, more precisely stated, is this. Just as you accept on testimony a great many things about the corporeal and incorporeal worlds you already know something about, so you should accept on testimony a great many things about the God whom you already know. Thus understood, Augustine's argument is on the road again. What could be more reasonable than relying on others for many things we cannot find out by ourselves in religion, even as we rely on others for many things we cannot find out by ourselves about the present physical world, about the objects of mathematics, and even about the complexities of morality?

Arguments for the Authority of Scripture

But now another question becomes most acute. Once we have accepted the way of authority, we have to decide which authority to accept. As Augustine himself says in *Of True Religion*: "But reason is not entirely absent from authority, for we have got to consider whom we have to believe" (xxiv, 45). Because that question comes up regularly in daily life, we should expect it to come up in religion as well. And just as we might expect Augustine to begin with examples of how we evaluate authority in everyday life, we should expect him to evaluate Scripture in a similar way. Surprisingly, however, he does not begin explicitly with such examples drawn from everyday life, except in one important instance, as we shall see. What he characteristically does is to offer his reasons for accepting the testimony of Scripture as if they are good reasons quite apart from whether they also function as reasons for accepting testimony in general. Of course, we can easily fill in the analogies to everyday life, to see that Augustine's reasons for accepting Scripture really do resemble those reasons we have for accepting testimony in general.

Monotheism.   Let us begin with what Augustine says in answer to his own question as he formulates it in *Of True Religion*. He repeats this answer as something that is our *duty*: "It is our duty to consider what men or what books we are to believe in order that we may rightly worship God, wherein lies our whole salvation" (xxv, 46). He initially offers two criteria in support of believing the testimony of Scripture. First, we should "follow those who summon us to worship one

God" (xxv, 46); and second, "those are to be believed who proclaimed miracles, which only a few had actually seen, and yet were able to persuade whole peoples to follow them" (xxv, 47).

The monotheistic criterion is striking. It calls on us to evaluate the testimony of Scripture by considering its teaching, not the character of its authors. Because the writers of Scripture believe in only one God, what they say should be believed. This argument presupposes, however, that we know (or believe) independently of Scripture that monotheism is true, for if we believe that monotheism is true on the testimony of Scripture, the reasoning will be circular. Fortunately, as I argued earlier, Augustine does hold that we have such a natural knowledge, prior to and independent of our considering the testimony of Scripture, that God exists and that he is one. Unfortunately, Augustine does not himself bring in his view concerning this natural knowledge of God to undergird his use of the monotheistic criterion for accepting the authority of Scripture. He does refer, briefly, to polytheists who agree on the supremacy among their deities of one who "rules all things"; but this only alludes to the presence of such natural knowledge in human beings. He also goes on to argue: "In the realm of nature there is a presumption of greater authority when all things are brought into unity. In the human race a multitude has no power unless by consent, i.e., agreement in unity. So in religion the authority of those who summon us to unity ought to be greater and more worthy of being believed" (xxv, 46). Thus Augustine here defends the authority of Scripture in a way that parallels how we might reasonably defend the authority of any book whatever, viz., by showing how its teachings are known (or believed to be true) independently of the book itself. That is the strength of his argument.

Still, the monotheistic criterion is too broad to support the special authority of the Bible, which is what the Christian Augustine needs to defend. Why is the Bible to be preferred to the *Koran,* or the *New Testament* believed in addition to the *Old Testament?* Why should the heretical *Epistle of Manichaeus Called Fundamental* have no authority at all? Of course, Augustine did not have to consider the *Koran.* Still, he now introduces a second criterion, that of miracles, including the fulfilment of prophecy. This criterion allows him to extend religious authority beyond the *Old Testament* to the *New* (which addresses Judaism) and also, when supplemented by a third criterion, the consent of a multitude, to restrict such authority to the Bible (which addresses Manicheanism). Let us look at both miracles and consent.

Miracles.   In an important section of *The Usefulness of Belief,* Augustine brings these two criteria together and shows their relationship, although he there addresses the problem not of other religions but of heresy—in particular, the heresy of Manichaeanism. He writes:

> Christ himself . . . demanded faith above everything else and before everything else. . . . What was the purpose of so many great miracles? He said himself that they were done for no other purpose than that men should believe in him. . . . Christ, therefore, bringing a medicine to heal corrupt morals, by his miracles gained authority, but his authority deserved faith, by faith drew a multitude, thereby secured permanence of the tradition, which in time corroborated religion. (xiv, 32)

What Augustine does not do in this case, as he began to do for monotheism, is to argue for the validity of miracles as an appropriate attestation to authority in general.

So we need to ask whether a similar criterion plausibly supports the acceptance of authority in everyday life. What about the wonders worked by modern science and technology? Although these wonders are not miracles in the technical sense, it seems that we respect the authority of science largely because of these wonders, which are quite beyond the understanding of most of us. If modern science did not lead to such amazing things, it is doubtful that it would attain the impressive authority it has achieved in modern culture on the basis of its theoretical discoveries alone. When, then, Augustine traces the authority of the Church to that of the Gospel, and the authority of the Gospel authors to the authority of Christ, and the authority of Christ to his miracles and his own miraculous birth and resurrection from the dead (xv, 33), his argument compares favorably with the familiar one for the authority of modern science. It is a basic feature of human experience that working wonders attracts the respect of the multitudes and establishes an authoritative tradition in their midst.

Consent. Hence Augustine puts his faith in the authority of Scripture instead of in the Manichean appeal to reason, for Scripture has become established as an authority among the multitudes. He says, rather dramatically:

> I confess I have come to believe in Christ, and to hold that what he said is true, though supported by no reason. . . . I see that I owe my faith to opinion and report widely spread and firmly established among the peoples and nations of the earth, and that these peoples everywhere observe the mysteries of the Catholic Church. Why, then, should I not rather ask most diligently of

them what Christ taught, seeing that I was brought by their
authority to believe that what he taught was profitable? ... This
[the very existence of Christ] I have come to believe on the
ground of a report confirmed by its ubiquity, by its antiquity,
and by the general consent of mankind. (xiv, 31)

The issue of the relative position of Church and Scripture in Augustine, which divides the Catholic from the Protestant interpretations of
Augustine, is one which can be argued either way. B. B. Warfield, in
his *Studies in Tertullian and Augustine*, surveys the issue and argues for
the Protestant interpretation (178–225). He draws the distinction,
derived from John Calvin (*Institutes* I, vii, 3), "that Augustine was not
setting forth the source whence the Gospel derives its authority, but
the instrument by which men may be led to recognize that authority"
(207). Warfield elaborates on this distinction: "The unbeliever ... may
well be brought to trust the Gospel by the consent of the Church; but
the believer's trust in the Gospel finds its authority not in the Church
but in the Gospel itself, and this is logically prior to that of the
Church, though no doubt, it may be chronologically recognized last
by the inquirer" (207). Warfield's distinction echoes the Augustinian
distinction between the priority of faith and the priority of reason.
The authority of the Church's testimony is prior to the authority of
the Gospel in *time*, but the authority of the Gospel as God's word is
prior to the authority of the church in the order of *reality*. Hence I
favor the Protestant interpretation.

Moral Effect.   But even the miraculous is not as such a sufficient
criterion for the validation of Scripture. For, continues Augustine in
The Usefulness of Belief "there are two kinds of miracle. Some there are
which merely cause wonder; others produce great gratitude and good
will" (xvi, 34). As examples of these two kinds, Augustine cites a man
flying, "which brings no advantage to the spectator beyond the spectacle itself," in contrast to the miraculous healing of "some grave and
desperate disease," in response to which "love of one's healer will
surpass wonder at one's healing" (xvi, 34). Thus Augustine narrows
down the criterion of miracles to those that do us some great good. It
is interesting that he selects those that heal sickness and disease, for
such miracles also provide a metaphor for one more criterion that
Augustine appeals to for the authority of Scripture, namely, that it
offers to do us some *moral* good we cannot do for for ourselves. This
moral good Augustine frequently describes in the language of the
healing of disease, whether by miracle or medicine.

As we saw earlier, Augustine is deeply convinced that we cannot hope to know God as we should without the moral cleansing and purification of our minds and lives. He repeats this theme in the context of the passages we have been discussing from *The Usefulness of Belief*: "To wish to see the truth in order that you may purge your soul is a perverse and preposterous idea, because it is precisely in order that you may see, that it has to be purged" (xvi, 34). The further criterion for accepting the authority of Scripture, then, is its moral power.

Expert Ability.   There are better and worse ways of addressing the moral problems of life that we are unable to solve. Here, at last, Augustine explicitly argues for the authority of Scripture from an experience of everyday life. In seeking things that can do us good, we look to experts in those things. Consider again Augustine's autobiographical account in the *Confessions*:

> By believing I could have been healed, so that my mind's clearer sight would be directed in some way to your truth. . . . But as often happens, just as a man who has had trouble with a poor physician fears to entrust himself even to a good one, so it was with my soul's health. In truth it could never be healed except by believing, but lest it believe what was false, it refused to be cured and it resisted the hands of you who have compounded the remedies of faith, and have applied them to the diseases of the whole world. (VI, 4, 6)

Augustine understands the state of his mind prior to his conversion by analogy with a disease in the body. The structure of his argument is this. Just as we should entrust ourselves to the best physician to restore our health when we are ill, so we should entrust ourselves to the best religious authority to restore our minds to moral purity. He found that authority, of course, in Scripture, as it was expounded by Bishop Ambrose on behalf of the Church (VI, 4, 6).

In *The Usefulness of Belief* Augustine brings together the last three criteria (consent, moral effect, and expertise) when he exhorts his friend Honoratus to abandon the Manicheans. Honoratus should accept the *Old Testament* (which they reject) because it is accepted by the Church. The Church, of course, by Augustine's day, consisted of multitudes: "Christians are more numerous than Jews and idolaters combined" (vii, 19). Honoratus should imagine himself "for the first time inquiring to what religion we are to entrust our souls for purification and restoration," noting that "the question of truth does not . . . concern us just now" (vii, 19). Augustine means that, although Honoratus is searching for truth, he must start his search "from scratch" (vii, 16). That implies that he should pay attention to what impresses the multitudes, even as a student of oratory should listen to what they say. Following the multitudes will lead such a student to Cicero. And why? Augustine answers: "Everyone wants to study Cicero's works because they are established by the authority of our ancestors. The crowds of the unlearned endeavour to learn what is prescribed for their learning by a few learned men.... Perhaps true religion is something like that" (vii, 16; cf. vi, 13 for a similar argument from the authority of Virgil).

There follows an autobiographical section that parallels his account in the *Confessions* referred to earlier. As Augustine was about to break with the Manicheans, he recognized the conflict between "so many dissentient voices"; still, because he desired to find the truth, "I made up my mind to continue a catechumen in the Church in which I had been brought up by my parents until either I discovered the truth I was seeking or was persuaded that nothing was to be got by seeking" (viii, 20). Augustine thus sees in himself a model for his advice to Honoratus.

Human Authority and Divine Authority

The model is one of following established human authority—in Augustine's own case, the authority of his parents and of the Church. This authority leads him to Scripture, just as the teachers of rhetoric lead the student of rhetoric to the writings of Cicero. But notice what Augustine's example from rhetoric implies for religion. Just as students go to Cicero because of the authority Cicero enjoys among the people, so he *went* to Scripture on the basis of the authority it enjoyed with the multitude of Christians; just as students stay with Cicero because they find in him what they seek, so he *stayed* with Scripture because he found there the truth he was seeking. Although he could not *know* ahead of time when he was acting on human faith that he would find the truth in Scripture, when he did find it there and stayed with the Scripture, this must have been for a reason different from those reasons he offers for *coming* to Scripture in the first place. Those reasons are its monotheism, its miracles, the consent of many, it moral effect upon them, and its expertise. The reasons are persuasive to *attract* him (and Honoratus) to Scripture, but not sufficient for him to *adhere* to it. For this, he needs more; he needs to *find* there what he seeks. What he seeks is God himself.

In "On Obstinacy in Belief" C. S. Lewis makes a similar distinction, with an eye on the relevance of evidence to belief:

We must beware of the confusion between the way in which a Christian first assents to certain propositions and the way in which he afterwards adheres to them.... Of the second it is true, in a sense, to say that Christians do recommend a certain discounting of apparent contrary evidence.... But so far as I know it is not expected that a man should assent to these propositions in the first place without evidence or in the teeth of evidence. (17)

Augustine's "reasons" for initially accepting the authority of Scripture parallel C. S. Lewis "evidence," which can be offered someone "in the first place." Although insufficient for *adhering* to Scripture, such reasons seem appropriate and even necessary for initially attracting the unbeliever to Scripture.

In other words, human authority must finally yield to divine authority; human faith to divine faith. At some point the believer no longer believes the testimony of human beings but the revelation of God. Already in *Divine Providence and the Problem of Evil*, one of his earliest works, Augustine explicitly makes the crucial distinction: "Authority is, indeed, partly divine and partly human, but the true, solid and sovereign authority is that which is called divine" (II, 9, 27). The distinction governs his thinking from that time on. For example, he says in *The City of God:* "The expression, 'City of God,' which I have been using is justified by that Scripture whose divine authority puts it above the literature of all other people and brings under its sway every type of human genius" (XI, 1). Again, in the anti-Pelagian treatise, *On Nature and Grace*, he puts the authority of Scripture above even that of the Church Fathers, with respect to whose writings he feels himself "free to use [his] own judgment (owing unhesitating assent to nothing but the canonical Scriptures)" (lxxi). In the same vein he writes in a *Letter:* "We are not obliged to regard the arguments of any writers, however Catholic and estimable they may be, as we do the canonical Scriptures (*Letter 148*, to Fortunatianus).

What, finally, is the basis for his accepting Scripture as divine? Not the arguments we considered earlier, from monotheism, miracles, consent of the people, moral effect, and expertise; for, although they are all reasonable arguments in support of authority and have parallels outside of religion, at most they attract the seeker to Scripture. The certainty with which Augustine accepts its authority as divine must arise from his discovery in it of God himself. For human faith to become divine faith, it must be changed to faith in God. God alone gives the understanding and salvation that faith seeks, and he gives it in his own word. As Augustine states it in the *Confessions*, meditating on Psalm 4:

Oh, if they [who seek God in outward things] would only grow weary of their hunger, and say, "Who will show us good things?" Then we would say, and then they would hear, "The light of your countenance, O Lord, is signed upon us," for we are not "the light that enlightens every man," but we are enlightened by you, so that we who were heretofore in darkness may be light in you. Oh, if they would only see that inner eternal light, which I had tasted. (IX, 4, 10)

The author of these words is no longer accepting the authority of Scripture on the testimony of the Church nor the existence of God on the testimony of the authors of Scripture; he is, with them, hearing God for himself in the words of Scripture. Having begun with faith in human authorities, he now has faith in divine authority and is beginning to see God as only the pure in heart can see him and to attain the understanding his faith seeks.

To summarize Augustine's doctrine of the knowledge of God: whether that knowledge is manifested in the converted Christian or in someone apart from Christian conversion, it consists in a direct and original intellectual vision and is not derived first of all by way of proof or argument. As such, it is like all initial knowledge of corporeal and incorporeal things. Thus it is to be distinguished from faith, which is accepting something about such things on the testimony of another person, human or divine. Believing God, that is, what God reveals in Scripture, incorporates, renews, corrects, and supplements the natural knowledge of God that human beings possess apart from that revelation. Thus, the most important differentiation of the knowledge of God that human beings manifest is owing to the presence or absence in them of Christian faith, with all the noetic and moral transformations which accompany that faith.

The directness or immediacy of human knowledge of God is a legacy that Augustine inherited both from Plato's account of knowing the Good and from the Bible's assumption that we know God prior to its command to believe in him. It is the legacy he, in turn, left to the Middle Ages. There, however, the legacy was obscured by the ascendancy of natural theology, in which St. Thomas Aquinas played a central role. The legacy was revived by the Protestant Reformers, notably John Calvin. Calvin elaborated the Platonic and biblical teachings on knowledge and faith as they were combined by Augustine, although in his own original way. I will now examine his thought, for it forms the immediate inspiration of Plantinga's contemporary Reformed epistemology.

6   The Universal Awareness of God: John Calvin

John Calvin's *Institutes of the Christian Religion*, says John T. McNeill, "is justly regarded as a classical statement of Protestant theology" ("Introduction," Battles translation, 1). In *Calvin's Doctrine of the Knowledge of God*, T. H. L. Parker observes:

> The chief source for our understanding of Calvin's doctrine of the Knowledge of God is therefore the 1559 *Institutio*, his last word, so to speak, on the subject. . . . The *Institutio* needs also to be compared with Calvin's other writings, and particularly with the Commentaries. There is nothing in the Commentaries that does not also come in the *Institutio*, but at the same time there are a good many things which he expresses far more forcefully and sometimes more fully in them. (3)

Unlike Augustine, who elaborates his theme of faith seeking understanding in widely scattered works, Calvin systematically sets forth his view of of faith and knowledge in this one comprehensive theological treatise. Hence we can concentrate our study on the *Institutes*.

Immediacy and Vitality

What, then, is Calvin's main theme with respect to the knowledge of God? Although his commentators disagree on many issues arising from Calvin's discussion of faith, reason, knowledge, and revelation, they agree that Calvin emphasizes two characteristics of the human knowledge of God: its *immediacy* and its *vitality*. Thus, on the former, McNeill writes: "At the beginning of the *Institutes* [Calvin] deals impressively with the theme: How God is known. The whole work is suffused with an awed sense of God's ineffable majesty, sovereign power, and immediate presence with us men" ("Introduction," li). John Baillie, in *Our Knowledge of God*, has done more than most of Calvin's followers to elaborate this concept of immediacy (Ch. 3, 4). Edward Dowey, in *The Knowledge of God in Calvin's Theology*, discusses the accomodated, correlative, existential, clear, and comprehensible character of our knowledge of God, but surprisingly omits its immediacy (3–40). He clearly assumes it, however, when he later discusses the *sensus divinitatis*, the witness and illumination of the Spirit, and the "problem of natural theology" in Calvin (50–56, 89–124 and 172–180, 131–147).

On the vitality of the knowledge of God in Calvin, McNeill says: "This awareness of God is for him neither a product of speculative thinking nor an incentive to it. He rejects the intellectual indulgence of detached speculation. . . . It is not what God is in Himself—a theme in his view beyond human capacity—that concerns his mind, but what God is in relation to His world and to us" ("Introduction," l). "In relation to us" God is first of all our *creator*, so that knowing him should evoke our response of *piety*, which Calvin defines as "that reverence joined with love of God which the knowledge of his benefits induces." In his famous words, "we shall not say that, properly speaking, God is known where there is no religion or piety" (I, ii, 1). Dowey calls this the "existential" characteristic of our knowledge of God, and mentions other useful synonyms for it: *moral, religious, practical, nonspeculative, nonneutral* and *nondisinterested* (24–31). I call this second feature the *vitality* of human knowledge of God to use a word that can refer both to this *proper knowledge* of God, which is characterized by the response of piety, and to what I will call the deficient knowledge of God, which is characterized by fear, disobedience, and idolatry. For, as we shall see, there is no knowledge of God for Calvin that is not differentiated among human beings by these two opposed religious or moral responses.

Although the commentators generally agree on this latter point, they sometimes obscure it by their other disagreements over the interpretation of Calvin. For example, Dowey argues that the overarching theme of the *Institutes* is a twofold knowledge of God consisting of knowing him as Creator and Redeemer. He notes that Calvin himself marks it out in I, ii, 1 (Ch. 2). Parker disagrees with Dowey and argues that there is, indeed, a twofold knowledge in Calvin, but that it is the knowledge of God and ourselves, which Calvin marks out in the very opening sentence of the *Institutes* (I, i, 1). According to Parker, knowing God and ourselves is the more fundamental theme that entails knowledge of God as Creator and Redeemer (117–125). Dowey and Parker argue vigorously for their different interpretations; each interpretation can be supported from the text, and each has interesting implications for understanding the outline and organization of the four books that make up the final edition of the *Institutes*. One advantage of Parker's approach is that it directly implies the second aspect of the knowledge of God, which I have called its *vitality*. For if the knowledge of God and of ourselves are "closely interwoven," as Parker says, it will follow that the knowledge of God is such that it must "make a difference" to us. The difference it makes is momentous, as we shall see.

Calvin's view of our knowledge of God as something *vital* and *momentous* calls to mind William James's analysis of the characteristics of religious "options" as "1, *living* or *dead;* 2, *forced* or *avoidable;* 3, *momentous* or *trivial*." In *The Will to Believe* James says: "We may call an option a *genuine* option when it is of the forced, living, and momentous kind" (3). There are at least two important differences between Calvin and James, however. First, for Calvin, the knowledge of God *itself* compels the "genuine option," whereas for James the option is created by *any* two *beliefs about God* between which one must choose. Second, for Calvin, every human being has already made a basic response to God that, apart from divine grace, determines the fundamental character of our present and future responses to God; for James, on the other hand, the will is *undetermined* in the face of alternative beliefs that create the genuine options for us. The implications of these differences, needless to say, are far-reaching and profound.

I believe that the overarching themes of Calvin's *Institutes* are the *immediacy* and the *vitality* of all human knowledge of God. I will support this claim by examining the relevant passages in which Calvin elaborates each one. The theme of immediacy is evident in his teaching of the the universal awareness of God (*sensus divinitatis*) and of the testimony (or illumination) of the Holy Spirit. The theme of vitality is evident in his teaching that there is a "proper knowledge" of God in the Christian believer and a "deficient knowledge" of God in the unbeliever.

Faith as Knowledge

I propose to begin, however, with Calvin's conception of faith, which has received less philosophical scrutiny than it deserves. Instead of carefully distinguishing faith from knowledge in the manner of St. Augustine and other medievals, let alone attempting to define knowledge in terms of belief as Plato does in the *Theaetetus*, Calvin defines faith in terms of knowledge. This move would seem like an abrupt departure from the tradition, marking an end of the medieval efforts to distinguish between between Greek philosophical and biblical religious ideas. That is why I propose to begin with Calvin's definition of faith. It will give us some general sense of his religious epistemology and force us to determine whether his conception of faith really does depart significantly from the Augustinian view. To do this, however, we must immediately plunge deeply into the *Institutes*, into Book III, in fact; for that is where Calvin discusses the nature of faith.

Here is Calvin's definition of faith as knowledge: "Now we shall possess a right definition of faith if we call it a firm and certain knowledge of God's benevolence toward us, founded upon the truth of the freely given promise in Christ, both revealed to our minds and sealed upon our hearts through the Holy Spirit" (III, ii, 7). There seem to be two different ways of analyzing Calvin's identification here of Christian faith as knowledge. He may have wanted to claim that faith is literally a kind of knowledge; in this case it appears that he thought of such knowledge as unique, unlike any other kind. Or, he may have wanted only to emphasize the certainty of faith; in this case his definition can be brought into line with the traditional Augustinian (and medieval) views that keep faith and knowledge distinct. Let us examine each possibility.

A New Sense of Knowledge?   On the "unique" approach, Calvin's contribution to epistemology would be more dramatic than Augustine's. For although Augustine only brings together the established Greek and biblical ideas into a combination not previously discovered by philosophers, Calvin (on this approach) goes one step further by introducing the novel view that faith, or Christian faith at least, is knowledge itself. T. H. L. Parker elaborates and defends this view. "To believe in God is to know God: the knowledge of God is a knowledge of faith" (105). He goes on: "The knowledge of God cannot be regarded as one of the branches of epistemology, but differs fundamentally from all other forms of knowing" (106). Parker then cites several passages from Calvin's *Institutes* and *Commentaries* that support his interpretation (108).

He also offers his own arguments for the view. First he argues that knowledge of God must be unique because of God's transcendence. Transcendence implies a complete "discontinuity" between man and God, the knower and the known; revelation alone can bridge this discontinutiy. This revelation can be known only if God gives us another mind equal to the revelation, as Calvin writes in his *Commentary* on Ephesians 4:23: "There is an implied contrast between the spirit of our mind and the Divine and heavenly Spirit, who produces in us another and better mind." The difficulty in this argument is that it implies the inherent inadequacy of our natural faculties, even as restored from their fallen state by divine grace. Parker realizes this difficulty, but in trying to meet it he gives up the force of his interpretation, for he says: "Calvin did not mean that our natural faculties are destroyed when we believe and new faculties given us by the Spirit. . . . It is indeed the human soul which knows God but it is the soul enlightened by the Holy Spirit" (108). But he cannot have it both ways: either our natural faculties are restored, so that they are made capable again of knowing God properly; or they are incapable of knowing God properly, so that the proper knowledge of God is attained in some unique way. It seems that Parker favors the latter alternative when he concludes by saying that "the knowledge of God is not a common act of cognition but the unique act of faith" (109). Calvin himself, however, invites Parker's interpretation, for (as we shall see later) Calvin fails to explain exactly what he thinks grace implies for the renewal of human reason. The result of this failure is clear. We may be tempted to take faith and revelation as unconnected to our created noetic nature, and thus as constituting an entirely novel way of knowing God.

Second, Parker argues that the knowledge of God is unique because it is a "pious knowledge" involving our affections as well as our intellect: "For Calvin it is unthinkable that one part of man could be in a true relationship with God while another was totally unaffected by Him" (107). Parker's claim is correct, but it does not prove that the knowledge of God is unique, only that it is "vital," as I have called it, analogous to the knowledge we have of other things that makes a practical difference to us and therefore affects our emotions and our will. Actually, this argument undermines the uniqueness it is designed to support, implying as it does that our affections as well as our intellect—both "parts" of human nature—are involved in the knowledge of God and not, therefore, some supernatural faculty added to them. I conclude, then, that these arguments for taking Calvin's definition of faith as *knowledge* in some novel sense are unconvincing.

Knowledge as Certainty.   There remains the alternative approach, which is that Calvin defines faith as knowledge only to emphasize the *certainty* of faith. I once suggested this approach, without arguing for it, in "Faith and Reason in Calvin's Doctrine of the Knowledge of God" (37). Since then Arvin Vos has argued for this interpretation in *Aquinas, Calvin, and Contemporary Thought*. In addition, Vos shows how the interpretation brings Calvin's view into line with that of the medievals, especially St. Thomas Aquinas.

What we must do, Vos suggests, is to examine carefully Calvin's own analysis of his definition of faith as knowledge. Says Calvin in this analysis: "When we call faith 'knowledge' we do not mean comprehension of the sort that is commonly concerned with those things which fall under human sense perception. For faith is so far above sense that man's mind has to go beyond and rise above itself in order to attain it" (III, ii, 14). Although that latter sentence suggests Parker's interpretation of the knowledge as unique, the former distinguishes knowledge from comprehension. The question is, Why does Calvin makes that distinction? He tells why:

> Even where the mind has attained, it does not comprehend what it feels. But while it is persuaded of what it does not grasp, by the very certainty of its persuasion it understands more than if it perceived anything human by its own capacity. . . . From this [some Scripture passages he quotes] we conclude that the knowledge of faith consists in assurance rather than in comprehension. (III, ii, 14)

So by "the knowledge of faith" Calvin means assurance, not comprehension. Vos explains:

> This distinction between assurance and comprehension is surprising and even puzzling at first sight. By *assurance* Calvin means what we often call "certitude," and by *comprehension* he means "understanding" in its common usage. Typically we become certain about a matter when we understand it: assurance follows upon comprehension. (4)

Noting the emergence of this distinction in Calvin's analysis leads Vos to ask the important question: "But if comprehension is not the basis of assurance or certitude, then what is?" (5) The answer is, of course, the divine nature of the authority on which the believer believes the "content of faith" (5).

Vos does not focus upon this answer as the essence of the solution to the problem in his ensuing discussion; instead, he probes a number of other issues such as the effect of divine illumination on the mind, the role of the heart (which Calvin identifies with the will), the difference between faith and opinion, the relation of faith to Scripture, and the possibility of retaining the word *knowledge* for the "content of faith" (7–9). These issues are all relevant, of course; but their relevance to the source of the *certainty* of faith is only implicit. After presenting Aquinas's view of faith and knowledge, and in the course of comparing it with Calvin's, however, Vos concludes that for Calvin, as for Aquinas, the certainty of faith arises from the reliabilty of God, on whose authority the believer believes what he believes:

> A person who does not understand a matter might nevertheless accept it as true, but will do so only on the basis of some exter-

nal authority. If the authority is completely reliable, belief can be certain. This is the meaning of *to believe* that is complementary to the sense of *to know* as comprehension. Of course, in common usage, we often speak of knowing things we do not ourselves understand but have simply accepted on the authority of others. In this case *to know* indicates an assurance or an absence of doubt grounded in authority. (19–20)

Although Calvin does not explicitly consider this sense of *to know*, I agree with Vos "that it is implicit in his contrast of the knowledge of faith with the knowledge of things known through the senses" (18–19).

I conclude that, when Calvin defines *faith* as knowledge, he is not really introducing a brand new kind of knowledge into the world but emphasizing the certainty of the content of Christian belief, certainty which is based on the authority of God who speaks in Scripture. This interpretation also comports well with the rest of what Calvin says in the definition, viz., that the knowledge of faith is "founded upon the truth of the freely given promise in Christ, both revealed to our minds and sealed upon our hearts through the Holy Spirit" (III, ii, 7). In other words, the Christian believer is *certain* "of God's benevolence toward us" (the content of faith) because the Holy Spirit (God himself) is the authority on whose word he believes it, *not* because he *knows* it by having seen or comprehended it with his own mind. The interpretation brings Calvin's view of faith into line with Augustine as well as with Aquinas.

This alignment between Calvin and Augustine allows us, I note incidentally, to assimilate their view of divine faith to my own justified true belief theory of knowledge, outlined at the end of Chapter 1. If the concept of knowledge can be extended to those true beliefs warranted by the reliability of the authority on whose testimony they are accepted, believing what God says will count as knowledge indeed. That way of defining knowledge in terms of true belief is not, of course, what Calvin has in mind when he identifies faith as knowledge; for he is no more aware of such an approach to a theory of knowledge than is Augustine. If Calvin's thought can be aligned with that of Augustine, then he also distinguishes faith (in what God says) from knowledge (of God himself) as two rather different states of mind. Although both faith and knowledge may be accompanied by certainty, the certainty arises in different ways. We can now explore further just how, for Calvin, the knowledge of God differs from faith.

Creation, Fall, and Redemption.   In keeping with Calvin's biblical orientation, it is necessary to examine the immediacy and vitality of the knowledge of God by frequent reference to the biblical themes of creation, fall, and redemption. The questions that keep arising are, First, what in our knowledge of God is owing to our nature, that is, to our being the kind of being God created us to be? Second, what are the effects of the fall on that natural knowledge of God? Finally, what are the effects of grace and redemption on that fallen natural knowledge of God? Calvin gives his answers to all these questions early in the *Institutes*, in the first seven chapters of Book I. Later he elaborates on each answer, especially at three specific points (I, xv; II, i–iii, and III, ii).

The Immediacy of Our Knowledge of God

Calvin is justly famous for his claim: "There is within the human mind, and indeed by natural instinct, an awareness of divinity" (*sensus divinitatis*; I, iii, 1). I will discuss this awareness of divinity under the following topics: its immediacy, its naturalness, its content, its implication for natural theology, and finally, its differentiation among human beings as determined by the presence or absence of Christian faith.

Immediacy. The term *awareness* (Latin: *sensus*) is drawn from the language of our sensation of physical objects, and suggests therefore that Calvin thinks of our knowledge of God by analogy with our acquaintance with these objects. The important parallel is the *directness* or the *immediacy* of our knowledge of God. The directness and immediacy of such knowledge is to be contrasted with the indirectness and remoteness that characterize both the conclusions derived from reasoning and proof (the hallmark of natural theology) and the beliefs acquired on the testimony of other human beings. If Calvin is clear on anything, it is that knowledge of God is first of all a knowledge by direct acquaintance with him. God is, for Calvin, directly *present* to human minds, analogous to the way in which sense objects (and Augustine's incorporeal objects) are present. The only difference between Calvin and Augustine (in our discussion so far) is that Calvin uses the language of experience signified by the term *awareness*, not the language of reason and rational vision of Augustine.

The Term Natural. Calvin's awareness of divinity is, like sensation and reason, *natural* to human beings. "There is within the human mind, and indeed by natural instinct, an awareness of divinity" (I, iii, 1). Here, and elsewhere, Calvin preserves the concept of *nature* and the *natural* that was his legacy from Greek and medieval thought. The world of nature and human life are *objectively given* to the human mind that seeks knowledge of both; the world (including its human beings and their minds) has a structure that is both intelligible and good. The world is both intelligible and good because it is a creation of God; that is the way God made it. Here Calvin shows his agreement both with the classical realist philosophical tradition and the biblical view, which identifies this nature of things as originating from God.

Sometimes Calvin uses the term *natural* to describe the present, *fallen* condition of humankind. He is careful, however, to distinguish this sense from the traditional ontological sense:

> Therefore we declare that man is corrupted through natural viti-ation, but a vitiation that did not flow from his nature. We deny that it has flowed from nature in order to indicate that it is an adventitious quality which comes upon man rather than a sub-stantial property which has been implanted from the beginning. Yet we call it "natural" in order that no man may think that any-one obtains it through bad conduct, since it holds all men fast by hereditary right. (II, ii, 11)

As McNeill indicates in a footnote, "once this double use of 'nature' is understood, Calvin's meaning at a given place is easily determined by context" (I, i, 2, n. 7).

Some of Calvin's modern followers quite ignore this ontological concept of nature in Calvin when they interpret his epistemology. John Baillie, for example, writes: "The truth is that there is in man no *nature* apart from *revelation*. Human nature is constituted by the self-disclosure to this poor dust of the spirit of the living God" (41). This absorption of an ontological idea (nature) by an epistemological one (revelation) is a typically modern development reflecting the influ-ence of subjectivistic idealism; such idealism threatens the integrity not only of the philosophical concept of nature but the theological concept of creation. Such confusion is entirely foreign to Calvin. For him the ontological status of human nature and of the universe in which that nature has a place is *confirmed* by the revelation of God in Scripture, according to which both are objective realities that God cre-ated distinct from himself.

Similarly, some of Calvin's modern followers obscure the *natu-ral* knowledge of God in Calvin by construing his awareness of God as a "natural revelation." John T. McNeill reflects this tendency in the very first footnote he supplies to the first book of the *Institutes*. The title of this book is "The Knowledge of God the Creator." Says McNeill, "The word 'knowledge' in the title, chosen rather than 'being' or 'existence' of God, emphasizes the centrality of revelation in both the structure and the content of Calvin's theology." (35, n. 1; see also 43, n. 1). McNeill's suggestion disposes the unwary reader mistakenly to think that the knowledge of God, for Calvin, is originally by revelation. But Calvin himself does not even use the word *revelation* to describe the knowledge of God in the first four chapters of Book I, and these chapters are central to his teaching on the knowledge of God. The term *general revelation*, which has come to designate what Calvin calls our natural knowledge of God, does not appear in the Reformed tradition until the nineteenth century. John Baillie, in *The Idea of Revelation*, explains how the concept of general revelation came to replace the concept of natural knowledge of God in modern theology (Ch. 1). And G. C. Berkouwer, in *General Revelation*, suggests something of the ferment of ideas that affect Protestant theology today as a result (Chs. 1, 7). In his recent *Revelation in Religious Belief* George Mavrodes also assimilates Calvin's natural knowledge of God to revelation (63–74), but not without questioning the propriety of doing so (5).

T. H. L. Parker argues that Calvin's awareness of God, interpreted as a natural revelation, makes any argument for the existence of God unnecessary. "The problem of the knowledge of God," he says, "is the problem of revelation," not a problem in natural theology, as it is in St. Thomas Aquinas (7–9). But this conclusion quite obscures the basic difference between Aquinas and Calvin. The issue between them is not over the necessity of revelation for the *proper* knowledge of God, but over the character of our *natural* knowlege of God. Calvin holds that this knowledge is *immediate*, as his "awareness of God" implies, while St. Thomas holds that it is *inferential*, on the model he provides with his own "Five Ways" in the *Summa Theologica* (I, Q.2, A.3). To be sure, St. Thomas does not deny a natural and immediate knowledge of God: "To know that God exists in a general and confused way is implanted in us by nature, inasmuch as God is man's beatitude" (I, Q.2, A.1, R.O.1). The difference between St. Thomas and Calvin, however, is that for St. Thomas this knowledge is only "general and confused" whereas for Calvin (as we shall see presently) it is quite specific and clear.

How does Parker reach his conclusion that Calvin's natural awareness of God is a natural *revelation*? He does so by starting with the following claim about revelation: "Revelation implies not only the impossibility of knowledge without it but also the will of God to be known and his ability to make himself known, as well as the capability of man to receive revelation (even if this capability is caused by revelation itself)" (12). Parker offers no argument, however, to support his claim that revelation (divine testimony) implies the impossibility of any other kind of knowledge of God. The claim simply begs the question and, in any event, it is contradicted by the opening chapters of the *Institutes*, in which Calvin clearly delineates a natural human knowledge of God. For Calvin, this awareness of God originates quite differently from the knowledge made possible by revelation:

> Men of sound judgment will always be sure that a sense of divinity which can never be effaced is *engraved upon men's minds*. Indeed, the perversity of the impious, who though they struggle furiously are unable to extricate themselves from the fear of God, is abundant testimony that this conviction, namely, that there is some God, is naturally inborn in all, and is *fixed deep within*, as it were *in the very marrow*.... From this we conclude that it is not a doctrine that must first be learned in school, but one of which each of us is master from his mother's womb and *which nature itself permits no one to forget*, although many strive with every nerve to this end.
>
> Besides, if all men are born and live to the end that they may know God, and yet if knowledge of God is unstable and fleeting unless it progresses to this degree, it is clear that all those who do not direct every thought and action in their lives to this goal degenerate from *the law of their creation*. (I, iii, 3; emphasis added)

Thus, instead of invoking the concept of revelation, Calvin repeatedly attributes the awareness of God to human *nature*, that is, to the kind of being God *created* when he made human beings, not to the way in which he *revealed* himself, through Scripture and Incarnation, both of which (he clearly holds) are partly *supernatural* in nature and origin.

Content. We should now consider the content of this natural knowledge of God, and this will lead us to the role of reason. The content of the natural awareness of God is both definite and momentous: "that there is a God and that he is their Maker" (I, iii, 1). How does the awareness of God come to contain these very important propositions? Edward Dowey observes that the *sensus divinitatis* "is not very closely defined in Calvin's thought." In particular, it does not seem to be a "special organ or faculty of the soul" (50). This claim is supported by the fact that Calvin does not return to the *sensus divinitatis* except when he identifies it as the "seed of religion" (I, iii, 1–3; see also I, xv, 6). It is not one of the faculties of the soul; for an account of these Calvin consciously follows Plato (I, xv, 6, 7). He takes fantasy (perception), reason and understanding to be "three cognitive faculties of the soul." How, then, is the awareness of God connected to reason as a faculty? Though Calvin does not say, it must be that reason *formulates* for its understanding the *content* of the awareness of God in specific propositions. Two of these propositions have already been mentioned: that God exists and that he is our Maker; others that Calvin includes are that God is majestic, that he ought to be worshipped, and that he is just one being, not many (I, iii, 1; x, 3).

These are the main propositions that express the knowledge of God that all human beings possess by natural reason alone, that is, by the reason that formulates the content of their immediate awareness of God. Although Calvin does not thus explicitly link the awareness of God to reason, he gives us warrant for doing so by what he says about reason. For one thing, he sees no conflict between the function of natural reason and the knowledge of God: "The more anyone endeavors to approach to God, the more he proves himself endowed with reason" (I, xv, 6). Elsewhere, he declares that reason's highest and final purpose is to know God: "Man in his first condition excelled in these pre-eminent endowments, so that his reason, understanding, prudence and judgment not only sufficed for the direction of his earthly life, but by them men mounted up even to God and eternal bliss" (I, xv, 8). Like Augustine, Calvin sees reason as one of God's great gifts to human beings.

It is sometimes suggested that sin, for Calvin, destroys the natural awareness of God. Nothing that Calvin says later, however, about the effects of sin on human reason supports this claim (II, ii, 12–17). When he says in his famous statement that "the greatest geniuses are blinder than moles," he refers exclusively to the knowledge of *piety* (II, ii, 18). Calvin does say that, since the fall (and even before the fall), humankind's natural endowments require the addition of "supernatural gifts" to issue in *this* knowledge of *piety*. "Stripped" of these gifts by the fall, the "natural gifts" became corrupted and remain so until they are "recovered through the grace of regeneration." This recovery requires the reinstatement of these supernatural gifts (II, ii, 12). The distinction between this knowledge of piety and a deficient knowledge due to the fall is part and parcel of Calvin's teaching, and we shall discuss it further in a moment. The difference between the two types of knowledge arises because of the fall and the redemption from the fall. But the fall and redemption do not obviate the doctrine of a natural knowledge of God; they actually presuppose it.

Workmanship of the Universe.   God created human beings with an awareness of himself for the purpose of piety and happiness. He also placed them within a marvelously constructed universe for the same purpose. We need now to consider the relationship between the awareness of God and the awareness of this universe as they are ordered to this same end. That these two, the awareness of God and of the "workmanship of the universe," function together is clear: "Lest anyone, then, be excluded from access to happiness, he not only sowed in men's minds the seed of religion of which we have spoken but revealed himself and daily discloses himself in the whole workmanship of the universe" (I, v, 1). It may be thought that Calvin's use of the term *revealed* here supports the claim I rejected earlier that Calvin's natural knowledge of God is to be taken as a revelation. But this is to place too much weight on the appearance of the term in this passage, which is also its first occurrence in the *Institutes*. For Calvin is not here discussing the idea of revelation or its necessity, but the role that our natural awareness of the universe plays in our knowing both that God exists and something of what he is like. As I mentioned earlier, Calvin first introduces the idea of revelation and its necessity later still, in I, vi, 14.

Natural Theology.   It may appear in this chapter on the workmanship of the universe that Calvin is reasoning from such workmanship to the existence of God, but that is not really the case. How, then, do we come to know God from the universe around us? Calvin says that we come to know God from its order and beauty. The order and beauty of the world serve as "marks" of his glory, or as a sort of "mirror in which we can contemplate God, who is otherwise invisible," or as "evidences . . . that declare his wonderful wisdom," or, finally, as "signs of divinity" (I, v, 1, 2, 4). The universe bears all these marks, signs, and evidences of God quite simply because the universe is not God himself, but his creation—an effect of which he is the cause (I, v, 6). So God is known not *in* his creation but *from* it, as from a *sign* to *what is signified*. Now the question is, How does that work?

The natural theologian will claim that this can work only by inference from premise (evidence) to conclusion (God exists). This is a plausible interpretation of Calvin's language, at least on a first reading; it is the way I interpreted the passage in "Faith and Reason in Calvin's Doctrine of the Knowledge of God" (20–23). One sense of knowing just is by way of evidence, by way of reasoning from premise to conclusion. It is also the classical way of interpreting the function of signs. As we also saw earlier, however, one of Augustine's claims to fame is his theory that signs can sometimes function noninferentially when we come to know from them what they signify. This theory opens the door to interpreting Calvin not as a natural theologian arguing (if only implicitly) from the order of the universe to the existence of God but as teaching that we come to know God, his universe, and their relationship immediately and simultaneously.

Calvin certainly does not formulate proofs in the manner of Aquinas's "Five Ways." To be sure, he uses the word *proof* at one point: "We see that no long or toilsome proof is needed to elicit evidences that serve to illuminate and affirm the divine majesty" (I, v, 9). But here Calvin does not reject the proofs of natural theology, one of which infers the existence of its creator from the order and beauty of the world; what he rejects is the need to prove the existence of the evidence itself, viz., the order and beauty. This is the proof he says is unnecessary, because the order and beauty of the world "are so very manifest and obvious that they can easily be observed with the eyes and pointed out with the finger" (I, v, 9). Those who are trained in "the liberal arts penetrate with their aid far more deeply into the secrets of the divine wisdom. Yet ignorance of them prevents no one from seeing more than enough of God's workmanship in his creation to lead him to break forth in admiration to the Artificer" (I, v, 2). Hence this passage offers no support for the claim that Calvin is not doing natural theology.

The argument for the claim goes instead something like this. Human beings are, by the *sensus divinitatis*, already directly aware of God "as their Maker" in the *sensus divinitatis*; hence, an inference to his existence as the cause of the universe is unnecessary. Indeed, recalling Augustine who holds that knowing words as signs presupposes knowing the objects they signify, we can take Calvin as holding that knowing the universe as a sign of God presupposes knowing God himself as the creator whom it signifies. And to anticipate the next chapter, Alvin Plantinga explains how knowledge of God from the workmanship of the universe can be immediate and noninferential in his theory of belief in God as a "properly basic proposition."

Worth discussing here, however, is the interesting term that John Baillie, the Reformed theologian, uses in his examination of the topic. Baillie describes our knowledge of God through the order of nature as a *mediated immediacy*. The term is original with Baillie, I believe; at any rate, it captures what Calvin means by knowing God *from* the universe. In *Our Knowledge of God* Baillie elaborates:

> Yet, although we are more directly and intimately acquainted with God than with any other presence, it does not follow that He is ever present to us *apart* from all other presences. And, in fact, it is the witness of experience that only 'in, with and under' other presences is the divine presence ever vouchsafed to us....
>
> I believe the view to be capable of defense that no one of the four subjects of our knowledge—ourselves, our fellows, the corporeal world, and God—is ever presented to us except in conjunction with all three of the others. (178)

Baillie's explication of his "mediated immediacy" in the Lutheran language describing the Eucharist is deliberate: "Nature is not an argument for God, but it is a sacrament of Him" (178). Baillie develops these ideas in an eloquent autobiographical account of how a Christian child comes to his knowledge of God not only from the testimony of his parents, the Church, Scripture, and his fellow human beings but also from his experience of the natural world. To this account Baillie adds a review of the implications of this Reformed approach for evaluating various other theological traditions. As might be expected, he is more sympathetic to the Augustinian, Bonaventurian, and Lutheran traditions than to the Thomistic. What he does less well, perhaps, is to "resolve the apparent self-contradictoriness of this phrase," *mediated immediacy* (181). One place to begin, perhaps, is to note the striking parallel to our knowledge of sense objects; for that, too, is an immediate acquaintance with those objects mediated by the elements of sensation (e. g., shapes and colors). In any event, Baillie is a good example of the typically Reformed effort to avoid natural theology in the interest of defending the priority of a noninferential way of knowing God from our experience of the world.

The Vitality of Our Knowledge of God

We have said enough to focus on the *immediacy* of the natural knowledge of God in Calvin. It remains to point up its *vitality*. By the "vitality" of the knowledge of God I mean that Calvin includes in it not only the propositions that express its intellectual content but also the affective and volitional responses that accompany that content. More precisely, Calvin teaches that the intellectual content of the knowledge of God nowhere concretely manifests itself among human beings without a moral and affective response; and that the nature of this response, in turn, is determined by the presence or absence of Christian faith.

Without such faith, Calvin says, "vanity joined with pride can be detected in the fact that, in seeking God, miserable men do not rise above themselves as they should, but measure him by the yardstick of their own carnal stupidity, and neglect sound investigation; thus out of curiosity they fly off into empty speculations" (I, iv, 1, see also 2–4; II, ii, 12, 18–25). We should not conclude from Calvin's rhetorical extravagance in this passage that he thinks no unbeliever can know anything of God or even show some admirable piety. Calvin himself points out that some pagan philosophers are closer than others to the truth about God, and that they even acknowledge the *vitality* of our knowledge of God in so far as that consists of piety. For example, he finds that Plato anticipates his own definition of the proper knowledge of God as "pious knowledge" (I, iii, 3).

In his *Principles of Sacred Theology*, Abraham Kuyper provides an example of such natural piety apart from Christian faith:

> In the negro, who trembles before his Fetish, there is more of the fear of God than in the proud philosopher, who reasons about the gods (or about *to theion*) as about powers, of which he will determine what they are. In the negro there is still a considerable degree of vitality of the seed of religion, while in the self-sufficient philosopher it is dead. He reasons; in however imperfect a way, the negro worships. (304–305)

Kierkegaard makes a similar point, for the Lutheran tradition, in a famous passage in his *Concluding Unscientific Postscript:*

> If one who lives in the midst of Christendom goes up to the house of God, the house of the true God, with the true conception of God in his knowledge, and prays, but prays in a false spirit; and one who lives in an idolatrous community prays with the entire passion of the infinite, although his eyes rest upon the image of an idol: where is there most truth? The one prays to God though he worships an idol; the other prays falsely to the true God, and hence worships in fact an idol. (179–180)

It is clear from Kuyper and Kierkegaard that the Protestant tradition has not lost sight of an estimable natural piety, however deficient it is because of the fall. Calvin certainly reminds his followers that it is deficient; even "Plato, the most religious of all and the most circumspect, . . . vanishes in his round globe" (I, v, 11). The point is, however, that the fall has extinguished neither the intellectual content of the natural knowledge of God nor its vitality as this appears in some admirable expressions piety.

Christian faith, however, begins to restore this fallen natural knowledge of God into the properly pious knowledge of God that characterized human beings before the fall: "Here indeed is pure and real religion: faith so joined with an earnest fear of God that this fear also embraces willing reverence, and carries with it such legitimate worship as is prescribed in the law" (I, ii, 2). This passage, incidentally, contains the first use of *faith* in the *Institutes* (for the next ones, which make the same point, see I, v, 14; vi, 1–2). Calvin's language on the salutary effects of faith in these early references to faith in the

Institutes is rhetorically restrained. By the time he has defined faith and analyzed his definition in Book III, however, he is far more eloquent about these effects:

> But how can the mind be aroused [by faith] to taste the divine goodness without at the same time being wholly kindled to love God in return? For truly, that abundant sweetness which God has stored up for those who fear him cannot be known without at the same time powerfully moving us. And once anyone has been moved by it, it utterly ravishes him and draws him to itself. (III, ii, 41)

So Christian faith transforms the affective and volitional response in particular by adding to the intellectual content of what is believed about God. For by faith in God's own testimony (revelation), the believers not only confirm their natural awareness that he is one, majestic, and is their Maker; they also learn that he is gracious, triune, incarnate, and their redeemer (I, ii, 1; see also II, ix–xvii).

Knowledge of God and of Ourselves. The vitality of the knowledge of God arises, for Calvin, directly from the intimate connection between the knowledge of God and the knowledge of ourselves. Adapting a term from Paul Tillich, Dowey calls this the "correlative character of the knowledge of God and man" (pp. 18–24). Calvin devotes the entire first chapter of his *Institutes* to this theme, which he summarizes in the very opening sentence: "Nearly all the wisdom we possess, that is to say, true and sound wisdom, consists of two parts: the knowledge of God and of ourselves" (I, i, 1). The fact that knowing God makes a momentous difference to human beings stems from the fact that human happiness—and human misery, it may be added—is rooted in the connection between the knowledge of God and self-knowledge. These connections are based on who God and human beings are and how they are related by the doctrine of creation. The theme is also a conspicuously Augustinian theme, and it is puzzling that Calvin does not acknowledge Augustine in his elaboration of it. For Augustine is his favorite Church Father. He writes, in *Concerning the Eternal Predestination of God*: "As for St. Augustine, he agrees so well with us in everything and everywhere, that if I had to write a confession upon this matter it would be enough for me to compose it from evidences drawn from his books" (61). Instead of citing Augustine in his opening discussion, however, he waits until the opening of Book II to make a classical reference suitable to the theme; then, however, he does not cite Augustine but the Delphic oracle,

Know thyself. Still, the parallel between Calvin and Augustine on the knowledge of God and ourselves is very close (compare the *Institutes* I, i; xv, 1; II, i, 1 with Augustine, *Soliloquies,* esp. I, ii, 7; and *Confessions,* VII, x, 16; xvii, 23; I, xx, 29).

A careful examination of the opening chapter of the *Institutes* reveals two different ways of analyzing Calvin's view of the intimate connection between the knowledge of God and the knowledge of ourselves. The two types of knowledge are connected both logically and psychologically. Logically, there is a mutual entailment between knowing God and knowing ourselves. The conceptual link is supplied by piety. For what is piety? It is "that reverence joined with love of God which the knowledge of his benefits induces" (I, ii, 1). Notice here that just as Calvin defines the proper knowledge of God in terms of piety (the right response to God), so too he defines piety, this response to God, in terms of a knowledge of God's *benefits* to us—in his words, "what is to our advantage to know of him" (I, ii, 1). So, to know God is to know him as the author of what is good for us, and to know what is good for us is to know ourselves. The converse also holds. To know ourselves is to know what is good for us, and to know what is good for us is to know who is the author of that good. Thus reverence of God's greatness and gratitude for his goodness, two main aspects of piety, make it conceptually unthinkable that we should know God without knowing ourselves and that we should know ourselves without knowing God.

On the psychological or causal connection, Calvin observes: "Which one precedes the other is not easy to discern. First, no one can look on himself without immediately turning his thoughts to the contemplation of God." For when we look at ourselves, we see especially two things: "the mighty gifts with which we are endowed," which "are hardly from ourselves"; and our "miserable ruin," "the feeling of our own ignorance, vanity, poverty, infirmity, and—what is more—depravity and corruption," which prompt us likewise "to contemplate the good things of God. . . . Accordingly, the knowledge of ourselves not only arouses us to seek God, but also, as it were, leads us by the hand to find him" (I, i, 1). Conversely, "it is certain that man never achieves a clear knowledge of himself unless he has first looked upon God's face, and then descends from contemplating him to scrutinize himself" (I, i, 2). What we see in God is his absolute goodness and greatness, his glory and majesty. And this vision leads us to see not only that the "mighty gifts with which we are endowed" originate in him alone as their source, but also that our "miserable ruin" is miserable indeed, and is owing to our own pride and wickedness:

For we always seem to ourselves righteous and upright and wise and holy—this pride is innate in all of us—unless by clear proofs we stand convinced of our own unrighteousness, foulness, folly and impurity. Moreover, we are not thus convinced if we look merely to ourselves and not also to the Lord, who is the sole standard by which this judgment must be measured.... [However,] suppose we but once begin to raise our thoughts to God, and to ponder his nature, and how completely perfect are his righteousness, wisdom and power—the straitedge to which we must be shaped. Then, what masquerading earlier as righteousness was pleasing in us will soon grow filthy in its consummate wickedness. (I, i, 2)

Knowing God is thus particularly required for leading us to this aspect of self-knowledge, viz., our sin and misery.

Knowledge and Virtue; Virtue and Happiness. Calvin elaborates upon the intimate connection between self-knowledge and the *proper* knowledge of God. But piety is built into this proper knowledge of God; therefore one who has such knowledge has virtue also. This is a striking Christian version of Plato's doctrine that knowledge is virtue. The important difference between Calvin and Plato is that wrongdoing for Calvin arises not from ignorance but with a knowledge of God, deficient though that knowledge is. Calvin does not elaborate upon the corresponding intimate connection between such *deficient* knowledge of God, typically characterized by *impiety,* and the impairment of self-knowledge. He gives some hints, however, in I, iv and related passages. Thus the deficient knowledge of God is not so deficient that human beings utterly fail to recognize their sin, guilt, and ingratitude; moreover, the deficient knowledge of God is the cause, and in turn also the result, of their knowledge of their guilt and misery.

The Platonic tradition also sees a close connection between virtue and happiness. This connection also has its Christian version in Calvin. Just as the deficient knowledge of God expresses itself in the vices of fear, distrust, and disobedience, which in turn produce misery and punishment (unhappiness), so the proper knowledge of God leads human beings to the virtues of love, trust, and obedience, which in turn produce the joy of divine salvation.

In a footnote to Calvin's definition of the proper knowledge as piety, McNeill interprets Calvin as saying that piety is a "prerequisite" to knowing God (I, ii, 1, n. 1). This term suggests that piety is a precondition, a first step, toward knowing God; but this does not seem to be Calvin's meaning. Instead, he means that piety is an essential characteristic of that knowledge; whatever looks like knowledge of God but lacks this characteristic of pious response is not, "properly speaking," knowledge of God. Consider again Calvin's descriptions of the *proper* knowledge of God:

> Now, the knowledge of God, as I understand it, is that by which we not only conceive that there is a God but also grasp what *befits us and is proper to his glory*, in fine, what is *to our advantage* to know him. . . . Moreover, although our mind cannot apprehend God without rendering some honor to him, it will not suffice simply to hold that here is One whom all ought to honor and adore, *unless we are also persuaded that he is the fountain of all good, and that we must seek nothing elsewhere than in him.* (I, ii, 1; emphasis added)

Here it is clear that the proper knowledge of God for Calvin consists not only in its intellectual content but also in an affective and volitional response, including a vivid appreciation of the divine gifts (note the emphasized phrases). Thus to say that these responses "accompany" the knowledge of God is misleading. Calvin seems to teach, as we just saw, not only that the proper knowledge (of God) is virtue, but also that virtue (piety) is its own reward (happiness). Hence the *vitality* of properly knowing God is manifested in piety and happiness.

The Effects of the Fall

We should now explore more systematically the effects of the fall on human beings who were created for knowing God in the way discussed earlier. The fall, for Calvin, consists in "original sin," which is an "hereditary depravity and corruption of our nature, diffused into all parts of the soul, which first makes us liable to God's wrath, then also brings forth in us those works which Scripture calls 'works of the flesh'" (II, i, 8). Although present in all people, original sin stems from the disobedience of Adam, which was occasioned by the temptation of the devil, and freely chosen in an act of the will (II, i, 4–11; iii, 5). Given the central role that Calvin ascribes to *faith* in redemption, it is essential to observe that he locates the root of sin and disobedience in *faithlessness* (II, i, 4). Such faithlessness cannot consist in ignorance; it must, like faith, presuppose the natural awareness of God that we have discussed. Disbelieving and distrusting God, like believing and trusting him, presuppose knowing him. What are the effects of the fall, of faithlessness, on this natural knowledge of God? We will answer this question first by looking at Calvin's account of human noetic faculties after the fall and then by considering his account of the actual knowledge that human beings still possess in their fallen state.

Our Noetic Faculties after the Fall.   Calvin follows Augustine by distinguishing between our natural and supernatural gifts, the latter being "adventitious and beyond nature." The natural gifts include "soundness of mind and uprightness of heart" (II, ii, 12). It must be remembered that for Calvin *heart* is often a synonym for "will" (II, ii, 27; iii, 6–10). The supernatural gifts include "the light of faith as well as righteousness, which would be sufficient to attain heavenly life and eternal bliss." The effect of the fall, according to Calvin, is "that the natural gifts were corrupted in man" and "that the supernatural gifts were stripped from him" (II, ii, 12); or, as he states it in an earlier passage, "vitiated as he is in every part of his nature and shorn of supernatural gifts" (II, ii, 4). Calvin seems to distinguish here between our faculties and their exercise. As *faculties*, reason and will "could not be completely wiped out" because they are "inseparable from man's nature"; but faith, as an *exercise* of these faculties, is "adventitious" and therefore can be quite "extinguished" (II, ii, 12).

Thus the loss of faith in the fall is complete and unambiguous—nothing is left of believing what God says, of trusting him, or of the assurance of God's favor. There is a certain paradox in all this, for it was precisely the loss of such faith that was the *cause* of the fall; but now that loss of faith is also said to be an *effect* of the fall. A paradox similarly pervades Calvin's lengthy discussion of the corrupted will. He quotes St. Bernard of Clairvaux approvingly:

> "Thus the soul, in some strange and evil way, under a certain voluntary and wrongly free necessity is at the same time enslaved and free: enslaved because of the necessity; free because of the will. And what is at once stranger and more deplorable, it is guilty because it is free, and enslaved because it is guilty, and as a consequence enslaved because it is free." (II, iii, 5; see also ii, 26, 27. The quotation is from St. Bernard, *Sermons on the Song of Songs*, lxxxi, 7, 9).

Calvin might also have quoted any number of passages from Augustine, who was the first to struggle deeply with the paradox of the free will being enslaved by its own free choice.

Much more straightforward is Calvin's account of the corrupted reason. For "earthly things" like "government, household management, all mechanical skills and the liberal arts," he observes that "no man is without the light of reason" (II, ii, 13). In one paragraph, often quoted, he notes how "we cannot read the writings of the ancients on these subjects without great admiration," adding only that we recognize "at the same time that it comes from God," and exhorting his fellow Christian believers to learn "how many gifts the Lord left to human nature even after it was despoiled of its true good" (II, ii, 15). With respect to "heavenly things," however, the situation is different: "This spiritual insight consists chiefly in three things: (1) knowing God; (2) knowing his fatherly favor in our behalf, in which our salvation consists; (3) knowing how to frame our life according to the rule of his law. In the first two points—and especially in the second—the greatest of geniuses are blinder than moles!" (II, ii, 18). This passage is as famous as any other in Calvin. It requires careful interpretation, and for help in this we need to turn to Calvin's account of the actual knowledge of God that human beings possess in their fallen state.

Our Knowledge of God after the Fall.   First and foremost, it must be noted that the "blindness" of which Calvin here speaks refers to the *proper* knowledge of God, the knowledge of piety. Otherwise he might be taken to deny all knowledge of God whatsoever in fallen human beings. This is not his intention at all, for he grants immediately "that one can read competent and apt statements about God here and there in the philosophers"; although he quickly adds, "these always show a certain giddy imagination." More important, he refers to the philosophers' natural awareness of God: "As was stated above, the Lord indeed gave them a slight taste of his divinity that they might not hide their impiety under a cloak of ignorance" (II, ii, 18). That this natural knowledge of God persists after the fall and is sufficient to leave human beings without excuse is a recurring theme in Calvin: "All excuse is cut off because the fault of dullness is within us"; we cannot "pretend ignorance" (I, v, 15).

Still, the natural knowledge of God after the fall is *deficient*. The deficiency has both a conceptual (propositional) and a moral (practical) component. As we saw earlier, fallen human beings, in virtue of their natural awareness of God, still know that God exists, that he is their creator, that he is majestic in power and deserving of their worship and obedience (I, ii, 1). Reason still formulates this knowledge in their minds; for as a natural faculty, it has only been corrupted, not destroyed. This corruption of reason has two consequences. First, it can no longer find, in the natural *sensus divinitatis*, that knowledege of God which it would formulate as his triune nature, his incarnation, and his gracious attitude to fallen human beings; these characteristics of God it can receive only by faith in the divine revelation. Second, reason after the fall tends to "fly off into empty speculations" about the nature of God. Indeed, Calvin sometimes seems less impressed with the "droplets of truth" in the writings of the pagan philsophers than with the "many monstrous lies that defile them" (I, iv, 1; II, ii, 18). Calvin directs his famous opposition to "speculation" not only against this corrupted exercise of reason in fallen human beings but also against the thinking of those who have been redeemed. In the latter case, it creates a special problem; we shall therefore postpone our discussion of it until we come to the noetic effects of grace.

Fallen human beings manifest the moral or practical implications of this deficient knowledge (its *vitality*, as I have called it) in their moral and religious lives. Though they are still religious by nature (I, iii), they no longer worship God as he is but falsely, in idolatry and superstition (I, iv; xi; xii). Nor do they obey God out of love for him or seek him as the fountain of all good. Instead, they fear his wrath and attempt, unsuccessfully, to suppress their knowledge of him, to their own disadvantage and misery. Hence their radical need of redemption.

The Effects of Grace

The origin of redemption consists, insofar as it is a conscious and noetic experience, in faith. The object of faith, as we saw earlier, is twofold, even as faith itself is both trust and belief. Thus God is the object of trust and what he says is the object of belief—what he says he has done and will do for the redemption of human beings. He reveals this in his word, the Scriptures, and acts in the incarnation of his Son and the illumination of his Spirit. Faith arises in human beings after the fall only as a gift of God (III, ii, 7), by the "grace of regeneration" in the elect only (III, i, 2; iii, 9), and upon their hearing the gospel, which is his Word (I, vi). Even before the fall, as we have seen, faith was present in human beings as an essential ingredient in their proper knowledge of God. Here I will focus only on Calvin's doctrines of *revelation* and *illumination* as the special conditions that make faith possible *after* the fall, and I am interested especially in the bearing of these two divine activities on the relation between faith and reason.

Revelation. Calvin first develops his ideas about revelation in the context of the natural knowledge of God as Creator (Book I), not in connection with faith (Book III). The point he makes there is that, although the deficient knowledge of those without Christian faith is a knowledge of the Creator and "is more than enough to withdraw all support from men's ingratitude," still, for the *pious* knowledge of God the Creator, "it is needful that another and better help be added to direct us aright to the very Creator of the universe." This help is "the light of his Word" by which he becomes "known unto salvation." This Word also assists believers in knowing God as Creator from his creation, even as a pair of spectacles helps those with weak vision to read the writing of "a most beautiful volume." In Scripture God assists the "mute teachers" of creation when he "also opens his own most hallowed lips" (I, vi, 1).

Two points are already clear in this early discussion of revelation. First, even though Calvin postpones his analysis of faith until Book III, he correlates it here with revelation (divine testimony): "For by his Word, God rendered faith unambiguous forever, a faith that should be superior to all opinion" (I, vi, 2; there is only one earlier reference to faith, as the essence of "pure and real religion" [I, ii, 2]). Second, Calvin regards revelation not only as necessary for the knowledge of God as Redeemer, which he takes up later, but also as a supplement and corrective for the natural awareness of God as Creator, which is inadequate apart from faith.

Divine Illumination.   A third point is even more important. It is that the Scriptures will *fail* to function as revelation, either as the spectacles for seeing the universe more clearly as the work of God or as the basis for faith in Christ the Mediator of redemption, unless they are taken to be God himself speaking: "Hence the Scriptures obtain full authority among believers only when men regard them as having sprung from heaven, as if there the living words of God were heard" (I, vii, 1). How is it possible for a human being to hear God himself speaking in Scripture? Calvin answers this question in two ways. The first is, by divine witness or testimony:

> Since for unbelieving men religion seems to stand by opinion alone, they, in order not to believe anything foolishly or lightly, both wish and demand rational proof that Moses and the prophets spoke divinely. But I reply: the *testimony of the Spirit* is more excellent than all reason. For as *God alone is a fit witness* of himself in his Word, so also the Word will not find acceptance in men's hearts before it is sealed by the *inward testimony of the Spirit*. (I, vii, 4; emphasis added)

The second is by divine illumination: "Therefore, *illumined by his power*, we believe neither by our own nor by any one else's judgment that Scripture is from God; but above human judgment we affirm with utter certainty (just as if we were gazing upon the majesty of God himself) that it has flowed to us from the very mouth of God by the ministry of men" (I, vii, 5; cf. III, ii, 33; emphasis added). Except for the fact that Calvin is here explaining divine revelation and not our natural knowledge of God, the parallel between his ideas and Augustine's is striking. His testimony of the Spirit recalls Augustine's inner teacher, his divine illumination, Augustine's light of the mind. Both testimony of the Spirit and divine illumination also resemble the *sensus divinitatis* in their immediacy to the mind, and Calvin defends them against the indirectness of both human reasoning ("rational proof") and human testimony ("any one else's judgment").

Against those who want rational proof of the divine authority of Scripture Calvin first admits that there are "arguments . . . that would easily prove—if there is any god in heaven—that the law, the prophets, and the gospel came from him" (I, vii, 4), and even lays out such arguments himself (I, viii). He goes on, however, to say that "they who strive to build up firm faith in Scripture through disputation are doing things backwards" (I, vii, 4). As earlier for the natural awareness of God, so here for God's revelation, Calvin rejects an inferential approach. Believers hear God speak to them in Scripture as directly as they (and all human beings) are naturally aware of him in the *sensus divinitiatis*. Indeed, it is easy to conclude from Calvin's discussion that believers *recognize* the God who speaks to them in Scripture on the basis of the natural knowledge of him they already possess. How else? How would they know that He who speaks to them in Scripture is God unless they already knew him independently of their hearing him speak there? Calvin himself does not reach this conclusion, but it seems to be the obvious way to relate his concept of revelation to his concept of the *sensus divinitatis*. For we must distinguish what the believer knows from what the believer believes. What the believer knows is *that* it is God who speaks; what the believer believes is the *content* of what God says. The "credibility of doctrine is not established until we are persuaded beyond doubt that God is its Author" (I, vii, 4). And who persuades believers that God is the Author? God himself: "Thus, the highest proof of Scripture derives in general from the fact that God in person speaks in it" (I, vii, 4). And which God is that? The God the believer already knows.

Against those on the other hand who, citing Augustine, claim that the divine authority of Scripture rests on the authority of the church, Calvin's objection is crystal clear:

> But a most pernicious error widely prevails that Scripture has only so much weight as is conceded to it by the consent of the

church. As if the eternal and inviolable truth of God depended upon the decision of men! ... Yet, if this is so, what will happen to miserable consciences seeking firm assurance of eternal life if all promises of it consist in and depend solely upon the judgment of men? (I, vii, 1)

Calvin's analysis of Augustine, to which we referred in Chapter 5, follows in I, vii, 3. Again, his objection to the adequacy of human authority reflects his conviction of the immediacy (and vitality) of believers' own direct knowledge of the one whom they believe, when they believe what God says to them in Scripture. Such knowledge is in sharp contrast with the secondhand nature of the testimony of other human beings, even of the church, that it is God who speaks in Scripture. Such testimony, Calvin thinks, can only lead to a believer's uncertainty. The church can and does function, of course, as "an introduction through which we are prepared for faith in the gospel" (I, vii, 3). Believers' believing with certainty what Scripture says, however, require their knowing God himself. And so, instead of either rational proof or human authority, Scripture is "self-authenticated" (I, vii, 5), by which Calvin can mean only that believers themselves know God, whose word it is.

Faith Seeking Understanding

All the preceding ideas on faith bring Calvin into line with Augustine. Faith lacks knowledge in the sense of comprehending what is believed on God's authority. God himself, however, is known. He is not known clearly or completely, of course; for some of the things he says about himself are, certainly at first (and perhaps even at last, in this earthly life), beyond understanding in the sense of comprehension. For Augustine, the certainty of faith does not obviate, however, a search for such understanding. Indeed, it is his basic theme that faith *seeks* understanding, both because of the natural desire of reason to know and understand what it believes and because of a duty imposed by Scripture itself (i.e., by God himself). But here Calvin does not follow Augustine. The Augustinian theme of faith seeking understanding is almost entirely absent from Calvin's thought. This is in part, as we shall see, because Calvin fails to work out the noetic consequences of redemption as clearly as he does the noetic consequences of the fall.

First let us note two passages in which Calvin does seem to adumbrate the theme of faith seeking understanding. One passage is found in the context of his attack on "implicit faith" (see Vos 1985,

21–28). Implicit faith believes revealed truths only on the authority of the church. Calvin condemns such faith as "heedless gullibility," error, and ignorance (III, ii, 3). He does not want to "turn over to [the church] the task of inquiring and knowing." Citing Romans 10:10, he declares "that it is not enough for a man implicitly to believe what he does not understand or even investigate" (III, ii, 2). Still, he recognizes a correct sense of implicit faith, according to which it *does* seek such understanding: "We certainly admit that so long as we dwell as strangers in the world there is such a thing as implicit faith; not only because many things are as yet hidden from us, but because surrounded by many clouds of errors we do not comprehend everything" (III, ii, 4). Precisely because we lack understanding, we are to avoid a thoughtless acceptance of what the church says and seek such understanding for ourselves, as he goes on to say:

> The height of wisdom for the most perfect is to go forward and, quietly and humbly, to strive still further. Therefore Paul exhorts believers that, if some disagree with others in any matter, they should wait for revelation [Phil. 3:15]. . . . And in our daily reading of Scripture we come upon many obscure passages that convict us of ignorance. With this bridle God keeps us within bounds, assigning to each his "measure of faith" [Rom. 12:3] so that even the best teacher may be ready to learn. (I, vii, 4)

Thus believers are to seek understanding both because of disagreements among themselves and because of ignorance. Calvin cites biblical examples in support. Peter and John were rewarded for their faith (little as it was) by seeing an empty tomb; the ruler whose son was ill was rewarded for his faith when he found him healed; and the faith of the neighbors of the Samaritan woman was rewarded when they saw and heard Jesus for themselves. Says Calvin in conclusion:

> This teachableness, with the desire to learn, is far different from sheer ignorance in which those sluggishly rest who are content with the sort of "implicit faith" the papists invent. For if Paul severely condemns those who "are always learning but never arrive at a knowledge of the truth" [2 Tim. 3:7], how much greater ignominy do those merit who deliberately affect complete ignorance! (I, vii, 5)

The other passage in which Calvin suggests that faith is to seek understanding is found in a discussion of divine illumination. As we have already seen, "without the illumination of the Holy Spirit, the

Word can do nothing" (III, ii, 33). Unfortunately Calvin does not connect this illumination with the faculty of human reason. Referring to 1
Corinthians 2:9, he emphasizes that the truth revealed in Scripture is
such that "neither eye nor understanding can grasp" (III, ii, 34). Still,
he does not entirely overlook that faith involves the mind: "In both
ways, therefore, faith is a singular gift of God, both in that the mind of
man is purged so as to be able to taste the truth of God and in that his
heart is established therein" (III, ii, 33). So Calvin does not completely
ignore that what God says in Scripture is for the *mind* as well as for
the heart. Nevertheless, it has to be said that the Augustinian dynam-
ic of faith seeking understanding is absent.

Noetic Effects of Grace. For all the attention Calvin gives to the
noetic effects of the fall, he gives surprisingly little to the noetic effects of
grace and redemption. In the *faithless*, God restrains the corrupting
effects of the fall (II, iii, 3). Calvin's followers have extensively developed this idea in the doctrine of common grace (Hodge 1872, II, Part III,
xiv, 3; Kuyper 1902). Curiously, neither Calvin nor his followers have,
with the same vigor, developed the noetic effects of grace in the *faithful*.
This anomaly stems from Calvin's failure to pick up the Augustinian
theme of faith seeking understanding. Calvin misses this theme for two
reasons: one inherent in his thought; the other in his temperament.

First, Calvin does not link his theory of divine illumination in the
believer with *reason*, the faculty of the mind whose function it is to
know and understand. This gap is aggravated by the way in which
Calvin distinguishes between supernatural and natural gifts. Counting
faith as a supernatural gift, Calvin sees it as completely stripped from
us by the fall, whereas reason, which is a natural gift, is only corrupted
(II, ii, 12). Thus when faith is restored in the believer, it sits separate
from reason, "adventitious, and beyond nature," as Calvin puts it. But
redemption is supposed to involve a *restoration* of the natural gifts,
which were corrupted in the fall. Yet Calvin is silent on just how grace
enables reason once again to attain the "spiritual insight" it lost in the
fall, especially for "(1) knowing God" and "(2) knowing his fatherly
favor in our behalf, in which our salvation consists"—the two points on
which Calvin holds that "the greatest geniuses are blinder than moles."

To be sure, Calvin *hints* at some great effect of grace on reason
when he writes "that we have been endowed with reason and understanding so that, by leading a holy and upright life, we may press on
to the appointed goal of blessed immortality" (II, i, 1). But he does not
follow through on this hint. How does the illumination made possible
by faith, the supernatural gift, rekindle the powers of *natural* reason
that has been restored, so that it "may press on to the appointed goal

of blessed immortality"? Calvin does not say; he suggests instead that knowing God and his benevolence toward us is self-contained within the replaced supernatural gift that had been entirely lost, the gift of faith. This separation of faith as a *supernatural* gift from reason as a natural faculty helps to explain the disappearance in Calvin's thought of a faith that seeks understanding.

Speculation. In addition to this structural difficulty in his anthropology, Calvin has a deep personal aversion to what he calls *speculation.* Calvin describes speculation as *thinking* about God without being properly *affected* by the thoughts we have:

> We are called to a knowledge of God: not that knowledge which, content with empty speculation, merely flits in the brain, but that which will be sound and fruitful if we duly perceive it, and if it takes root in the heart. For the Lord manifests himself by his powers, the force of which we feel within ourselves and the benefits of which we enjoy. We must therefore be much more profoundly affected by this knowledge than if we were to imagine a God of whom no perception came through to us. Consequently, we know the most perfect way of seeking God, and the most suitable order, is not for us to attempt with bold curiosity to penetrate to the investigation of his essence, which we ought more to adore than meticulously to search out, but for us to contemplate him in his works whereby he renders himself near and familiar to us, and in some manner communicates himself to us.
> (I, v, 9)

In this passage and others like it Calvin seems to frown upon the kind of philosophical inquiry and search for understanding implied in the Augustinian formula and modeled so well by Augustine himself.

Calvin's point is, of course, that the pious knowledge of God made possible by faith requires such attitudes as fear, praise, trust, obedience, and worship. But it does not follow from this point that attitudes of inquiry and search for clearer knowledge and fuller understanding are necessarily in conflict with these attitudes of piety. Still, that may be his fear, since he does not explore the possibility of a *pious inquiry*, an inquiry that exercises the powers of reason but does so precisely as another one of the believer's proper responses to God. Augustine would certainly agree with Calvin that any inquiry into the nature of God divorced from piety is inherently inadequate. According to Augustine, faith as the foundation of such piety may never be left behind in the believer's search for the rational understanding of God and his revelation. Augustine's own thinking is a model of the harmony possible between the attitudes of inquiry and seeking and those of trust, certainty, obedience, and worship.

Calvin offers Epicurus as an example of speculation, inquiry into the nature of God divorced from fear and reverence:

> What is God? Men who pose this question are merely toying with idle speculations. It is more important for us to know of what sort he is and what is consistent with his nature. What good is it to profess with Epicurus some sort of God who has cast aside the care of the world only to amuse himself in idleness? What help is it, in short, to know a God with whom we have nothing to do? Rather, our knowledge should serve first to teach us fear and reverence; secondly, with it as our guide and teacher, we should learn to seek every good from him, and, having received it, to credit it to his account. (I, ii, 2)

By contrast, Calvin offers Plato (as we have seen) as an example of pious rational inquiry into the nature of God:

> It is clear, that all those who do not direct every thought and action in their lives to this goal degenerate from the law of their creation. This was not unknown to the philosophers. Plato meant nothing but this when he often taught that the highest good of the soul is likeness to God, where, when the soul has grasped the knowledge of God, it is wholly transformed into his likeness. (I, iii, 3)

Still, Calvin fails to find in Plato, to say nothing of Augustine, a model for the believer's own pious rational inquiry under the lead of faith. As eloquent as he is proscribing idle speculation, he is not even prosaic in prescribing its pious counterpart.

Religion and Philosophy. Plato himself at one point avoids a speculative inquiry into the nature of the Good, which may be taken as his parallel for God (*Republic* 506–509); but this did not lead him to avoid philosophy. Plato saw no conflict between his religious attitude in the presence of ultimate reality and the pursuit of philosophical inquiry. Calvin really wanted no conflict between them either, as is evident from his *Commentary* on Col. 2:8: "Many have mistakenly imagined that philosophy is here condemned by Paul; [but he only] means everything that men contrive of themselves when wishing to be wise through their own means of understanding. . . . Under the term philosophy Paul has merely condemned all spurious doctrines which come forth from man's head" (180–181). Still, Calvin was personally disinclined to pursue philosophical questions, even those of great intrinsic interest and of significance for the Christian view of things. For example, he writes:

> I leave it to the philosophers to discuss these faculties [of the soul] in their subtle way. For the upbuilding of godliness a simple definition will be enough for us. I, indeed, agree that the things they teach are true, not only enjoyable, but also profitable to learn, and skillfully assembled by them. And I do not forbid those who are desirous of learning to study them. (I, xv, 6)

Thus, though he is open to philosophizing, he also seems to think it will obscure or hinder his own practical, pastoral aim, "the upbuilding in godliness." Partly, too, Calvin seems not to appreciate the complexity of philosophical quesions; for example, he thinks that the relationship of body and soul is "a topic of no great difficulty" (I, xv, 2).

Calvin's ambivalence toward philosophy arises also from Calvin's fear that philosophy may "go beyond" the divine will; and he is certain, as all believers are, that this will is the sole ground for human trust. Thus he elaborates on the nature of piety:

> For, to begin with, the pious mind does not dream up for itself any god it pleases, but contemplates the one and only true God. And it does not attach to him whatever it pleases, but is content to hold him to be as he manifests himself; furthermore, the mind always exercises the utmost diligence and care not to wander astray, or rashly and boldly to go beyond his will. It thus recognizes God because it knows that he governs all things; and trusts that he is its guide and protector, therefore giving itself over completely to trust in him. (I, ii, 2)

Because the pious mind is thus persuaded so completely and exclusively by God's revelation itself, Calvin is led to adopt his "one rule of modesty and sobriety" for all religious doctrine: "not to speak, or guess, or even seek to know, concerning obscure matters except what has been imparted to us by God's Word" (I, xiv, 4). But this rule, which expresses Calvin's pastoral concern, combined with his disinterest in philosophical questions and his fear of going astray, tends to create a cleavage between faith and philosophy. In *Christianity and Philosophy*, Etienne Gilson presses this tendency to its objectionable conclusion: "There then, is philosophy once again reduced to the

Word of God" (14). Gilson comments here on the link Calvin establishes between "the sum of what God meant to teach us in his Word" and what is "comprised in the Christian philosophy" ("Subject Matter of the Present Work," *Institutes*, 6).

We can now summarize our study of Calvin. Although Calvin does not distinguish faith (and hence belief) from knowledge, his definition of faith as knowledge can be interpreted in line with Augustine's distinction between seeing for ourselves (knowing God) and the certainty of faith (believing without doubt what God says in his revelation because he is absolutely reliable). All human beings know God in virtue of a natural awareness of him; but the manifestation of this knowledge is significantly differentiated among human beings by the absence or presence of Christian faith. Those who believe what God says in his revelation manifest a "proper knowledge" of God. This pious knowledge both incorporates further intellectual content (trinity, incarnation, grace) into that of the natural awareness of God (that he is one, majestic, our maker, and worthy of our obedience) and accompanies this content with affective and volitional expressions of reverence, worship, obedience, love and trust. Believers know God directly as a Holy Spirit who witnesses to them that what he says in Scripture is said by him, so that they believe what Scripture says on no merely human or ecclesiastical authority. This same Spirit illuminates their minds to begin understanding God through what he says about himself (e.g. that he is three persons in one being), what he says about his relationship to the universe (that he is its creator and redeemer), and about his relationship to human beings (that he is incarnate in one of them).

Calvin does not, however, incorporate into his position or into his thinking the Augustinian formula, faith seeks understanding. This is because he fails to spell out the noetic effects of grace on human reason and because he tends to cast doubt on the possibility of pious philosophical inquiry in the midst of his vigorous rejection of "idle speculation." Those who lack the Christian faith manifest a knowledge that is deficient both in intellectual content and in the accompanying moral and religious attitudes; but their knowledge is not so deficient that they are excused for their ignorance, idolatry, disobedience, or lack of reverence, love, and trust. The heart of Calvin's religious epistemology is the immediacy and vitality of human knowledge of God, in believer and unbeliever alike; and these characteristics are a development of Augustinian ideas, in particular of Augustine's doctrines of the divine illumination of the human mind and of the presence there of God himself as the ultimate teacher of all truth and goodness.

7 Properly Basic Beliefs: Alvin Plantinga

As we have now seen, Augustine distinguishes sharply between knowledge as seeing an object for oneself and belief as accepting the testimony of someone else about it. We have also seen that, although Calvin defines faith, and hence belief, as knowledge, what he means by this is not so very different from the Augustinian view. For what he means is that faith involves certainty about what is believed when it is believed on a completely reliable authority; and because what Christians believe on the basis of Scripture they believe on the authority of God himself, they are certain about what they believe. In this way Calvin's approach to knowledge, belief and faith can be aligned with that of Augustine.

Both Augustine and Calvin teach that there is a universal, immediate, noninferential knowledge of God in human beings, whether that knowledge is accompanied by Christian faith or not. Augustine describes this knowledge in the language of rational vision, Calvin in the language of awareness, and both use the language of divine illumination of the mind. Their theory of knowledge is thus a combination of Plato's approach to knowledge in the *Republic*, which defines knowledge as direct acquaintance with an object and his approach to belief in the *Meno*, which illustrates it as accepting a proposition on testimony. Neither Augustine nor Calvin considers the other Platonic approach in the *Theaetetus*, which defines knowledge as justified true belief.

The Revival of Knowledge as Justified True Belief

Alvin Plantinga is important (among other things) both for creating new interest in the Reformed or Calvinist approach on these matters and for restating them in the language of contemporary philosophy. A conspicuous feature of recent epistemology is its rejection of the *Republic* approach to to knowledge and the revival of knowledge as justified true belief. Plantinga has contributed his own theory of knowledge as justified true belief to this revival, and it therefore may not be very clear to everyone that his thinking is nevertheless Augustinian and

Reformed. How can a theory that rejects the restriction of knowledge to direct acquaintance that characterizes Augustine's and Calvin's thinking still be a continuation of their approach? There is an answer to that question, which will emerge in the course of this chapter.

Plantinga began his epistemological investigations not with a theory of knowledge as justified true belief but with a theory of *properly basic belief*. Because that theory shows the continuity of his thought with that of Augustine and Calvin, I turn first to it, as he sets it forth in "Reason and Belief in God."* Unlike Calvin the biblical theologian and more like Augustine the philosopher-theologian, Plantinga places his religious epistemology within the larger framework of epistemology generally. This has the great advantage of allowing some very general features of belief and knowledge to illuminate the nature of belief and knowledge in religion, as well as, in turn, allowing the claims of a religious viewpoint—specifically the Reformed viewpoint—to illuminate the nature of knowledge and belief in other, nonreligious areas of life.

Belief in God as Properly Basic

Belief In *vs.* Belief That.   The heart of Plantinga's thinking, so far as it reflects the influence of Reformed theological thought, is his claim that a person's belief in God can be a *properly basic belief*. By *belief in God* Plantinga means "belief that God exists"; and he distinguishes this, very much as we did in Chapter 2, from the other meaning of *belief in God*, viz., to "trust God":

> To believe that God exists is simply to accept as true a certain proposition: perhaps the proposition that there is a personal being who has created the world, who has no beginning, and who is perfect in wisdom, justice, knowledge, and power. . . . Belief in God means *trusting* God, accepting God, accepting his purposes, committing one's life to him and living in his presence. (18)

Furthermore, the two senses are related so that the latter presupposes the former. In Plantinga's words:

---

*This essay incorporates the ideas of several earlier articles: "Is Belief in God Rational?" "The Reformed Objection to Natural Theology," "Is Belief in God Properly Basic?" and "On Reformed Epistemology."

One cannot sensibly believe in God and thank him for the mountains without believing that there *is* such a person to be thanked and that he is in some way responsible for the mountains. Nor can one trust in God and commit oneself to him without believing that he exists; as the author of Hebrews says, "He who would come to God must believe that he is and that he is a rewarder of them of seek him." (Heb. 11:6) (18)

Plantinga's theory of a properly basic belief, then, is a theory of belief in its intellectual sense, belief that the proposition that God exists is true.

Plantinga offers another preliminary clarification about the claim that belief in God is properly basic: "Strictly speaking, however, it is probably not that proposition [God exists] but such propositions as [God is speaking to me, God has created all this, God disapproves of what I have done, God forgives me, and God is to be thanked and praised] that enjoy that status" (81–82). But these latter propositions "immediately and self-evidently entail" the proposition *that God exists*, so that it is convenient to speak of the latter as the central properly basic belief in question.

Basic vs. Nonbasic Beliefs. To understand the claim that belief in God is a properly basic belief, we must first understand the concept of a *basic belief*. A basic belief is a proposition that one believes without basing it on other propositions that one believes. "Let us say that a proposition is *basic* for me if I believe it and do not believe it on the basis of other propositions" (46). Some obvious examples come to mind: "I believe that $2 + 1 = 3$, for example, and do not believe it on the basis of other propositions. I also believe that I am seated at my desk, and that there is a mild pain in my right knee." What characterizes our assent to such beliefs is the immediacy of the assent. We do not assent to these beliefs by having first assented to other beliefs as their basis. Beliefs that we do affirm by basing them on other beliefs are *nonbasic beliefs*. Plantinga gives two simple examples:

I believe the word "umbrageous" is spelled u-m-b-r-a-g-e-o-u-s: this belief is based on another belief of mine, the belief that that is how the dictionary says it is spelled. I believe that 72 times 71 = 5112. This belief is based upon several other beliefs I hold: that 1 times 72 = 72; 7 times 2 = 14; 7 times 7 = 49; 49 + 1 = 50; and others. (46)

The reader will notice that Plantinga applies the characteristics *basic* and *nonbasic* to both beliefs and propositions. But if, as we saw in

Chapter 1, the term *belief* may be used to designate either a mental attitude or the object of that mental attitude, it may be asked, "To which sense of belief does the contrast between basic and nonbasic apply?" The answer, it seems, is that what is basic and nonbasic is not, strictly speaking, the propositions themselves but the mental attitudes of the person towards them. Thus, in the example, my *attitude* of assent to a proposition that states how a word is spelled is based on the *attitude* of assent to another proposition that states how the dictionary spells it. Otherwise we would have the unacceptable position that propositions that are *taken* to be based on others *really are;* but this may be mistaken. If the dictionary spells a word differently from what I believe, the proposition itself which I believe is not based on the dictionary spelling; but my attitude toward my spelling is based on another attitude I have toward the dictionary spelling. *Basing* certain (nonbasic) beliefs upon other (basic) beliefs is a *mental operation* that may or may not be in accord with the way things are between the propositions themselves that are believed. In other words, the attitude that constitutes the mental operation of basing one proposition on another has a third proposition also as an object, viz., that the one proposition *is based on* the other; and *that* third proposition may be true or false. When we speak of beliefs as basic or nonbasic, then, we should understand what is meant in this more precise way.

Noetic Structure.   Thus beliefs (that is, attitudes toward propositions) come in these two kinds; and as one is the complementary class of the other, they are mutually exclusive and exhaustive kinds. They are related to one another, in a person's mind, in such a way that they form what Plantinga calls a *noetic structure.* "A noetic structure is the set of propositions he believes, together with certain epistemic relations that hold among him and these propositions" (48). The essential relation, of course, is that the person believes some propositions *on the basis* of others.

A person would not have to do this, of course. It is "abstractly possible," says Plantinga, that a person could hold none of his beliefs as basic beliefs, or all of them so. In the former case, however, with everyone based on another one, there would be no point to taking one belief as based on another one to be significant in any special way, because the latter belief will be based on still another, with the basing relationship coming to no end. But if the basing relationship has no end, there seems to be no point in calling the set of beliefs a structure at all, there being no ultimate difference between basic and nonbasic beliefs whatever. In any event, it seems obvious to Plantinga, and has been obvious to most philosophers in the tradition, as well as to common sense, that the human noetic structure (when taken simply as a set of beliefs) is actually a structure composed of the two different kinds of belief and the relationship of *being based upon* that relates them.

Foundationalism. Now all of these ingredients in our noetic structure put together—the two different kinds of beliefs and the relationship between them—yield a theoretical model of the intellectual workings of the human mind. These days this model is called *foundationalism,* for on this model our total system of beliefs is so organized that some of them rest upon others, the nonbasic beliefs upon the basic ones, and thus we get the picture that the basic ones provide the *foundation* for those that are nonbasic. An alternate model has been proposed, viz., coherentism, according to which there is a noetic structure of beliefs, but it is a structure of their coherence rather than of some being basic to others. The issues between these two models are very wide and deep and reflect the opposition between realistic and idealistic theories of knowledge and reality. Plantinga has dealt with some of these issues in "Replies" (390–393) and "Coherentism and the Evidentialist Objection" (109–138). I leave those issues aside here to focus on the central issue that divides foundationalists among themselves; for Plantinga's thesis that belief in God is a *properly* basic belief is not a coherentist thesis but a foundationalist one.

The Central Issue. A division arises between foundationalists over the question of which beliefs it is *proper* or *correct* for us to hold as basic beliefs. Thus the issue is a *normative* one, very much like questions in morality. Just as debates over morality concern, among other things, not how human beings do behave but how it is correct and proper for them to behave to *be moral,* so the debates over basic beliefs concern not whether people hold certain beliefs as basic but which of these beliefs it is correct and proper for them to hold to *be rational.* Thus what it is for human beings to be reasonable or rational in their beliefs turns out to involve *standards,* just as it does for them to be moral in their actions. Furthermore, some failures in rationality may be excused, for, just as in some cases of moral failure, the failure may be owing to some sort of "intellectual deficiency" and not to a willful transgression of norms, so that the proper response is "one of sympathy rather than censure" (39). Nevertheless, general agreement on the nature of human rationality will be as difficult to achieve as it is for the question what it is to be moral. In other words, the *appeal to reason* for establishing the nature of rational belief is as unpromising as it is for establishing the nature of morality, for the nature of reason itself is at stake today in a way that it was not for ancient and medieval philosophers.

Reformed Foundationalism. This rather pessimistic state of affairs becomes especially evident when the issues are engaged between theists and nontheists. In the following passage, Plantinga acknowledges this state of affairs and also offers a glimpse of the divisions that have arisen between foundationalists:

> A former professor of mine for whom I had and have enormous respect once said that theists and nontheists have different conceptions of reason. At the time I did not know what he meant, but now I think I do. On the Reformed view I have been urging, the deliverances of reason include the existence of God just as much as perceptual truths, self-evident truths, memory truths, and the like. It is not that theist and nontheist agree as to what reason delivers, the theist then going on to accept the existence of God by faith; there is, instead, disagreement in the first place as to what are the deliverances of reason. (90; for an elaboration of this autobiographical passage, see Plantinga's "Self-Profile," [3–36]. The professor is William Harry Jellema.)

The issue, it will be recalled, is what constitutes a *properly* basic belief. From a Reformed point of view, the issue comes to a head over the status of belief in God—belief that God exists. Plantinga claims that it is "entirely acceptable, desirable, right, proper, and rational to accept belief in God without any argument or evidence whatever" (39). Indeed, belief in God is a "deliverance of reason" itself, just as much as "perceptual truths, self-evident truths, memory truths and the like."

That claim is the heart of *Reformed* foundationalism, which Plantinga distinguishes from a long philosophical tradition. In his earlier essay, "Is Belief in God Rational?" he observes: "Foundationalism has had a long and distinguished career in the history of philosophy, including among its adherents Plato, Aristotle, Aquinas, Descartes, Leibniz, Locke, and, to leap to the present, Professor Roderick Chisholm" (13). I have always thought it significant that Plantinga omits from this list the great name of St. Augustine. I believe the omission is justified, because Augustine is not really a traditional foundationalist like the others whose names are on the list. For, as we have seen, unlike them, Augustine teaches that belief in God is an immediate deliverance of reason. Although Augustine's language (of rational vision and divine illumination) differs from Plantinga's, his conception of knowing God sets him off from the ancient foundationalist tradition of natural theology. Thus the roots of Plantinga's views go deeper than the Reformed tradition out of which he writes, even to the Christian Platonism of St. Augustine.

Evidentialism. The major division between Reformed foundationalists and other foundationalists, then, is between those who hold
that belief in God can be a properly basic belief and those who do not.
What shall the latter be called? Non-Reformed foundationalists? That
would not be a very good name, because it suggests that the division
exists primarily between Christian theological traditions, which is not
the case. Philosophically it is more illuminating to draw the lines in a
different way. Plantinga uses the the term *evidentialism* for all such
non-Reformed foundationalist positions (1983, 17–39).

This term makes room for both other theological traditions and
agnostic positions which insist that belief in God, to be rational, must be
based on argument and evidence. Thus natural theology is evidentialis-
tic, in so far as it regards belief in God as a nonbasic belief that needs to
be *based on* other beliefs which are either themselves properly basic or in
turn based upon those that are. But agnostics and atheists (*atheologians,*
as Plantinga calls them) are typically evidentialists also, as Plantinga
shows, for such representatives like Bertrand Russell, W. K. Clifford,
Brand Blanshard, Michael Scriven, and Anthony Flew (17–39). In fact,
the most common defense of agnosticism and atheism is that the *evidence* with respect to belief in God is either insufficient or counts against
it, whereas the central point of natural theology is that the evidence justifies the belief. As a recent example of agnosticism, Anthony Kenny, in
Faith and Reason, shows how finding the evidences of natural theology
inadequate combined with failing to find belief in God properly basic
leads him to a carefully defined ("contingent") agnosticism.

Classical Foundationalism. Let us now sketch in the larger contours of traditional foundationalism. One of the advantages of
Plantinga's philosophy of religion, as noted earlier, is that he has
developed it within the context of the broader issues of epistemology.
The major division within philosophical foundationalism divides
ancient and medieval philosophers from the moderns. Ancient and
medieval philosophers typically (of course, there are exceptions, as I
have argued that Augustine is one) restrict properly basic beliefs to
what is evident to the senses and what is self-evident. What marks
ancient and medieval foundationalism is not the descriptive claim
that such beliefs are basic beliefs, but the normative claim that these
two kinds of beliefs are the *only* kind of beliefs that can be *properly
basic beliefs.* All other beliefs, including the belief in God, to be rational, ultimately must be based on either or both of those (39–48).

Modern foundationalism agrees with ancient and medieval foundationalism on the self-evident truths of reason, but rejects what is *evident* to the senses in favor of what *appears* to the senses. This is a radical

shift, for it revives the skepticism about the senses that goes back to the ancient Greeks—Gorgias, Protagoras, Pyrrho, and even Plato himself. The revival of ancient skepticism and its impact on modern philosophy has become a fertile field of exploration (Popkin 1979; Burnyeat 1983). What *appears* to the senses is different from what is *evident* to the senses by being "incorrigible." When the "incorrigible" propositions expressing the way things appear to us (e.g., it seems to me that I see a tree) are combined with those that are self-evident as the only two kinds of "properly basic beliefs," the modern version of foundationalism is the result. As important as this difference between the "ancients" and the "moderns" may be from the point of view of skepticism over the nature and existence of the external world, the two foundationalisms agree in sharing a *restrictive criterion* for what constitutes a properly basic belief, for what kind of propositions properly belong in the foundation of a rational noetic structure. Plantinga therefore lumps them both together under the label of *classical foundationalism* (58).

   The Collapse of Classical Foundationalism.   Plantinga rejects classical foundationalism. He begins by distinguishing two parts in the criterion it lays down for properly basic beliefs: "First, a proposition is properly basic *if* it is self-evident, incorrigible, or evident to the senses, and second, a proposition is properly basic *only if* it meets these conditions. The first seems true enough; suppose we concede it. But what is to be said for the second?" (59). Not very much, as Plantinga procedes to show, by two different arguments. First, he offers *counterexamples* of beliefs that certainly appear to be properly basic, but are ruled out from being so by classical foundationalism. For example, our beliefs that minds other than our own exist and our memory beliefs seem generally to be properly basic, but neither kind is either self-evident, evident to the senses or incorrigible. Thus the second part of the criterion is overly narrow and restrictive, and therefore false.

   Second, Plantinga argues that the classical foundationalist's criterion for a properly basic belief is *incoherent*. For this criterion is itself a proposition that the classical foundationalist believes. But what is the basis of that belief? If one could believe it on the basis of other propositions that are ultimately self-evident, evident to the senses, or incorrigible and truly do support it, one would be rational; but "no foundationalist has provided such an argument." If, on the other hand, it is itself properly basic, it must be either self-evident, evident to the senses, or incorrigible. But

   clearly [the proposition] meets none of these conditions. Hence it is not properly basic for [the classical foundationalist, who] is then self-referentially inconsistent in accepting [it]; he accepts [it] as basic, despite the fact that [it] does not meet the condition for proper basicality that [it] itself lays down" (60–61)

And thus classical foundationalism is incoherent.

These two arguments against classical foundationalism are powerful indeed, and certainly pave the way for considering belief in God as a properly basic belief. For if classical foundationalism is false and no less restrictive version has been successfully proposed to replace it, nothing has been shown that excludes belief in God from being among the properly foundational beliefs of our noetic structure. Plantinga's arguments, of course, do not warrant the inclusion of theistic belief in these foundations. Even if certain properly basic beliefs fall outside the restrictive criterion of classical foundationalism, it does not follow that belief in God is among them. That has to be shown on its own merits.

Bavinck and Calvin. It is at this point that Plantinga appeals to the Reformed tradition, especially to Herman Bavinck and Calvin himself. Bavinck is particularly clear. Plantinga finds five distinct points in Bavinck's *The Doctrine of God* (not to be confused with the more famous "five points of Calvinism," set forth by the Synod of Dort and memorialized by generations of Calvinists in the acronym TULIP). First, "typically the believer does not believe in God on the basis of arguments." Second, "argument is not needed for *rational justification.*" Third, "the arguments of natural theology just do not work." Fourth, "there is nothing by way of proofs or arguments for God's existence in the Bible; that is simply presupposed." And fifth, "Bavinck points out that belief in God relevantly resembles belief in the existence of the self and of the external world" (Plantinga 1983, 64–65).

What can be said of these five points? Plantinga agrees with the first point, that "arguments or proofs are not, in general, the source of the believer's confidence in God" (64). Assuming that Plantinga means to speak here, according to his earlier distinction, of the belief that God exists, not "confidence in God," his agreement on the first point only confirms that Christian belief in God is *basic*, not that it is *properly* basic. So more will have to be said. Plantinga also agrees with the second point, that argument is not *needed* for belief in God to be *rationally justified.* If, however, belief in God can be properly basic, that by itself will show that we do not need argument for the belief to be rationally justified. Third, Plantinga agrees that the arguments of natural theology do not work as proofs and acknowledges Bavinck's efforts to show this. In *God and Other Minds* Plantinga conducts his own detailed examination of the proofs for the existence of God; like Bavinck, he concludes that they are unsound. (In a later work, *The Nature of Necessity*, he offers a carefully circumscribed exception in a modal version of the ontological argument [Ch. 10]). Thus Plantinga has made up any serious lack of such an examination in the writings of Reformed theologians. Of course, it does not follow from the failure of natural theology that theistic belief is properly basic, so again, more must be done.

Fourth, Scripture offers no arguments for God's existence but presupposes it, a point we have already had occasion to make (Chapter 2). Plantinga asserts that "the same should be true of the Christian believer" (65). Although this is not an argument, it is an altogether appropriate appeal to authority—that of the Bible, which is the supreme authority of the Christian religion. Finally, Plantinga agrees with the fifth point, "that belief in God relevantly resembles belief in the existence of the self and the external world—and, we might add, belief in other minds and the past (65). To fill out this argument, of course, the relevant resemblance needs to be shown.

Plantinga follows these five points in Bavinck to stake out the Reformed objection to natural theology. He goes on to discuss Calvin's claims for a natural, universal awareness of God and the way in which this "disposition to believe in God," as he calls it, is "triggered or actuated by a widely realized condition," viz., a recognition of the workmanship of the universe (65). As we saw in the previous chapter, Calvin's claim for such an awareness of God combined with an experience of the workmanship of the universe renders natural theology unnecessary. So, too, does Plantinga's claim that belief in God is properly basic.

The Problem of a Criterion. Plantinga develops the argument from Bavinck that belief in God relevantly resembles other properly basic beliefs that fall outside the criterion of classical foundationalism. Before we turn to that argument, let us consider his discussion of the most conspicuous difference between theistic belief and these other properly basic beliefs. This difference is simply that not nearly everyone who agrees that those other beliefs (e.g., memory beliefs, beliefs in the past, and beliefs in other minds) are properly basic in spite of being excluded from being so by classical foundationalism also agrees that the same is true for theistic belief. Plantinga answers the objection based upon this fact in a way that is reminiscent of his argument that classical foundationalism is incoherent. For what these objectors are doing, in effect, is to modify the criterion laid down by classical foundationalism in the following way. "*P* is properly basic for S if and only if *p* is self-evident or incorrigible or evident to the senses for S, or is accepted as basic by nearly everyone" (62). Plantinga argues that *this* proposition is incoherent, because it does not meet any of the several parts of the criterion it lays down, especially not the last part, which was added to rescue the situation. For "not nearly everyone takes [it] as basic; I do not, for example" (62); nor, he could add, does anyone in the Reformed tradition, and perhaps not in the Augustininian tradition either.

This reply effectively wards off any appeal to *agreement* for discovering a more satisfactory criterion to replace that of classical foundationalism. How, then, should we approach the problem of the criterion for proper basicality? Plantinga has an answer. "The proper way to arrive at a criterion [for proper basicality] is, broadly speaking, *inductive*" (76). By this he means that "criteria for proper basicality must be reached from below rather than from above; they should not be presented *ex cathedra* but argued to and tested by a relevant set of examples. But there is no reason to assume, in advance, that everyone will agree on the examples" (77). Significantly, the clearest example of such disagreement is that between Christians and agnostics—which is a deeply *religious* disagreement:

> The Christian will of course suppose that belief in God is entirely proper and rational; if he does not accept this belief on the basis of other propositions, he will conclude that it is basic for him and quite properly so. Followers of Bertrand Russell and Madelyn Murray O'Hare [sic] may disagree; but how is that relevant? Must my criteria, or those of the Christian community, conform to their examples? Surely not. The Christian community is responsible to *its* set of examples, not to theirs. (77)

In other words, epistemology is not a religiously neutral inquiry. It is not the arbiter of the legitimacy of religious belief; religious belief is the arbiter (or one of the arbiters) of epistemology.

How Belief in God Resembles Other Properly Basic Beliefs. Plantinga goes further. Christians may hold that their belief in God is properly basic even if they have *not* developed a "full-fledged criterion of proper basicality." But without such a criterion in hand, how can they reject the proper basicality of irrational beliefs, for example, a belief in the Great Pumpkin? They can, says Plantinga, and the reason why leads us to the most interesting and innovative, if also the most controversial, aspect of Plantinga's theory of properly basic belief. The reason why theistic belief is properly basic and therefore rational, and belief in the Great Pumpkin is not properly basic and therefore irrational, is that it is *not groundless:*

> The central point here, however, is that a belief is properly basic only in certain conditions; these conditions are, we might say, the ground of its justification and, by extension, the ground of the belief itself. In this sense basic beliefs are not, or are not necessarily, *groundless* beliefs.
>
> Now similar things may be said about belief in God. When the Reformers claim that this belief is properly basic, they do not mean to say, of course, that there are no justifying circumstances for it, or that it is in that sense groundless or gratuitous. (80)

Just as we can point to the grounds of our memory beliefs, our beliefs in other persons, and our beliefs in physical objects, so we can point to the grounds of our belief in God. Theists can point to "conditions that justify and ground belief in God" (78) in the same way that we all can do the same thing for those other properly basic beliefs. The argument for this resemblance has been called the *parity argument.* Its significance is that it enables theists to answer two objections at once: both the objection that belief in God is not relevantly similar to other properly basic beliefs that fall outside the criterion of classical foundationalism, and the objection that belief in God is too close for comfort to irrational beliefs like belief in the Great Pumpkin.

We shall presently return to the grounds of properly basic beliefs, because they constitute, as Plantinga says, their *justification* and thus provide a link between the idea of properly basic beliefs and a theory of knowledge as justified true belief. For now, enough has been said to see the essential continuity between Reformed thought and Plantinga's epistemology. Belief in God for Plantinga, like Calvin's natural awareness of God and testimony of the Holy Spirit, is entirely rational and proper for human beings not only because it is, like some other important properly basic beliefs, immediate and based on no other beliefs that offer evidence for it, but also because, like them, it is not arbitrary and groundless.

Knowledge vs. Belief.

The most important difference between Plantinga's Reformed epistemology and that of the Reformed tradition, as noted at the outset, is that Plantinga has replaced its acquaintance theory of knowledge with a theory of knowledge as justified true belief. For Calvin does not, like Plantinga, begin with *belief in God* and then develop a theory of justification; he begins with the (implicit) theory of knowledge as acquaintance, and claims that all human beings possess knowledge of God so defined. What human beings have, says Calvin, is not justified belief, or properly basic belief, but a natural *awareness* of God. Furthermore, *all* human beings have such knowledge, even agnostics and atheists, who when they deny knowing that God exists are really only suppressing a natural mental state of knowing God. And what all Christians have in addition to such natural awareness is a *revelation* of God himself in Scripture, which they believe because it is the testimony of God himself.

Now the main point of Plantinga's early writings, as we have seen, is to show that it is *rational* or *proper* to *believe* in God (that God exists) as a basic belief. To show this is not to show the stronger point that it is *irrational* or *improper* not to believe in God as a basic belief. If, however, it could be shown that belief in God as a basic belief can be *knowledge* itself, then it certainly might be irrational or improper *not* to believe in God. In other words, if I am "within my rights" to believe in God as a basic belief, it does not follow that I *know* that God exists. But it does not follow either that I do *not* know that God exists. If, when I believe that God exists, the conditions under which I believe it are such that I also *know* that he exists, it would be irrational or improper for me not to believe it. So we need now to pursue Plantinga's explanation of how justified belief constitutes knowledge, to see both how his theory contrasts with the acquaintance theory of Augustine and Calvin and how it can neverthelesss incorporate their approach. I anticipated this prospect earlier in Chapter 1, when I chose the lead of Plato's *Theaetetus* approach over his *Republic* approach and argued that the former approach can incorporate the latter. It will become evident that Plantinga's justified true belief approach can incorporate the acquaintance theory of the Reformed tradition and that his approach thereby highlights the contribution this tradition makes to the contemporary epistemological discussion.

Grounds vs. Evidence. The critical point we have reached in Plantinga's theory of what justifies properly basic beliefs is that these beliefs are not groundless. Properly basic beliefs are formed under "conditions that confer justification on one who accepts them as basic. They are not therefore groundless or gratuitous" (82). It is important, first of all, to indicate that Plantinga uses the term *grounds* in a very special way, not to be confused with evidence. Evidence and grounds both function as *justification*, but they do this in substantially different ways. The difference is that evidence consists of *beliefs* on the basis of which other, nonbasic beliefs are held (and thereby justified), whereas grounds are not beliefs at all, but *conditions* or *circumstances* that occasion properly basic beliefs, and thereby justify them *without being formulated as beliefs*. In other words, both nonbasic and basic beliefs need justification; but, although nonbasic beliefs receive their justification from other beliefs on which they are based, basic beliefs receive it, when they do, from grounds. Again, to have *evidence* for a belief is to hold that belief on the basis of other *beliefs* which one consciously takes as *supporting* it. To have *grounds* for a belief, however, is to hold it in such a way that there are conditions in which it arises and that justify it, even though the believer may typically be *unaware* at the moment of what those conditions are. Being unaware of them, one does not formulate beliefs about them on the basis of which he holds the belief, which is precisely what makes that belief a *basic* belief. One may, of course, be able to point to some of these grounds for one's basic beliefs if asked, but that is a different matter.

Plantinga illustrates what he means by grounds with examples drawn from perceptual beliefs, memory beliefs, and beliefs about mental states of other persons—all of which are typically basic beliefs. Here is his example of a perceptual belief:

> Upon having experience of a certain sort, I believe that I am perceiving a tree. In the typical case I do not hold this belief on the basis of other beliefs; it is nonetheless not groundless. My having that characteristic sort of experience—to use Professor Chisholm's language, my being appeared treely to—plays a crucial role in the formation of that belief. It also plays a crucial role in its *justification*. (79)

Now there are three essential points in this picture of the justification of a basic belief. First, justification does not consist in a *belief* but in some "characteristic experience"; an experience (of which one may be quite unaware) constitutes the *ground of* the basic belief by contrast with one's (consciously) having or giving *evidence* for it. Second, "being appropriately appeared to . . . is not sufficient for justification; some further condition—a condition hard to state in detail—is clearly necessary" (80). So there is more to justification than what is captured by the Chisholmian language of appearance; what that is Plantinga develops in his later writings, in his theory of the proper working of our noetic faculties. With that more complete theory of justification (as we will see later), Plantinga provides a theory of *knowledge* that is already implicit in the present account. The main point of the present account, as Plantinga says, is "that a belief is properly basic only in certain conditions [and that] these conditions are . . . the ground of its justification and, by extension, the ground of the belief itself" (80; cf. also 93, n. 41).

"Now similar things may be said about belief in God," says Plantinga (80). He gives examples of the sorts of circumstances or experiences, drawn from Calvin himself, that provide the grounds or the justifying circumstances for a properly basic belief in God: "guilt, gratitude, danger, a sense of God's presence, a sense that he speaks [for example, on hearing the Bible read], perception of the various parts of the universe. A complete job would explore the phenomenology of all these conditions and of more besides" (81). It seems clear that Plantinga's conception of the grounds of religious belief requires a further investigation of the nature of religious experience. Stephen Evans, in "Kierkegaard and Plantinga on Belief in God," challenges some stereotypes of each philosopher that may have prevented readers from considering them together and argues "that a good part of this fuller phenomenology of the ground of belief in God has been provided for Plantinga by Kierkegaard" (34). And William Alston, in "Christian Experience and Christian Belief" and other articles, explores the question how religious experience can offer grounds for religious belief.

Proper Basicality and Truth.   We now have in hand an enriched concept of a properly basic belief. It is a belief not based on any other belief but nevertheless grounded in conditions or circumstances that justify it. These conditions or circumstances, however, may or may not guarantee the truth of the basic belief. For all that we have seen so far, Plantinga's theory of justification falls short of that. So far, the point of that theory is to show only that belief in God, like belief in external objects, can be *properly basic;* it is not yet a theory of *knowledge* as justified true belief. Still, we can already tell the fundamental shape that the concept of justification will take in Plantinga's later thought. The justification of properly basic beliefs has two fairly clear characteristics. First, it is *external*, not internal. I first alluded to this difference in Chapter 1. I noted there that Plato, in his *Theaetetus* approach, assumes that one who knows can *give* an account of one's true belief. In that connection I quoted from William Alston, who distinguishes between *being justified* and *being able to give a justification.* The latter implies that the knower has access to, and can therefore produce the justification of his or her belief; it is thus *internal* to the knower's mental attitude. The former, however, does not imply such access, for the reason that the justification of one's belief may be *external* to one's state of mind.

We can now observe this difference again in the distinction Plantinga makes between *evidence* and *grounds*. Evidence consists of beliefs to which someone may be expected to have access and to give (or be able to give) in support of other beliefs; beliefs that count thus as evidence are beliefs that one consciously holds and are thus internal to one's noetic structure. (For example, the natural theologian formulates beliefs about the orderliness of the universe and infers from these beliefs the belief in God.) Grounds, by contrast, are conditions or circumstances in which someone forms a properly basic belief without having to formulate beliefs about such conditions or circumstances at all, or about the role such conditions or circumstances play in justifying a properly basic belief; thus the conditions or circumstances are external to the belief system that constitutes the believer's noetic structure. (For example, recall John Baillie's concept of the mediated immediacy of our knowledge of God from the workmanship of the universe; an experience of the starry heavens above mediates my immediate awareness of God.) Justification of belief by evidence is *internalistic*, by grounds, *externalistic* justification.

Second, Plantinga distinguishes between prima facie and ultima facie (or "all-things-considered") justification. Plantinga illustrates this new distinction with the same perceptual belief cited earlier:

> My being appeared to treely gives me a *prima facie* right to take as basic the proposition *I see a tree*. But of course this right can be overridden; I might know, for example, that I suffer from the dreaded dendrological disorder, whose victims are appeared to treely only when there are no trees present. If I do know that, then I am not within my rights in taking as basic the proposition *I see a tree* when I am appeared to treely. (83).

In other words, the grounds for a properly basic belief may be overridden by evidence that counts against its being *true*. The example is a bit contrived, of course. Plantinga actually holds that properly basic beliefs generally have more warrant as properly basic than if they are believed on the basis of evidence, as he argues in "The Foundations of Theism: A Reply" (304–306). Still, the contrived example of being appeared to treely highlights an important point, viz., that even properly basic beliefs are not proof against being false. That is, they are not prima facie, at any rate, to be equated with knowledge, which cannot be false. If properly basic beliefs do constitute knowledge, therefore, it will only be upon "all-things-considered," or ultima facie. Thus the justification of properly basic beliefs, as so far discussed, is not quite sufficient for understanding those beliefs *as knowledge*. They *may* constitute knowledge, but we do not yet have a *theory* to explain when, or why, or under what circumstances they are to be so understood.

Weak vs. Strong Justification.   Plantinga can also be seen as reaching for a theory of knowledge in the distinction he makes between weak and strong justification. Still employing the same example, he writes:

> *Being appeared to treely* may confer on me, not merely the *prima facie* right to believe that there is a tree present, but the more impressive epistemic condition of being such that if the belief in question is true, then I *know* it. Call that condition *strong justification.* Being thus appeared to may perhaps also lay obligations on me; perhaps in those conditions I am not merely within my rights in believing that there is a tree present; perhaps I have a *prima facie* obligation to do so. (85)

Here Plantinga adds to the grounds that confer on someone the right to believe there is a tree present the essential condition of knowledge that the belief is true *and* the further condition that an *obligation* is laid on him to believe it. The tentative language he uses ("perhaps...; perhaps...") suggests that he has not worked out all these ideas yet at this stage. Still, it does seem that if I *know* something, I will be more *compelled* to believe it than if I only have a right to believe it. If I know something, it seems that I am *obliged* to believe what I know, although it is hard to say in what feature of knowing the obligation consists. Still, the term *strong justification* implies that something more than we have seen so far is required for the concept of justification to constitute knowledge, in the account of it as justified true belief.

Belief on Testimony vs. Belief on Appearance.   At one point Plantinga says that to believe on *testimony*, which is prima facie or weakly justified, is to be in a "less favorable epistemic condition" than to believe on one's own acquaintance with something, which is (presumably) to be strongly justified in one's belief:

> If I ask you your name and you tell me, I have a *prima facie* right to believe what you say. A child is within his epistemic rights in believing what he is taught by his elders.... You may believe that the Kröller-Müller museum is in Gelderland, Netherlands....
> As I have said, testimony confers a *prima facie* right to believe; but in the typical case the epistemic condition one is in vis-a-vis *p* by virtue of having been *told* that *p* is not as favorable as the

condition one enjoys vis-a-vis a proposition—2 + 1 = 3, say
—that is apparently self-evident. (85)

The claim is interesting because in it Plantinga echoes Plato's ancient
assumption, picked up by Augustine, that belief on testimony is inferi-
or to knowing by acquaintance. On the latter view, it will be recalled,
this inferiority is so significant that both Plato and Augustine deny
that belief on testimony is knowledge and reserve that term for cases
where the mind is in direct touch with reality. This inferiority becomes
the motivating force behind Augustine's formula, faith seeking understanding. It is not clear from Plantinga's language here that he, too,
wishes to deny the status of knowledge to everything we believe on
testimony, but the tenor of his language suggests it. I have argued that
believing on testimony can—and certainly does, in the "typical" examples cited by Plantinga—constitute knowledge, simply because testimony can provide an adequate justification for true belief.

Plantinga offers another typical example of moving from belief
on testimony to belief grounded in one's own experience:

> One who has been brought up to believe in God has a *prima facie*
> right to do so; but perhaps one who is brought up to believe and
> then finds himself in one of the circumstances mentioned above
> ["guilt, gratitude, danger, etc."] has (*prima facie*) strong justifica-
> tion for believing in God. Perhaps his condition is such that
> (given that his belief is true and given the absence of contraven-
> ing conditions) he *knows* that God exists. (86–87)

But why could not a person's belief in God based on testimony alone,
given that the belief is true and given the absence of contravening
conditions, be such that one *knows* that God exists? Such a believer
will not know that God exists by his or her own acquaintance with
him, mediated by the relevant conditions and circumstances; but to
say one will not know that God exists on reliable testimony that God
exists just begs the question as to whether reliable testimony can provide in its own way an adequate justification for true belief such that
it constitutes that true belief as knowledge.

Perhaps the issue here is only over what Plantinga means in the
earlier quotation by one epistemic condition being "more favorable"
than another. To know that God exists by "being in certain circumstances" can certainly be a *more favorable* way of knowing that he exists
than knowing that he exists only on the reliable testimony of one's parents; the former may even be God's own preferred way of being
known, because it makes possible an acquaintance with him and a

response to him not possible by accepting his existence on testimony alone. That, at any rate, is the central thrust of Reformed epistemology.

In any event, Plantinga says of his discussion of these examples that he intended only to "suggest some hints for further study" (85). As we have seen, in the article we have discussed, "Reason and Belief in God," Plantinga aims to give an account only of properly basic belief, not of knowledge as justified true belief. For that, we must turn to his more recent writings.

Noetic Faculties Working Properly

Plantinga first outlines his theory of knowledge as justified true belief in the article, "Justification and Theism." What is knowledge? "According to an ancient and honorable tradition, knowledge is *justified true belief*" (403). Indeed, as we saw in Chapter 1, the tradition goes back to Plato's *Theaetetus*. We also saw, in our study of Augustine and Calvin, that this tradition disappears from the main classical and medieval tradition, which favors Plato's *Republic* approach. We would have noticed its absence also if we had followed the Aristotelian tradition that culminates in St. Thomas Aquinas. Although the Platonic-Augustinian and Aristotelian-Thomistic epistemologies differ in important ways from one another, neither of them is a theory of justified true belief.

There is, however, an ancient tradition that keeps alive the approach to knowledge as justified true belief, although neither Platonists nor Aristotelians will likely regard it as an "honorable" tradition. That is because this tradition is to be found mainly among the skeptics. They were the first thinkers to develop the view when they took over the Academy under the lead of Arcesilaus, who became its head in 260 B.C. As the skeptics developed the idea of justified true belief, it was not, of course, a theory of knowledge, for they held that the truth cannot be found, that nothing can be *known*. Their theory, therefore, is not a theory of justified *true* belief, but of what is most *probable* or *like* a truth.

Carneades, who became head of the Academy about a hundred years after Arcesilaus, is one of the most significant figures in this development. As Sextus Empiricus makes clear in *Against the Logicians*, Carneades works out his view as an answer to the practical objection that, if nothing can be known, the skeptic has no guide for life: "Yet, as [Carneades], too, himself requires a criterion for the conduct of life and for the attainment of happiness, he is practically compelled on his own account to frame a theory about it, and to adopt both the probable presentation and that which is at once probable and irreversible and tested" (I, 166). Carneades thus offers a threefold criteria for justified belief. A belief must first be probable, by which he means *like a truth* (or *verisimile*, as Cicero later describes it and Augustine picks it up again in *Answer to Skeptics*). Because, however, what looks like a truth may be turn out to be false, which shows that it has no clear mark that distinguishes it from the false, we must (second) see whether it coheres with other beliefs. If it does, this will incline us against "reversing" the belief:

> For example, he who receives the presentation [probable belief] of a man necessarily receives the presentation both of his personal qualities and of the external conditions—of his personal qualities, such as color, size, shape, motion, speech, dress, footgear; and of the external conditions, such as air, light, day, heaven, earth, friends, and all the rest. So whenever none of these presentations disturbs our faith by appearing false, but all with one accord appear true, our belief is the greater. (I, 176–178)

Finally, we must "test" all these beliefs and their concurrence, which means "scrutinizing attentively" each of the beliefs to verify that the "judgment" it represented at first sight (prima facie in Plantinga's language) holds up after (ultima facie) a second and even a third look at the object that gave rise to it. Clearly, however, Carneades intends to give a theory of justified *belief*, not of *knowledge* as justified *true* belief.

Nevertheless, his approach reflects the framework of Plato's *Theaetetus* approach. It begins with belief, and with what at least *looks like* a true belief, and proceeds to justify it by comparing it with other beliefs with which it should be consistent and then by checking out once again the original experience that gave rise to the belief. Notice that the approach makes no room for the bearing of *testimony* on the justification of belief. Indeed, like Plato before them, skeptics distrust hearsay. This distrust is owing mainly to the conflict in human testimony, which, very much like the "Modes" of skepticism (developed first, it seems, by Aenesidemus c. 100 B.C.?), should lead to a suspension of belief (*epoche*) because of the equivalence (*isosthenia*) of contrary evidence or testimony. "The main basic principle of the Skeptic system," writes Sextus in *Outlines of Pyrrhonism*, "is that of opposing to every proposition an equal proposition" (I, 12). Nothing is more impressive to the skeptic than the conflict between human opinions and perceptions and between the doctrines of "dogmatic" philosophical systems.

So there is an ancient tradition that approaches the topic of knowledge and belief by way of the *justification* of belief. It has been, however, a minority tradition in the history of philosophy until modern times. Richard Popkin, in *The History of Skepticism from Erasmus to Spinoza*, recounts the influence of skepticism on the beginnings of modern philosophy. Even so, the explicit resort to the justification of belief as the framework for understanding the nature of knowledge did not occur until our century. Roderick Chisholm, whom Plantinga calls "the dean of contemporary epistemologists and surely one of the finest of that breed our century has to offer" (*Warrant*), opens his *Theory of Knowledge* with the claim: "The theory of knowledge could be said to have as its subject matter the *justification of belief*, or, more exactly, the justification of *believing*" (5). It is significant that Chisholm turns to Carneades as his guide for "a solution to our problem," the problem of the justification of sense knowledge. In contrast to Carneades, Chisholm develops a theory of *knowledge* and has no problem accepting the *truth* of what is evident to the senses (although he calls what is evident to the senses the *indirectly evident*, to distinguish it from the *directly evident*, in which he includes only "self-presenting states"—the incorrigible propositions of appearance beliefs and the self-evident "truths of reason"). Thus, although Chisholm is not a skeptic, the framework of his theory of *justification* is still that of Carneades and the skeptical tradition.

So the tradition of knowledge as justified true belief is ancient, but as it was earlier developed in an attentuated, skeptical form, there will be those who question whether it is an honorable tradition. The issue is whether the skeptical framework of the tradition as it developed in the Academy after Plato necessitates a skeptical conclusion. Plato certainly does not explore the idea of knowledge as true belief with an account in order to give skepticism a footing. Neither does Chisholm, when he consults Carneades; nor does Plantinga, as we shall see later. Nor do I in Chapter 1 when I take Plato's *Theaetetus* approach as a springboard for my own theory of knowledge as justified true belief.

Internalism vs. Externalism.   There are currently a great many different theories of knowledge as justified true belief. Observes Plantinga in "The Justification of Theism": "It is widely agreed that true belief, while necessary for knowledge, is not sufficient for it" (404). The major issue is over the theory of justification. Plantinga rues the confusion that exists on the contemporary scene:

> Contemporary epistemologists, sadly enough, do not . . . speak with a single voice. . . . Some claim that justification is by *epistemic dutifulness*, others that it is by *coherence*, and still others that it is by *reliability*. The differences among these views are enormous; this is by no means a case of variations on the same

theme. Indeed, disagreement is so deep and radical it is sometimes hard to be sure the various disputants are discussing
approximately the same issue. (403)

The theories can be divided roughly into the three categories Plantinga refers to here. They can also be divided into internalist and externalist theories. An *internalist* theory, as mentioned earlier, proposes a
justification that a believer can *give* for a belief; an *externalist* theory
proposes a justification that justifies the believer's belief even though
he or she is *unable to give* it, because, although it exists, the believer
may not even be aware of it.

This way of contrasting the two types of theory is oversimpli-
fied, of course; but it will do for our purposes here. Internalist theories typically involve deontological ingredients such as duties, per-
missions, obligations, and rights—terms that appear, as we saw, in
Plantinga's account of the justification of properly basic beliefs. In his
theory of knowledge as justified true belief, however, he moves away
from these internalist notions toward more externalist ones, similar to
those at the center of reliabilist theories. For the reliabilist, justification
arises from "a reliable belief producing mechanism or process" (423).
Clearly such a process can occur and produce a belief without the
believer being aware of the process or being able to describe it if
asked to do so. Plantinga acknowledges that his later theory of justification is "closer to reliabilism" than to either the internalism of
Chisholm or the coherentism of Lehrer and Bonjour (423). Let us see
how this is the case, as least with respect to internalism.

Three Elements of Justification.   The resemblance of Plantinga's
theory to reliabilism is evident from its central idea, the idea of our
noetic faculties working properly. The proper working of our noetic faculties is one of three elements that jointly constitute "positive epistemic status." Plantinga now prefers this term to *justification,* precisely
because it lacks internalist connotations. Positive epistemic status is
the important characteristic "enough of which distinguishes mere
true belief from knowledge" (404). Its second element is that these
noetic faculties must be working properly in *an environment* to which
they are "properly attuned" (407). Third, "the strength of the impulse
towards believing a given proposition" will vary for different beliefs
(e.g., the rules of logic vs. the memory of events in one's distant past),
so that positive epistemic status comes in *degrees* (409).

The Connection between the Earlier and Later Accounts.   The notion
of our faculties working properly in an environment to which they

are attuned was already implicit in Plantinga's earlier account of properly basic belief. His example of failing to see a tree because of "the dreaded dendrological disorder" turns on a disorder of some faculty (or faculties) that so affects the whole *process* that it results in the *mistaken* belief that one sees a tree. If, however, our "cognitive equipment" (407) is in proper working order and if we are on earth rather than on some planet revolving around Alpha Centauri, the environment of which has bizarre effects on earth-bound creatures like us, then the properly basic belief that we see a tree is *knowledge*. Likewise, Plantinga's earlier suggestion that properly basic belief in God can be knowledge of God in certain "appropriate circumstances" presupposes faculties in us which form the belief in an environment which provides the grounds for the belief.

We also found Plantinga in his earlier account invoking the notion of experience. Experience, too, is the result of our noetic faculties functioning in an environment. As he did earlier, Plantinga uses the term *experience* as the source of both our a priori and our a posteriori beliefs (406–407). Still, he acknowledges the difficulties in elaborating this vague and ambiguous term: "What we need here is a full and appropriately subtle and sensitive description of the role of experience in the formation of these various types of beliefs; that project will have to wait another occasion, as one says when one really has no idea how to accomplish the project" (407). Finally, by focusing on the faculties (reason and the senses) that give rise to our *experience*, Plantinga continues to suggest that belief on testimony may not count as knowledge. Be that as it may, it should be evident that his theory of noetic faculties working properly is continuous with his earlier theory of properly basic beliefs.

Reformed Anthropology

It should also be evident that such a theory requires the development of a complete philosophical anthropology. Just what are the noetic faculties that human beings possess? There is also an "ancient and honorable tradition" on the nature of these faculties, as we saw in our study of Plato, Augustine, and Calvin. For writers in the classical and medieval tradition typically do not explore the nature of knowledge, belief, and faith apart from discussing the nature of reason and the senses. Plantinga asks whether a nontheist can easily "make use of this notion of working properly" (411). Confidence in our noetic faculties is, of course, strongly supported by the Christian theistic belief that they were so *designed* by a God who is himself "an *intellectual* or *intellecting* being" who "has knowledge," who has "indeed . . . the maximal degree of knowledge," and who created us *"in his own image"* (405). He suggests that "this notion of proper functioning is . . . more problematic from a nontheistic perspective—more problematic, but by no means hopeless" (411). But is it really the case that confidence in our noetic faculties is especially linked to *Christian* theistic belief? It was Plato and Aristotle, after all, not Abraham, Moses, Isaiah, St. Paul, or even John Calvin, who first developed the notion of virtue, intellectual and moral, as the aim of *human nature*, as the goal of human reason, will, desire, and emotion all functioning properly in relationship to one another. Perhaps Plantinga's Reformed "working properly theory of human nature" is problematic only from a modern *skeptical* perspective. Descartes's rejection of belief in God as a properly basic belief is only part of that philosopher's primordial modern break from the classical and medieval view of reason and the senses; indeed, Cartesian skepticism implies by its nonconfidence in human knowledge a corresponding nonconfidence in the noetic faculties from which it was traditionally taken to arise.

This is an important point to pursue, for some have charged that Plantinga is himself a Cartesian or a Berkeleyan who bails out the senses (and reason, too, perhaps) by appealing to God. For example, in "'Reformed' Epistemology" T. A. Russman writes that Plantinga's "realism about sense perception is of a distinctly modern sort. It takes modern skepticism seriously and then claims to find a way around it by invoking the divine veracity" (198). But note that Plantinga responds to his own queries (earlier) by affirming that "the notion of proper functioning" is even from the nontheistic perspective "by no means hopeless," and asks:

> Can't anyone, theist or not, see that a horse, let's say, suffering from a disease, is displaying a pathological condition? Can't anyone see that an injured bird has a wing that isn't working properly? The notions of proper function and allied notions (sickness, dysfunction, disorder, malfunction and the like) are ones we all or nearly all have and use. (411)

Reformed thinkers have always held that the knowledge of human nature as consisting of faculties functioning either well or badly is available to anyone. Calvin himself, as we saw, adapted the pagan Plato's account of the faculties of the soul to his own Christian understanding of faith and knowledge.

In any event, Plantinga affirms that belief in God, on the Reformed view, is a "deliverance of reason." We saw that Augustine also holds such a view, but that Calvin is much less clear about the role of reason in our knowledge of God. That probably helps to explain why the charge of fideism arises periodically against Reformed epistemology. Fideism either ignores reason or disparages it in the interest of faith. Plantinga argues that Reformed epistemology does neither of these things. As he says in "Reason and Belief in God," he himself sees belief in God as a *deliverance of reason,* just as much as any other properly basic belief—"basic perceptual truths (propositions 'evident to the senses'), incorrigible propositions, certain memory propositions, certain propositions about other minds, and certain moral or ethical propositions" (89).

But just how does reason "deliver" the properly basic belief that God exists, and more particularly, how does reason deliver that belief in such a way that it is *knowledge,* on a par with other properly basic beliefs when they, too, constitute knowledge? And what are the noetic effects of sin on the function of reason for the knowledge of God, as well as the noetic effects of grace and faith? These questions bring up the question of the role of the will. Though the will is not sharply in focus until Augustine, the Greek philosophers already presuppose analogous concepts of the will in their analysis of choice, voluntary action, moral virtue, and the bearing of these upon the exercise of reason in its search for truth. It was clear to these philosophers that, to account adequately for knowledge, belief, ignorance, error, and other epistemic states, they had to examine our moral disposition. For Augustine and Calvin, the disposition of the will for or against God is the chief determinant of how reason functions in its seeking after and attaining the knowledge of God.

Plantinga, however, minimizes the role of the will in the formation of belief. He says that a belief is "formed in us" rather than that "we form the belief;" indeed, "in the typical case we do not *decide* to hold or form the belief in question, but simply find ourselves with it" (406). He illustrates the point with a self-evident belief (the propositional equivalent of *modus ponens*), a perceptual belief (the belief, on being appeared to "in the familiar way," that there is a tree before me), and a memory belief (what I ate for breakfast this morning). His account here is a rather deterministic approach to the origin of human beliefs. But is belief in God just like all other properly basic beliefs in this respect? People do seem to deliberate about belief in God in a way in which they do not typically deliberate about self-evident or perceptual beliefs, and deliberation implies choice. Even Christians sometimes find themselves wondering whether God exists; and when one wonders whether an important belief like the belief in God is true, it becomes a matter of inquiry, reflection, and decision.

What must we do, what action shall we take, to settle such doubts? Sometimes, says Plantinga, the action we take for such deliberation and decision is to look more closely at the evidence, pro and con; he gives as an example a controversial scientific theory. But even then, "I still don't really *decide* anything: I simply call the relevant evidence to mind, try in some way to weight it up, and find myself with the appropriate belief" (406). But to understand our questions about belief that God exists in this model of scientific theorizing would reflect an evidentialism that conflicts with Plantinga's account of such belief being formed as a properly basic belief. More to the point, the analogy overlooks the central role of the will that, in the Reformed view, underlies both the Christian's occasional wondering whether God exists and the atheist's outright denial that he does.

So the relation of the will to belief in God requires further investigation. Plantinga recognizes that "an enormous amount" still needs to be said about the "noetic effects of sin": "Clearly (from a Christian perspective) sin has had an important effect upon the function of our cognitive faculties; but just how does this work and how does it bear on specific questions about the degree of positive epistemic status enjoyed by various beliefs?" (425). He begins to answer this question by distinguishing between the *proper* function of our noetic faculties and their *normal* function, "if we take the term 'normally' in a broadly statistical sense." For example:

> It may be (and in fact is) the case that it is not at all abnormal for a person to form a belief out of pride, jealousy, lust, contrariness, desire for fame, wishful thinking, or self-aggrandizement; nevertheless when I form a belief in this way my cognitive equipment is not functioning properly. It is not functioning the way it ought to. (408)

But the cardinal Reformed teaching on the noetic effect of sin is that precisely such moral dispositions as Plantinga mentions here adversely affect the proper functioning of our noetic faculties with respect to belief in God. And because these moral dispositions involve the will, it cannot be the case that the formation of belief in God occurs in the same way as the formation of self-evident and perceptual beliefs. Likewise, the opposite moral dispositions (love, humility, obedience, self-sacrifice, etc.) that are made possible by Christian faith have an opposite, salutary effect on these noetic faculties with respect to belief in God—an effect that must be missing in those without such faith. Plantinga recognizes, of course, that he has not worked out in detail these implications, either of the noetic effects of sin or those of faith, for his theory of belief in God. When he does, it seems that he will need to modify his generally determinist theory of the formation of belief by his indeterminist theory of the will, as set forth in his famous "Free Will Defense."* Thus his theory of our noetic faculties working properly raises further important questions that require the development of a complete philosophical anthropology.

Reformed Metaphysics

What constitutes the *environment* to which our noetic faculties are *attuned?* What are the *objects* of our properly basic beliefs, when those objects are known? Plantinga offers an initial list:

> God has therefore created us with cognitive faculties designed to enable us to achieve true beliefs with respect to a wide variety of propositions—propositions about our immediate environment, about our own interior lives, about the thoughts and experiences of other persons, about our universe at large, about right and wrong, about the whole realm of abstracta—numbers, properties, propositions, states of affairs, possible worlds and their like, about modality—what is necessary and possible—and about himself. (405)

The list is not organized in a way that correlates the objects of our beliefs with the noetic faculty or faculties designed to achieve beliefs about them. Nor does the list reflect the important distinction between propositions and the states of affairs that propositions represent, which certainly are two different *kinds* of cognitive objects. As we saw in Chapter 1, the distinction between them is necessary for sorting out knowledge by acquaintance from knowledge by inference and testimony, because the former does not have a proposition but a state of affairs as its object, whereas the latter both have propositions, and only propositions, as their objects. Augustine, it will be recalled, organizes the objects of our knowledge together with our noetic faculties right from the start. In essence, he says, there are only two kinds of the former (corporeal and incorporeal) and only two kinds of the latter (the senses and reason). Reformed philosophers need to do the same kind of metaphysical sorting. Plantinga offers a start in *Does God Have a Nature?* and "How to Be an Anti-Realist." I will return to these metaphysical explorations in the Epilogue.

---

*In *God, Freedom, and Evil* (29–64) and *The Nature of Necessity* (Ch. IX).

To summarize: Plantinga's central position is that belief in God, that is, belief that God exists, does not require argument or evidence because it can be a properly basic belief. Indeed, for a fully rational human being, belief that God exists is in the foundations of the human noetic structure, just like beliefs that are self-evident to reason or evident to the senses, memory beliefs, and beliefs in other minds. Thus far Plantinga is in essential agreement with Augustine and Calvin, although he appeals only to Calvin (and his followers) for historical precedent and support. Diverging from (but thereby improving on) Calvin, who overlooks linking the faculty of reason to either the awareness of divinity or to faith and revelation, Plantinga takes belief in God (Calvin's natural awareness of divinity) as a foundational deliverance of reason itself. This brings him into company with Augustine; for like Augustine, who uses the language of seeing God, Plantinga's properly basic belief in God is a direct rather than an inferred deliverance of reason. Also like Augustine, who offers the quasi-ontological proof that God exists from the existence of truth, Plantinga offers a modal version of the ontological proof that God exists from his maximal greatness. Yet both Plantinga and Augustine have reservations about their proofs that render them less than proper models of natural theology. Unlike Calvin and Augustine, Plantinga does not, in the development of his theory so far, explore in detail the differences between the natural knowledge of God and knowledge of God by revelation, nor the noetic effects of sin and grace on the proper functioning of human reason and the will with respect to the formation of the belief in God.

Finally, the theme of "faith seeking understanding," which permeates the thought of St. Augustine, does not seem to characterize Plantinga's thinking any more than it does Calvin's. In Calvin this is in part because the focus of his thinking is on the certainty of faith and the moral implications of that faith for Christian life and service. In Plantinga it is (perhaps) because he writes in a context completely different from either of those in which Augustine or Calvin wrote. Augustine wrote to integrate Platonic philosophy with Christian faith; Calvin, to reform both Christian faith and the Church. Plantinga writes to defend the rationality of the core of theistic belief, the belief in the existence of God, in a secular culture deeply influenced by the "cultured despisers" (in Schleiermacher's familiar phrase) of that belief and religion itself. In the next chapter we turn, accordingly, to the implications of Reformed epistemology for apologetics.

8 Prepared to Make a Defense: The Apostle Peter

To offer an apology, in current usage, is to admit having offended someone by word or deed; its purpose is to restore an injured personal relationship. The original meaning of *apology* is just the opposite. It was to defend one's innocence for the purpose of being acquitted of charges of wrongdoing. The classic example is Plato's *Apology*, a record of the speech in which Socrates defends himself against the charges that had brought him to his infamous trial. This original sense of the term reappears in the New Testament, notably where the Apostle Peter writes: "Always be prepared to make a defense to anyone who calls you to account for the hope that is in you" (1 Pet. 3: 15). In these words Peter both authorizes and exhorts Christians to defend their faith.

Apologetics

In keeping with this apostolic mandate, a branch of theology known as *apologetics* has developed. The *American Heritage Dictionary* defines the task of apologetics as "the defense and proof of Christianity." The difference between defense and proof is currently reflected in the distinction made between "negative" and "positive" apologetics. Positive apologetics constructs arguments to *establish* the central Christian beliefs, that is, to show their *truth*; it is thus the same sort of enterprise as natural theology. Negative apologetics, by contrast, criticizes arguments brought against these beliefs; it aim, thus, is to *defend* Christian belief against attacks. What both kinds of apologetics share in common is the employment of the tools of reason and reasoning—concepts, propositions, and arguments—in the service of religious belief.

Now, as we have seen, Reformed epistemology involves a certain objection to natural theology and, hence, to positive apologetics. One thesis I will support in this chapter is that Reformed epistemology likewise involves a certain objection to negative apologetics. But that thesis seems flatly to contradict Peter's injunction that believers should be prepared to make a defense. I will resolve this apparent contradiction by distinguishing some very different objectives that the (negative) apologist may have in defending the Christian faith. I will argue that the legitimacy of defending Christian faith depends on the purpose of the defense. Having done this, I will reconsider the fate of positive apologetics—natural theology—in Reformed epistemology. This reconsideration will lead to my second thesis, namely, that beyond the Reformed objection to natural theology lies an entirely legitimate appropriation of natural theology which the objection has sometimes obscured, even for Reformed thinkers themselves. In short, having closed one door to reason and reasoning in natural theology and negative apologetics, Reformed epistemology opens another door to such reason and reasoning and thereby to the unique view of the *rationality of faith* that, as I see it, is the legacy of Reformed thought.

First I shall briefly take note of some disagreement among Reformed theologians over the role of reason in the service of faith in order to set a stage for outlining what I take to be the authentic Reformed approach. Then I shall examine Alvin Plantinga's discussion of (negative) apologetic defenses to distinguish between the several objectives that these defenses may be thought to achieve and determine which of these objectives are legitimate. Finally I shall follow the lead of two recent Reformed theologians, Auguste Le Cerf and Henry Stob, to elaborate this authentic Reformed approach, both to negative and positive apologetics.

Controversies over Apologetics

In "Apologetics" Benjamin Warfield, the great Princeton theologian of the early decades of this century, traces the first uses of the term *apologetics* to Planck (1794) and Schleiermacher (1811) (3). There has been no agreement on the task of apologetics, however, among Protestant—and even Reformed—theologians ever since. Two controversies in particular have been conspicuous among the latter, one between the Princeton theologians themselves and the Amsterdam school (as it was called) led by Abraham Kuyper and Herman Bavinck, during the early decades of the century; the other following upon the famous interchanges between Karl Barth and Emil Brunner after 1929 over the very possibility of apologetics.

Amsterdam vs. Princeton. Warfield develops a notion of apologetics essentially akin to natural theology. Its aim is more to *establish* the main doctrines of theism than to defend them against attacks: "Apologetics undertakes not the defense, not even the vindication, but the establishment, not, strictly speaking of Christianity, but rather of that knowledge of God which Christianity professes to embody and seeks to make efficient in the world, and which it is the business of theology scientifically to explicate" (3; see also 7–8). Notice how careful Warfield is to distinguish defense from support and subordinate the former to the latter. Defense of Christian belief against attack may be incorporated in apologetics as "ancillary portions of its structure"; apologetics proper, however, "does not derive its contents or take its form or borrow its value from the prevailing opposition" but "from the fundamental needs of the human spirit" (4). One of these needs as applied to a Christian believer is "to be able to give a reason for the faith that is in him." Hence "it is . . . the function of apologetics to investigate, explicate, and establish the grounds on which a theology . . . is possible; and on the basis of which every science which has God for its object must rest" (4).

Warfield's conception of apologetics thus assimilates it to the evidentialism against which Plantinga lodged the objections discussed in the previous chapter. As we saw there, Plantinga's Reformed objection to natural theology draws upon the views of Herman Bavinck. Accordingly, his "Reformed objection," like that of the Amsterdam school, also counts against some other Reformed thinkers who lapse into the assumptions of evidentialism and classical foundationalism.

Barth vs. Brunner.   Karl Barth initiated the second controversy in his famous rejoinder to Emil Brunner in 1929 entitled, "Nein!" (Brunner and Barth 1946). Brunner's position, as he later formulates it in *The Christian Doctrine of God*, is that "the mere act of 'bearing witness' remains sterile unless it can be integrated with the truth which the listener already possesses" (100–101). Barth, on the other hand, thinks that Brunner's position assumes a "'point of connection for the divine message in man,' undestroyed by sin, a 'questioning after God,' natural to man," as he states it in *The Doctrine of the Word of God* (29). Barth argues that such a point of contact compromises the noetic effect of sin in the unbeliever, and implies that "faith must take unbelief seriously and itself not quite seriously" (32). For Barth, proclamation of the Word of God, not the dialectics of reason, should characterize Christian faith and the theology in which it expresses itself.

Evidentialist Apologetics.   How are we to interpret these controversies among twentieth century Reformed theologians? Nicholas Wolterstorff gives us a helpful clue in his recent paper "The Migration of Theistic Arguments: From Natural Theology to Evidentialist Apologetics." Wolterstorff argues that "the evidentialist challenge to religious belief first became part of the mindset of Western intellectuals at the time of the Enlightenment" (38). He considers that John Locke first issued the challenge in a definitive way, "doing so as himself a Christian who thought that he could meet the challenge" (39). He shows, further, that the arguments Locke employs originate in the natural theology of the medievals, notably Aquinas. There, however, the apologetic function of these arguments was very much subordinate to two other more important functions: the "transmutation" of faith into knowledge and the development of *scientia*, more precisely, metaphysics.

Aquinas not only subordinated the apologetic function of natural theology to these other two functions, he also avoided making it foundational for faith. Locke, by contrast, takes natural theology as foundational for faith, for the very *rationality* of faith. "In consequence," observes Wolterstorff, "the believer was put on the defensive in the dialogue between belief and unbelief" (80). Being thus on the defensive, the believer is required by Locke not only to defend his or her faith against objections, but to construct prior arguments to *establish* its truth. After the Enlightenment, any *defense* of religious faith must include its prior *establishment* with the arguments of natural theology. (Positive) apologetics thus becomes a *prerequisite* to faith, instead of a *consequence* of it. We shall return to this important distinction later, and also to the projects of transmutation and *scientia*.

How, then, should we understand the Reformed controversies over apologetics? According to Wolterstorff, Barth's objections to natural theology "are relevant to the Enlightenment project of evidentialist apologetics; they are not relevant to the mainline medieval project of natural theology" (1986, 39). By the same token, we can add, Warfield's conception of apologetics betrays the influence on him of the Enlightenment approach, and it is to such conceptions that Barth's objections are relevant. His objections are not relevant, however, to the more authentic Reformed view represented by Brunner, his immediate opponent, and the Amsterdam school. The mainstream, authentic Reformed view of apologetics, I hope to show, lies between the evidentialist apologetics of Princeton on the left and the extreme "fideistic" reaction of Basel against all apologetics on the right. But first I shall examine Plantinga's discussion of negative apologetics, the defense of theistic belief against attacks.

Apologetics and the Justification of Belief

Should Faith Be Dogmatic? Having argued, in "Reason and Belief in God," that belief in God can be properly basic, so that it is is neither necessary nor even appropriate to rest it on the evidence and proofs of natural theology, Plantinga goes on to ask: "Suppose the fact is belief in God is properly basic. Does it follow that one who accepts it dogmatically is within his epistemic rights? Does it follow that someone who is within his rights in accepting it as basic *remains* justified in this belief, no matter what counterargument or counterevidence arises?" (83). He answers his question, "Surely not." There are at least three different questions, here, however, and Plantinga's answer is correct for only two of these. If by *dogmatic* is meant "arrogant," then surely Christian believers have no business being dogmatic in the face of attacks on their belief. If, however, by *dogmatic* is meant "unargued," then, again, surely, Christian believers have no business leaving their beliefs undefended in the face of the attacks upon them. But the further issue here is, What are the proper *objectives* of believers when they engage in these defensive arguments against the objections of unbelievers?

Plantinga claims that one of these proper objectives for defensive argumentation is to maintain the *justification* of the believers' properly basic theistic beliefs. This claim, I will argue, is a mistake. Having shown this, I will turn to two other possible objectives for apologetic arguments that Plantinga also endorses in the course of his discussion, love for the unbeliever and love for the truth. These are the two proper objectives for believers' engagement in defensive arguments against objections to their faith.

Plantinga begins his argument that apologetic defenses may be necessary for the justification of belief by distinguishing, as we saw in the last chapter, between prima facie and ultima facie justification. Prima facie justification can be overridden by contrary evidence. Recall his example:

> My being appeared to treely gives me a *prima facie* right to take as basic the proposition *I see a tree.* But of course this right can be overridden; I might know, for example, that I suffer from the dreaded dendrological disorder, whose victims are appeared to treely only when there are no trees present. If I do know that, then I am not within my rights in taking as basic the proposition *I see a tree* when I am appeared to treely. (83)

The example is clear-cut, for what overrides my justification for believing that I see a tree is something else I *know,* from which it follows (and I *see* that it follows) that I do not see a tree. "The same goes for the conditions that confer justification on belief in God," says Plantinga.

> Perhaps I have been brought up to believe in God and am ini-
> tially within my rights in so doing. But conditions can arise in
> which perhaps I am no longer justified in this belief. Perhaps
> you propose to me an argument for the conclusion that it is
> impossible that there be such a person as God. If this argument
> is convincing for me—if it starts from premises that seem self-
> evident to me and proceeds by argument forms that seem self-
> evidently valid—then perhaps I am no longer justified in accept-
> ing theistic belief. (83–84)

In other words, the justification of my belief now depends not only on
its being properly basic but also on my ability to refute arguments
against it.

Just as my properly basic tree belief loses its justification if I
should know both that I have the dreaded dendrological disease, and
that it follows from this that my tree belief is false, so my properly
basic belief in God may lose its justification if I am confronted by an
argument against his existence that "is convincing for me" (84). My
belief in God, though properly basic, will be insufficiently justified so
long as I am unable to refute such an argument: "Following John Pol-
lock, we may say that a condition that overrides my *prima facie* justification for *p* is [a] *defeating condition* or *defeater* for *p* (for me)" (84). Of
course, if I am able to refute the argument or arguments that are contrary to my properly basic belief in God, I will by force of my reasoning ability remain justified in that belief:

> Defeaters, of course, are themselves *prima facie* defeaters, for the
> defeater can be defeated. Perhaps I spot a fallacy in the initially
> convincing argument; perhaps I discover a convincing argument
> for the denial of one of its premises; perhaps I learn on reliable
> authority that someone else has done one of those things. Then
> the defeater is defeated, and I am once again within my rights in
> accepting *p*. Of course a similar remark must be made about
> defeater-defeaters: they are subject to defeat by defeater-
> defeater-defeaters and so on. (84)

But if I am unable to refute them, I will not remain justified in the
belief, even though it is still properly basic. Thus evidence and argument, when used to meet objections to religious belief, can become a
necessary ingredient in its justification.

The problem with this claim is that it involves the justification of
properly basic beliefs in the very entanglements of evidentialism
against which Plantinga lodged the Reformed objection to natural the-

ology. The question is, If the proper basicality of theistic belief makes the arguments of natural theology unnecessary and inappropriate to its justification, why does that proper basicality not make apologetic defenses of that belief equally unnecessary and inappropriate to its justification? Plantinga holds, on the contrary, that a properly basic belief in God that needs no evidence to *establish* its truth nevertheless does need the critical consideration of contrary evidence for the *defense* of its truth: "Many believers in God have been brought up to believe, but then encountered potential defeaters. ... If the believer is to remain justified, something further is called for—something that *prima facie* defeats the defeaters. Various forms of theistic apologetics serve this function (among others)" (84). One objective, then, of (negative) apologetics is to shore up the justification of theistic belief when it is under attack.

But this outcome both weakens Plantinga's theory of justification and misconceives the function of apologetics. Let us see how this is so. One of the most conspicuous objections to theistic belief is raised from the existence of evil in the world. Now the free will defense, from its original formulation by St. Augustine to its latest version in Plantinga, is an apologetic *defense* of theistic belief against that attack. The question is, however, Is such a defense a necessary component in the justification of theistic belief? Plantinga clearly thinks that it may be:

> Thus the free-will defense is a defeater for the atheological argument from evil, which is a potential defeater for theistic belief. Suppose I am within my epistemic rights in accepting belief in God as basic; and suppose I am presented with a plausible argument—by Democritus, let us say—for the conclusion that the existence of God is logically incompatible with the existence of evil. (Let us add that I am strongly convinced that there *is* evil.) This is a potential defeater for my being rational in accepting theistic belief. What is required, if I am to continue to believe rationally, is a defeater for that defeater. Perhaps I discover a flaw in Democritus' argument, or perhaps I have it on reliable authority that Augustine, say, has discovered a flaw in the argument; then I am once more justified in my original belief. (84)

But suppose I do not find a flaw in Democritus' argument or learn that other philosophical authorities have discovered a flaw in it; what am I to do then? It seems clear that Plantinga has allowed the defense of my belief in God to get entangled in the very inconclusiveness and uncertainty of evidentialism, avoidance of which was the whole point of his theory of justification by way of proper basicality. It is unnecessary and even inappropriate, says Plantinga, for the justification of my belief in God, either to *reach* or *establish* it by way of argument; but once that belief is in place as a properly basic belief, it may be necessary and appropriate for me to *maintain* its justification by defending it with argument. What has gone wrong here?

Epistemic vs. Nonepistemic Justification.   The answer, I think, lies in a confusion over the proper objective of (negative) apologetics. According to St. Peter, the believer is called on "to make a defense" to *someone else* "who calls [him] to account for the hope that is in [him]." I take Peter's words here to imply that the believer is *not* to make this defense to *himself*, because *he* is in doubt. In other words, the believer's defense of his faith arises not because he considers that his faith may be mistaken or in some other way inappropriate, but because, from the standpoint of his faith, the objections of the unbeliever are mistaken. Whether he can *show* by reasoning that they are mistaken is, of course, a further question; but how does the rationality, the justification, of his faith hinge upon its answer, any more than it hinges on whether he can establish his belief with the arguments of natural theology?

Plantinga says, however, that the believer is required to meet those objections, when convinced by them, by constructing counterarguments or citing some authority who has done so to *justify his own belief* that heretofore found its justification by simply being properly basic. Perhaps the problem lies in Plantinga's supposition that the believer can be *convinced* by atheological arguments against his belief. If he really can be thus convinced, the question arises whether he is a believer at all. In any event, Plantinga has allowed objections to theistic belief to ensnare its justification in the tangle of evidentialist arguments, which is quite inconsistent with the single-minded way in which he warded off the evidentialism of the natural theologian who sought the justification of theistic belief in argument.

Here we must be careful to observe that the kind of justification in question is *epistemic* justification. This is the justification that any belief—and in our present discussion, belief in God—can have in case it is proper, permissible, or warranted by the conditions or circumstances that give rise to it as a properly basic belief. This epistemic justification must be surely be distinguished from the justification of faith that Peter has in mind in his famous exhortation that believers are to be prepared to make a defense. For Peter is not there doing epistemology, but something else we shall consider in a moment. It may also be called *justification of belief*, of course; but let us call it *nonepistemic justification*, to distinguish it from the more technical *epistemic justification* that is the province of epistemologists. Earlier I distinguished the two kinds of justification in terms of their different objectives. What the two objectives share in common, of course, is the use of reason in defense of faith; they differ in the objective to be achieved by this use of reason in the defense of faith. The believer who defends a belief for the purpose of its epistemic justification tries to *maintain its rationality* in the face of objections to it, on the assumption that such objections threaten its rationality. This objective, I have argued, is unnecessary and inappropriate, because the rationality of the believer's belief may already be guaranteed by its being properly basic. Let us briefly consider the parallel on this point between religious and nonreligious basic beliefs.

The Parity Argument Again. Suppose, for example, that the (epistemic) justification of my belief in the external world required the same kind of defense against skeptical arguments that are raised against that belief as the (epistemic) justification of my belief in God requires (as Plantinga supposes) against skeptical arguments brought against it. (This is the correct analogy to theistic belief, and not Plantinga's very specifically circumscribed case of my seeming to see a tree, when I also *know* I have the dreaded dendrological disorder, which, of course, ruins the rationality of my believing there is a tree.) So I believe there is an external world of mountains, rivers, trees, planets, stars, and galaxies. How can I prove to Plato that this belief is true, when he suggests that we are living in a cave, and that all these objects are merely shadows of some other reality I have missed? How can I prove to Descartes that there is no evil genius who deceives me into my belief that there is an external world made up of such things as these? How can I prove that life is not a dream?

The fact is that I cannot *know* that any of these skeptical hypotheses is false, if by knowing is meant that I am required to *prove* it. I may, of course, be intellectually perplexed by skeptical arguments, and even unable to answer them satisfactorily. But believing the evidence of my senses is none the less rational for all that. Likewise, the theist may be intellectually perplexed by atheological arguments, and even be unable to answer them satisfactorily. But his continuing to believe "every word that proceeds from the mouth of God" (Matt. 4:4) may be nonetheless rational for that. As Cardinal Newman wrote in his *Apologia Pro Sua Vita*: "Ten thousand difficulties do not make one doubt" (184).* Thus the Christian's belief in God *is* dogmat-

---

*I thank Lynn C. Bartlett and "Chapter and Verse" (*Harvard Magazine*) for locating this quotation for me.

ic in the sense that it is unargued and does not *need* to be argued, either by arguments to establish it or by arguments to defend it against objections, just as the Christian's (and everyone else's) belief in the external world is dogmatic in the same sense, but no less rational for all that.

Knowledge of God Its Own Defense. The case against employing apologetical arguments for epistemic justification of theistic belief is stronger still. For in Plantinga's view, to believe in God is not only properly basic, it can also constitute *knowledge* of God. Typically, in fact, the Christian believer is one who *knows* that God exists, through *knowing* God himself by the direct acquaintance afforded one in Calvin's natural awareness of him, restored and enlarged by the revelation of God that one believes on God's own testimony. Or, in Plantinga's language, the believer's noetic faculties are functioning as they were designed to function, in an environment that includes all the fundamental realities there are to know; and God is one of these. Now if the believer *knows* God, and *knows* also that he is perfectly good, all-powerful, and all-knowing, the believer's apologetic defense (say the free-will defense) against the atheological objection to the existence of God based on the existence of evil can hardly be construed as constituting part of the (epistemic) justification of the believer's belief. Indeed, the believer's *knowledge* of God is *itself* a defense against the objection, and an altogether adequate defense.

In "The Foundations of Theism: A Reply," Plantinga offers an example that illustrates the point:

> I am applying to the National Endowment for the Humanities for a fellowship; I write a letter to a colleague, trying to bribe him to write the Endowment a glowing letter on my behalf; he indignantly refuses and sends the letter to my chairman. The letter disappears from the chairman's office under mysterious circumstances. I have a motive for stealing it; I have the opportunity to do so; and I have been known to do such things in the past. Furthermore an extremely reliable member of the department claims to have seen me furtively entering the chairman's office at about the time when the letter must have been stolen. The evidence against me is very strong; my colleagues reproach me for such underhanded behavior and treat me with evident distaste. The facts of the matter, however, are that I didn't steal the letter and in fact spent the entire afternoon in question on a solitary walk in the woods; furthermore I clearly remember spending that afternoon walking in the woods. Hence I believe in the basic way

(13) I was alone in the woods all that afternoon, I did not steal the letter.

But I do have strong evidence for the denial of (13). For I have the same evidence as everyone else that I was in the chairman's office and took the letter; and this evidence is sufficient to convince my colleagues (who are eminently fairminded and initially well disposed towards me) of my guilt. They are convinced on the basis of what they know that I took the letter; and I know everything they know. (310)

In this example Plantinga's memory belief counts as a basic belief because it is based on no other beliefs; presumably it is also properly basic. Furthermore, it is a case of knowledge, for we are told that what is remembered is true (that the letter writer *was* alone in the woods the afternoon his letter was found missing). Moreover, the letter writer has all the contrary evidence that everyone else has, and that evidence is impressive.

Now the question is, Must the letter writer take account of this contrary evidence? No, says Plantinga; and this is not because he can independently refute this contrary evidence and the argument based upon it (he probably cannot), but because, for the epistemic justification of his belief, his memory itself is sufficient.

The reason is that in this situation the positive epistemic status or warrant that (13) has for me (by virtue of my memory) is greater than that conferred upon its potential defeater [viz., that I was not in the woods but stealing the letter from the office] by the evidence I share with my colleagues. We might say that (13) *itself* defeats the potential defeater; no further reason for the denial of this defeater is needed for me to be rational. (311)

Can a theistic believer's belief be rational in the same way, without that believer's taking account of the evidence brought against it?

The answer, of course, is yes. Plantinga gives his own example: "When God spoke to Moses out of the burning bush, the belief that God was speaking to him, I daresay, had more by way of warrant for him than would have been provided for its denial by an early Freudian who strolled by and proposed the thesis that belief in God is merely a matter of neurotic wish fulfillment" (312). The case of Abraham offers an even better example, for Abraham had evidence of his own that counted against his believing what God said. However, as we saw in Chapter 2, Abraham did not counter that evidence with arguments in order thereby to remain fully rational in his belief in God, both in his belief that God exists and spoke to him or in his belief that God would do as he said he would do. This is because Abraham *knew* it was God who spoke to him, and this fact would have made arguments of both kinds, either natural theological arguments for God's existence or apologetic defenses against objections to his existence, unnecessary and inappropriate for the rationality of his faith.

It may be objected that no Christian believer today is an Abraham, a Moses, a prophet, or an apostle. True enough, but it does not follow that they had "more to go on," so to speak, than the Christian believer does today. At any rate, it does not seem that they had, or sought, or developed arguments against objections to their belief that counted toward the justification of it. So if their belief was fully rational without the arguments of natural theology or the defenses of (negative) apologetics, the belief of the Christian believer today can likewise be fully rational without the one or the other. If the Christian believer knows God, and knows that God reveals himself in Scripture, that knowledge must have more by way of epistemic warrant than any awareness of the potential defeaters of that knowledge, because these defeaters have only the weaker warrant of argument based on contrary evidence. As in the case of the letter writer whose knowledge defeats its potential defeaters, so the Christian's knowledge of God—that is, the direct acquaintance with God—defeats its potential defeaters. I conclude, then, that apologetic defenses are not necessary for the epistemic justification of Christian faith.

From recent conversations with Plantinga, I learned that he has moved toward this conclusion as well. For example, in a more recent article, "Epistemic Probability and Evil," he says:

> It could be that the theist is like someone who has substantial propositional evidence against the claim that pigeons are to be found near Devil's Tower, and no propositional evidence for it; in point of fact, however, he is in full view of the tower and sees several large flocks of pigeons flying around it. He may be like the person who shares with his accusers propositional evidence for the claim that he failed to mail his tax return; he himself, however, clearly remembers that he did. In such a case the belief in question has much by way of warrant or positive epistemic status, despite the propositional evidence against it; no doubt he knows that he mailed it in, despite the propositional evidence against it. And of course the same may be true for belief in God. Our question as to the warrant of theistic belief cannot properly be settled just by examining whether the propositional evidence

tells for or against it. We must look into the question what sort of nonpropositional warrant, if any, such belief enjoys. (583)

Such nonpropositional warrant is the kind possessed by properly basic beliefs, including belief in God, and we are back to Plantinga's account of this warrant as consisting, alternatively, in their *grounds* (the conditions and circumstances which give rise to them) or in their *being produced by our noetic faculties functioning properly* in an environment to which they are attuned.

The Necessity of Apologetics

Love of Neighbor.   Still, of course, apologetic defenses of Christian belief in God are appropriate and even necessary. Peter says clearly to his fellow believers, "always be prepared to give a defense" (1 Pet. 3:15). Defenses of faith must be appropriate and necessary, then, for some other reason or reasons. There are at least two such reasons, in fact. One of them is evident from the context of Peter's words. Christians are to love their neighbors. Christians should not return evil for evil, but bless the evildoer (3:9). They should "seek peace and pursue it" (3:11). They should be "zealous for what is right," even if they must suffer for it (13–14). Thus they should make their defense as a testimony to those who raise the objections, and they should do it out of faith, not fear, and "with gentleness and reverence" (15). Plantinga perhaps has something like this in mind when he rejects, as we saw him do earlier, the "dogmatic" assertion of Christian belief. For to be dogmatic in one sense is to be arrogant, which is contrary to the spirit of love. To act as if the objections of the unbeliever do not matter could be arrogant. For a believer to defend a belief against those objections, then, is to take the unbeliever seriously, which is part, at least, of what love requires.

The Barthian Objection.   But how can believers take the objections of unbelievers seriously without forsaking their own standpoint for that of the unbelievers? This is the question that Karl Barth asks of the believers who do natural theology. Barth objects to their doing natural theology because he thinks that believers, whenever they reason with unbelievers, are in danger of assuming *their* standpoint, the "standpoint of unbelief." More exactly, Barth claims in his *Church Dogmatics* that all such reasoning poses a dilemma for believers (vol. 2, pt. 1, 93–97). In "Reason and Belief in God" Plantinga formulates this dilemma succinctly in the following words: "Either the natural theologian accepts the standpoint of unbelief or he does not. In the latter case he misleads and deceives his unbelieving interlocutor and thus falls into bad faith. In the former case he makes his ultimate commitment to the deliverances of reason, a posture that is for a Christian totally inappropriate" (71). Barth might have posed the same dilemma for the believers who try to defend their faith against objections to it, who engage in negative apologetics.

In his rejoinder to the dilemma, Plantinga argues that even believers who reason with unbelievers from the evidences of natural theology can maintain their own standpoint as believers and still be helpful to the unbelievers, which is what love requires. His rejoinder to the dilemma is this:

> As a natural theologian she [the believer] offers or endorses theistic arguments, but why suppose that her own belief in God must be based upon such argument? And if it is not, why suppose she must pretend that it is? Perhaps her aim is to point out to the unbeliever that belief in God follows from other things he already believes, so that he can continue in unbelief (and continue to accept these other beliefs) only on pain of inconsistency. (71)

So believers do not need to accept the traditional rationalistic assumptions about reason. Still, they recognize that, so long as unbelievers accept these assumptions, they can, as believers, appeal at least to the possible inconsistency of the beliefs which unbelievers hold within the framework of this acceptance. For though the consistency of beliefs is not a sufficient condition of rationality, it is an essential minimal condition, and on that point believers and unbelievers can agree. It certainly does not follow from *this* agreement that believers have adopted the "standpoint of unbelief." They aim only at holding unbelievers to the consistency of *their* beliefs on *their own standpoint* as unbelievers, even as they also defend the consistency of their own (Christian) beliefs against the objections of unbelievers from their own standpoint as believers. If, as a result of such a discussion, unbelievers give up their objections, the apologetic believers have done something good for them, which is what love requires.

It does not follow, of course, that the unbeliever will give up his objection or be converted by such reasoning, either by the arguments of natural theology or by the defenses of (negative) apologetics. Still, such arguments and such defenses can be part of the believer's *witness* to the unbeliever, and this is the main point. As Plantinga says:

> We may hope this knowledge [which results from the examination of arguments] will lead him to give up his unbelief, but in

any event she [the believer] can tell him quite frankly that her belief in God is not based on its relation to the deliverances of reason [as the unbeliever understands these]. Indeed, she can follow Calvin in claiming that [anyone's] belief in God *ought* not to be based on arguments. (71)

In the Reformed view, then, believers' arguments—both those of natural theology and those of apologetic defense—can be part of their witness to unbelievers; and, when their purpose is correctly limited and understood, they do not compromise their faith. Apologetic defense is thus not only proper for believers, it may be morally necessary, being a duty flowing from their love for their unbelieving neighbors.

Scientia. If, as I have argued, defensive arguments are not necessary for the epistemic justification of the believer's belief, are they of any value to him or her at all? Of course they are. In his rejoinder to Barth, Plantinga tells us why even the arguments of natural theology may be of value to the believer: "If there *were* good arguments for the existence of God, that would be a fact worth knowing in itself—just as it would be worth knowing (if true) that the analogical argument for other minds is successful, or that there are good arguments from self-evident and incorrigible propositions to the existence of other minds" (73). Likewise, if there were good *defenses* against the objections to Christian faith, that would be something worth knowing in itself. If the free-will defense is a successful defense against the objection to theistic belief based on the existence of evil, that fact is worth knowing in itself.

But how will the believer know whether the arguments of natural theology are good ones or not, and whether the various defenses against objections to theistic belief are successful or not, without examining them? Such examination is by definition a part of the pursuit of knowledge for its own sake. Now the pursuit of knowledge for its own sake, that is, quite apart from its utility, has been advocated ever since the ancient Greeks; indeed, they were among the first to define it and to engage in it. Can Christians agree and join in? Just as Scripture is their charter for love, so it is also their charter for the pursuit of *scientia.* Reformed theologians are fond of citing the "cultural mandate" of Genesis: "Be fruitful and multiply, and fill the earth and subdue it; and have dominion over the fish of the sea and over the birds of the air and over every living thing that moves upon the earth" (1: 28). One aspect of this cultural mandate, say these theologians, is already fulfilled in Adam's naming of the animals. Giving names to things, to their properties and to their relationships is certainly the first step, not only toward finding our practical way in the universe, but also toward developing *scientia*, knowledge for its own sake.

Nicholas Wolterstorff, in *Reason within the Bounds of Religion*, says that the Christian "like everyone else ought to seek consistency, wholeness, and integrity in the body of of his beliefs and commitments" (76). The body of a Christian's beliefs will include the teachings of science and philosophy, in so far as he or she is aware of them or actively pursues them. The Reformed understanding of faith, therefore, does not obviate, let alone prevent, the believer's doing science, either natural, social or metaphysical; instead it equips one to do it even more correctly. One's faith does not eliminate one's desire for scientific knowledge, for this desire arises because of the noetic faculties that both the believer and the unbeliever have been given by God. Apologetic arguments can do for the believer just what metaphysics can do, viz., satisfy the natural quest for scientific truth. But science of any kind is a set of propositions about the nature and causes of things, and in many areas the truth of these propositions is in dispute. Many of the hypothetical and theoretical propositions of science are no less controversial than religious beliefs. Thus the apologetic arguments in defense of basic theistic beliefs may very well be defenses against those scientific theories and hypotheses that conflict with these theistic beliefs. This will be the case especially in the science of metaphysics, which seeks the ultimate nature and cause of the universe.

Apologetic defenses of Christian faith are thus necessary and appropriate, both for the believer and for the unbelieving objector. For the believer, these defenses contribute to the satisfaction of the natural desire for science and metaphysics, for acquiring and organizing the truth about the universe as a whole and in all of its aspects. These defenses are not necessary, however, for the epistemic justification of faith, any more than are the arguments of natural theology. For the objector, the defenses may be instrumental in helping one to come to terms with one's unbelief. Still, such defenses, like the arguments of natural theology, are neither necessary nor sufficient for the *conversion* of the unbeliever, even as they are neither necessary nor sufficient for the *foundation* or *rationality* of the believer's own faith.

The Reformed Objection to Natural Theology

It is important once more to review the Reformed objection to natural theology to see its critical limitation. Some Reformed theologians themselves have failed to appreciate this limitation, especially those on the right under the influence of Karl Barth. This failure will certainly obscure a correct Reformed view of both natural theology and (negative) apologetics. The Reformed objection to natural theology is essentially twofold, that it is unnecessary and that it is inappropriate.

Unnecessary. Natural theology, that is, an inferential approach to the existence and nature of God apart from revelation, is unnecessary, say Reformed thinkers, because God can be known, and originally is known, by the direct acquaintance of the mind. Reformed thinkers make this claim for a direct acquaintance of the mind with God not only for those whose minds have been revitalized by Christian faith, but also for those who are without such faith. This is the central teaching of the entire intellectual tradition we have studied: Plato's doctrine of the rational intuition of the the Good, to which he ascribes some of the central characteristics of God, namely, being the transcendent source of the existence, intelligibility, and goodness of the universe; the Bible's teaching of the immediate knowability of the God whose triune nature, activity in human history, and will for human life it claims to reveal; Augustine's synthesis of the Platonic and biblical ideas in his doctrine of the direct illumination of the mind by the divine light; Calvin's reformulation of Augustine's ideas in his doctrine of the universal awareness of God and the inner testimony of the Holy Spirit; and Plantinga's version of Calvin's teaching in his doctrine of belief in God as a properly basic belief, a belief that constitutes knowledge of God when it is formed in the human mind by its noetic faculties functioning properly in the appropriate environment.

The limitation of this Reformed objection to natural theology should be obvious. It does not follow from the claim that we have, by our very nature, a direct acquaintance with God that natural theology is *impossible*. For all the truth and significance of the central Reformed teaching on the natural awareness of God, it may still be within the capacity of human reason to infer correctly God's existence and something of his nature, and to do this in the various ways that have developed in the natural theology tradition—from the idea of him that is formed naturally in the mind (the ontological argument), from features of the universe such as its contingence and design (the cosmological arguments), or from the transcendence of the moral law (the moral argument). Let me use again the illustration from an earlier chapter. From the fact that I know my wife by a direct acquaintance with her it does not follow that I cannot correctly infer her existence, nature, and characteristics from her effects as I discover these by experience. At least the impossibility of such inferential knowledge would have to be shown on its own merits; it is not entailed by my knowing her in a noninferential way. Indeed, it seems clear that on some occasions the only way I can know of my wife's existence and whereabouts is by inference, as when I see her keys and her purse on the table, and conclude she has returned home from work, even though at the moment I have no direct way of knowing that, because she is not in the room where I discover her effects. So, for all of the Platonic, biblical, Augustinian, and Reformed claims to the immediacy of our knowledge of God, it does not follow that human beings cannot know him also by inference. Whether such knowledge is possible in one or several of its forms remains an open question that needs to be decided on its own merits.

My own view is that the various arguments of the natural theologian, in their most carefully worked out versions, are good arguments, which deepen our knowledge not only of God but also of ourselves and of the universe. It is not part of my purpose here, however, to try to demonstrate this claim, but only to show that the Reformed *objection* to such arguments does not in itself lead to their *rejection*. For if that point is clear, the way is clear to understand that the Reformed tradition, for all its critical stance toward natural theology, still appreciates such theology and can even incorporate its findings into its own philosophical activity. I elaborate on this important point later.

Inappropriate.   Second, according to the Reformed objection to natural theology, there is something quite inappropriate about reaching the existence of God by inference, if he is indeed directly present to the human mind. This is because of who God is. He is not only the transcendent origin of all things outside himself, and as such beyond human comprehension; he is also the very personal being who is the Creator and Lord of the human mind, who therefore seeks and rightly expects to be acknowledged as such. Thus any attempt to establish his existence by inference *in place of* such simple acknowledgement of him will be an affront to him, an insult, an irreverence.

Here, then, Reformed thinkers identify a *religious* objection to natural theology. To infer God's existence from something else—the idea of him in the mind, the contingency of the universe or its order and design, and so forth—is to imply that these other things are known more immediately than God himself. For that is the procedure of an inference, to begin with what is better known and move from that to what is less well known or not known at all. Unlike human beings, however, who are not always with us in the room, but whose recent presence in the room we can infer from their effects, God is omnipresent; immanent in the universe he has made, he is never absent from it or from us. Therefore, as Plantinga puts it: "Believing in the existence of God on the basis of rational argument is like believing in the existence of your spouse on the basis of the analogical argument for other minds—whimsical at best and unlikely to delight the person concerned" (1983, 67–68). So, just as I will offend my wife if I substitute an inference of her existence for an acknowledgement of her presence, likewise human beings will offend God if they ignore his immediate and inescapable presence to them and suppose they can first find him only, or find him best, at the end of a logical proof.

Still, it does not follow from this second aspect either of the Reformed objection to natural theology that its arguments are to be rejected. For it may also be insulting to God, if he has made us capable of inferring his existence, that we *ignore* what can be known of him in this *additional* way, even as my wife will be insulted that I did *not* infer from the dinner she has just prepared that she is even more creative in preparing food than I had earlier believed. So again, if natural theology is impossible, it will need to be shown in some other way.

There is a kind of corollary to the Reformed objection to natural theology. It is that natural theology can be misleading in certain ways. Calvin warned against the "vain speculations" of the philosophers. Augustine before him warned about the pride that can be engendered by the successes of reasoning. So reasoning about God seems to be misleading in at least two ways. It may tempt the reasoner to believe that the God found by inference is adequate to his or her religious needs, and it may ignite a foolish pride in achieving so great a thing by his or her own wit and effort. But if that belief is false and such pride vain, and both can be occasioned by natural theology, then the Reformed objection to it seems wise and just.

But, again, it does not follow from this corollary that it is essentially misleading to pursue an inferential knowledge of God. If the Christian faith is the proper antidote to vain speculations and pride, such faith need not reject natural theology; it may instead welcome and incorporate such theology into a comprehensive Christian philosophy. The fact that natural theology originated among the ancient Greeks apart from faith and revelation testifies to the failure of the willful suppression of truth to obliterate the knowledge of God entirely from the pagan mind. The authentic Reformed conclusion from all this is that natural theology, with all of its limitations and dangers, may well be an entirely natural way for Christian philosophers to pursue the knowledge of God, though only, of course, as a consequence of their faith, not as a prerequisite, foundation, or subsititute for it.

The main implication of this review of the Reformed objection to natural theology should now be clear. Nothing in the objection—or set of objections—counts against the *possibility* of natural theology. The Reformed objection to natural theology counts mainly against its serving the purpose of *evidentialist apologetics*. That is, natural theology is unnecessary and inappropriate and perhaps even misleading as the *basis for religious faith*, simply because human beings already have a natural, immediate awareness of God. This knowledge of God, which is diminished and even suppressed by the unbeliever, is presupposed, restored and enlarged by Christian faith. Hence none of the arguments of natural theology or knowledge of the evidence on which these arguments are based is required as the basis for that faith; and to suppose that it is ignores both the direct knowledge of God already in the foundation of human rationality and the directness of his revelation to which such faith is a response. To suppose that faith must be based on inference from evidence, then, from the Reformed point of view, is a critical and fundamental mistake.

When Christians believe in God, then, they do so because their natural awareness of him is enlarged by the testimony and illumination of the Holy Spirit to accept what he reveals of himself in Scripture and Incarnation. But once this happens, once people become Christian believers, the question of apologetics arises, May they defend their faith? I have argued that, just as there is a valid Reformed objection to natural theology, so there is a valid objection to *defending* belief in God (negative apologetics), if its point is thought to be the epistemic justification of that belief. I have also argued, however, that defending belief in God is altogether appropriate if its point is either to help the objector overcome objections or to help the believer in the pursuit of truth. Likewise, however, it seems clear that the pursuit of natural theology, the inferential approach to the existence and nature of God from evidence apart from revelation, is appropriate for the believer *after* he or she believes. If it is a mistake to do natural theology as a *prerequisite* for faith, it does not follow that it is a mistake to do it as a *consequence* of faith. There is no reason why the believer should be limited for the knowledge of God to the direct acquaintance with him possessed in virtue of a natural awareness of God and God's revelation in the Bible. In the Reformed view, the believer is open to the truth, also the truth about God, "wherever it may be found" (in Augustine's immortal phrase). The conclusions of natural theology, and reaching them by reason and reasoning, certainly seem to contain some of this truth.

Two Reformed Theologians on Apologetics

To show that the foregoing elaboration represents the authentic Reformed view of apologetics and of the entire landscape of *faith and reason*, I will consider now the thought of two lesser known, but not for that reason less incisive, Reformed theologians, Auguste Le Cerf and Henry Stob. Le Cerf writes in the setting of midcentury European Calvinism, Stob in the setting of midcentury American Calvinism. Both maintain and reformulate the approach of Kuyper and Bavinck, the classical representatives of the Amsterdam school.

A Middle Way. I want to consider Auguste Le Cerf at some length for two reasons. First, he develops his account of Reformed apologetics in response to the Thomist complaint on the left and the Barthian complaint on the right; and second, although he shares with other Reformed writers the well-known point that reason is corrupted by sin, he is more explicit than many of them are (and, as we saw, than Calvin himself is) on the less developed point that reason is also restored by faith. Moreover, it is noteworthy that his *Introduction to Reformed Dogmatics*, on which my discussion below is based, recently has been republished (1981; it first appeared in 1949).

First, then, Le Cerf takes up the charges of Etienne Gilson, which we discussed in Chapter 6, that, for the Calvinist, philosophy is impossible. Le Cerf sums up what he takes to be Gilson's objection:

> Philosophy is nature, that is to say paganism. It is natural rea-
> son. And on its own showing the entire effort of Calvinism is
> directed towards eliminating from theology every pagan ele-
> ment: it is condemnation of fallen nature, humiliation of inde-
> pendent reason. Naturally, it needs a theology, but it has no need
> for a philosophy. Even if it had the need, it would have no right
> to one. (204)

Next Le Cerf considers Barth's objection to apologetics, which he sums up as follows:

> The dogma of total corruption regards the natural man as inca-
> pable of judging spiritual things. Such is the teaching of Paul, as
> well as that of the Reformation. Now, to construct a system of
> apologetics is to establish that natural reason which you reco-
> gize to be incompetent, as judge of divine things. It is impossible
> to imagine a more palpable contradiction. (203).

Le Cerf's initial response to both objections is exactly like that of Wolterstorff. What Wolterstorff calls *evidentialist apologetics*, Le Cerf identifies in more traditional language as the "rationalism" of the seventeenth century, inaugurated by Descartes and culminating in thinkers like Leibniz. Karl Barth's objection is against such rationalism, and as such, says Le Cerf, "it is a useful reaction against an error of method which has arisen in Christian theology and even in the bosom of Calvinism during its decadence" (204). But Gilson, by affirming an area of autonomous reason, independent of faith, postulates "a principle utterly contrary to the primitive Reform [of Calvin], namely, that the affirmation of the existence of God and of the authority of Scripture is an object of science rather than an article of faith" (204).

Here Le Cerf overshoots his mark. For, although the Thomist affirms a certain integrity to natural theology apart from faith which the Calvinist denies, he also limits its scope; furthermore, he does not necessarily subject the authority of Scripture to the evidentialism of reason operating apart from faith. Aquinas, at any rate, is not a classical foundationalist in his approach to the rationality of faith, as Wolterstorff points out in "The Migration of Theistic Arguments" (80). Still, there is the danger of evidentialism in the Thomist affirmation of the (limited) integrity of reason apart from faith, and Le Cerf might better have restricted his criticism of the Thomistic approach to a warning against that danger.

Faith Restores Reason. My second reason for considering Le Cerf's views at some length is that he affirms the *restoration* of fallen reason by the act of faith. I believe he begins to make up for the imbalance in the Reformed view in favor of the noetic effects of sin over those of grace. The constructive part of Le Cerf's response provides a view of apologetics that both avoids its wholesale rejection by Barth on the right and affirms the possibility of "Reformed philosophy" against Gilson's strictures on the left. Note that the complaint in both Gilson's and Barth's objections arises from the Reformed doctrine of the corruption of our natural gifts, including reason, by the fall. This is one of the more conspicuous Reformed doctrines; no wonder, therefore, that it galvanizes both the reaction of the Thomist and that of some Reformed theologians themselves against finding a proper place for apologetics and philosophy itself in Reformed thought. I trace this coalescence of what I have called left and right reactions not to the Reformed teaching on the noetic effects of sin, however, but to the failure of Reformed thinkers, beginning with Calvin himself, to balance this teaching with the noetic effects of grace. If sin has corrupted the natural light of reason, and grace is the antidote to sin, then grace must restore this natural light.

Now faith is the principle effect of grace. What is faith? Here is Le Cerf's answer:

> It is not a supernatural faculty which God added to human nature considered in its state of integrity. The accidental disap-

pearance of this aptitude [because of the fall] has had the effect of modifying human nature profoundly. On the contrary, the *fides qua creditur* is a mode of intelligent sensibility in contact with God who reveals himself to it. (205)

In this short description, Le Cerf eliminates the two-level natural-supernatural distinction so prominent in Thomist thought and that still hovers over Calvin's own discussion. Faith is "not a supernatural faculty"; indeed, it is not a faculty at all, but instead an *aptitude* of "intelligent sensibility in contact with God who reveals himself to it." In this phrase Le Cerf links faith both to reason ("intelligent") and to Calvin's awareness of God ("sensibility"), both of which are aspects of *human nature*. Faith, in other words, restores, and becomes integral to, the nature that is so dear to the Thomist but is so corrupted by the fall for Barth (and Calvin). "Its [faith's] restoration involves nothing less than the commencement of the renovation of fallen nature. To believe, then, is not to renounce thought: it is to begin to think normally" (205–206).

The apologetic implication of this integration of faith and reason is that the defense of Christianity against "systems which assail it from without" is both appropriate and necessary (206). To affirm the truths of Christianity is to reject the falsehoods in nonChristian ways of thought. But "even if, *per impossible*, there were no such systems, it [faith] would be compelled by its own internal logic to examine the theoretical difficulties which array themselves against it under the form of intellectual temptations, starting from the principles by which it is dominated and determined" (206). Le Cerf here recalls the point made by Warfield that the rational articulation of faith does not depend on there being enemies that attack it; it is the natural disposition of the restored reason to find the truth, newly motivated in this disposition by faith itself. Le Cerf appropriately invokes the Augustinian formula as entirely consistent with and even flowing from the Reformed view of faith and reason: "To do this is to construct a certain apologetic, the apologetic of faith seeking to understand" (206). In contrast to Warfield, however, Le Cerf suggests that the natural reasoning of apologetics flows *from* faith, not *to* it. According to the distinction made earlier, reasoning and argument are not properly a *prerequisite* to faith but they are an entirely proper *consequence* of it.

Against the Scholastic View. Le Cerf further elaborates his conception of Reformed apologetics by considering, again, the two objections that may be raised against it from the scholastic and the evangelical camps he has already identified with Gilson and Barth. "In the first place, say certain scholastics, why cannot the reason which is supposed to be regenerate do what is impossible for fallen reason: namely, demonstrate religious truth?" (207) Le Cerf's response to the scholastic objection is twofold. First, he reiterates the Reformed objection to evidentialist apologetics:

> Faith is not the product of discursive reason. It arises when there has been revealed to a different faculty of reason, namely, intelligent sensibility, the fact that one must believe in something in order to accept life: that it would be folly to believe in something which was not essentially truth and the originating source of truth: in other words, in one who was not God. (207)

> Faith is therefore, in principle, a free act. It no more depends on logical constraint than on physical necessity....
> The Calvinist apologist must, therefore, never try to produce the initial act of faith by the constraint of the syllogism. (208)

Le Cerf thus reminds "certain scholastics" that faith never *rests on* reasoning. Reasoning is not a prerequisite for faith.

Note, by the way, in these passages, that Le Cerf also echoes two familiar Augustinian themes, the priority of faith and the significance of truth as the way to God. Human beings must "believe in something to accept life" (207), and what they most deeply believe in is the truth. Thus Le Cerf also strikes the "neo-Calvinist" note of the Amsterdam school that all philosophizing stems from a religious faith, if not that of the Christian religion, then that of some alternative faith which competes with it. The evidentialist believes, ultimately, in the powers of human reason as they operate apart from the renewing effects of divine faith. His ancient Augustinian counterpart was the Manichean, whom Augustine criticizes in his *Confessions* for "mak[ing] a mockery of credulity by rash promises of sure knowledge" (VI, 5, 7). Still, Augustine holds, whoever finds truth is on the way to finding God, who is "truth itself" (X, 24, 35). As for Augustine, so for the Calvinist, faith and reason are united in their search for truth; but only the Christian faith assures that reason will find God in the truth and the truth in God.

Faith and Philosophy. Having reiterated his objection to evidentialist apologetics, however, Le Cerf goes on, second, to point out to the scholastic that there is nothing philosophically anomalous in the Reformed view that Christian faith *informs* philosophical reason, once that faith has found its place in the human mind: "If faith cannot be, by its origin, the result of logical constraint, reasoning, with its constraining necessities, can and must be introduced into it" (208). Now Gilson would agree with this, of course, but he argues that such reasoning, because it proceeds from faith, can issue only in theology, that is, in the dogmatic theology of revelation, and that therefore such reasoning must preclude not only apologetics but philosophy itself. What Gilson fails to see is that nothing prevents reason thus renewed by faith either from affirming the truths of philosophy "wherever they are found," including the truths of natural theology, or from doing this for the very purpose of *scientia*, the science of metaphysics, the independence of which Gilson wants to maintain. The difference between them is this. For Gilson philosophy must be independent of faith, whereas for Le Cerf philosophy must only be distinguished from revealed theology; both alike share faith as their common spring.

Le Cerf therefore devotes an entire chapter to "Calvinism and Philosophy" to develop the thesis that philosophy can "be established side by side with dogmatics and with Christian and Reformed dogmatics in particular." By *philosophy* he means "a discipline sovereign in its own domain, independent of dogmatics and nevertheless specifically Christian and Reformed" (214). The heart of such a discipline is metaphysics, the explanation of the universe in terms of its ultimate principle or source. Le Cerf agrees with the advocates of natural theology that metaphysics as a science was created by the Greeks. He points out that one of the main things that Christian philosophy must oppose in Greek natural theology is its implicit pantheism; but it can do this only because of the new principle, "creation *e* [sic] *nihilo*," which Christianity introduced into philosophy and which can be accepted only by faith (225). "But when a pagan thinker expresses something true, beautiful or noble, our faith teaches that he does so under the supernatural action of common grace" (230). Having cited Calvin, he affirms that "the sciences cultivated by the pagans and the philosophical truths which they glimpsed are the magnificent result of the action of common grace" (230). Among these sciences, of course, is metaphysics; and the natural theology of the Greeks is a part of it.

Natural Theology and Metaphysics. It is only a short step, then, from Le Cerf's affirmation of *scientia* to the conclusion that the Calvinist philosopher, when pursuing metaphysics, does the *same kind of thing* the Greeks did when they did metaphysics. And just as their metaphysics, their search for the *archē*, led some of them without faith, but correctly, to natural theology, so, too, faith leads the Reformed philosopher even more correctly and clearly to God as the ultimate principle of all things. But the rational articulation of the *archē* that follows on faith is still metaphysics, not, as Gilson contends, dogmatic theology: "Dogmatics authenticates, catalogues, interprets, formulates, and relates genetically the revealed data. Christian religious philosophy takes these revealed data as matter for the meditations of reason or of the natural intelligence, but illuminated by faith" (226). Thus the Reformed philosopher follows the lead of Christian faith, examines the writings of the pagan philosophers, and brings their natural theology to its appropriate fulfilment, by correcting its mistakes and removing its deficiencies. Thus the Reformed philosopher can do metaphysics (including natural theology) as well as, and even better than, the pagan philosophers, because it is done in the additional light cast on its questions by faith. But it is still metaphysics, not dogmatic theology, that the Reformed philosopher pursues.

Le Cerf reminds us—and the Thomist—that metaphysics, wherever it has been done under the guise of a so-called autonomous reason, is fundamentally determined by "prejudices" that are conspicuously beyond the determinations of such an "unaided," autonomous reason to establish. One of these prejudices is the classical foundationalism discussed in Chapter 7, the very position that underlies both modern rationalism and, to some extent, the Thomist approach: that "autonomous reason is the only legitimate foundation on which to support his [the metaphysician's] convictions relative to the first principle of reality" (216–217). This prejudice "fails to consider that reason itself forms part of the phenomenon to be explained." It also fails to see that the difference between Christian philosophy and unbelieving philosophy is analogous to the differences between unbelieving philosophies themselves:

> Christians do not philosophize like philosophers: Which philosophers? Unbelieving philosophers? Surely that is obvious; but who has decreed that the sole legitimate manner of philosophizing is that adopted by the immanentist philosophers [i. e., those who begin with some other principle than the God revealed in Christian faith]? The philosophers of the school of Alexandria did not philosophize in the manner of Bacon, while Descartes had yet another method. Must they all be omitted from the history of philosophy for this reason? (217)

Le Cerf's point is simply that Christian revelation gives those who accept it by faith "a new vision of the world," one that is not only entitled to inform Christian metaphysics but required to do so, just as each of the multitude of other nonChristian visions has informed its alternative metaphysical system.

The impulse to philosophy and metaphysics arises, therefore, not from Christian faith, but from human nature itself. When the impulse is followed by Christians and informed by the intellectual content of their faith, their metaphysics is no less philosophical, since it is no less natural, for all that: "The Christian is thus in the position of a student who knows the solution of a problem in mathematics or physics, but still has to discover the reasons and the operations to be carried out in order to arrive at it. It is in this sense that he seeks, having already found" (219). Again Le Cerf invokes an Augustinian outlook to explain the nature of Reformed philosophy: "It is with his natural organs of knowledge that he will endeavor to understand the data of sensible reality and to relate them to a unique principle. But he cannot abstract from the fact that his faith makes him see this reality in a new light" (225). Reformed philosophy, like Augustinian philosophy, requires an integration of faith and reason.

Against the Barthian View. Reformed apologetics thus opens the door to Reformed philosophy. Still, apologetics is itself technically, Le Cerf claims, a part of dogmatic theology; he therefore also addresses the opposite objection from the evangelical side. He formulates the objection as follows:

> Calvinist apologetics, if it could give satisfaction to the scientific instinct of the believer, has still neither religious motive nor apostolic impulse. Not being religious, it is no longer a theological science. Not being addressed to unbelievers, it merely draws attention to the fact already suspected, that Calvinism has no aptitude for evangelization. (207)

Le Cerf answers the objection by pointing out that the three motives—defending faith against attack, scientific understanding, and evangelical witnessing to the unbeliever—do not necessarily conflict with one another; they can all feed on the same faith that has become "reflective" and "does not change its nature by becoming more profound" (208). Moreover,

> apologetics does not endeavour to destroy the adversary's disposition to attack merely in order to comfort the believer; but, by the intellectual defense of religious truth which it presents, it seeks to become an instrument in God's hands, a means of grace, that shall produce in the opponent himself a deep and favourable impression of the truth of religious doctrine. (208)

As we have seen, Plantinga also adopts this positive approach to the use of apologetic arguments for the benefit of those who object to theistic belief.

Le Cerf reminds us that faith began to combine "the methods of an apostle with motives of wisdom" already during the subapostolic age, in the writings of the Apologists. So also today, he says, God can "use the preaching and the apologetics to open the intelligent sensibility of the unbeliever or sceptic to the victorious action of grace. This action is not merely subliminal; it is also intellectual. 'God does not work in us as in trunks of trees'" (209). Thus preaching the faith, defending it, and working out its implications for philosophy are all of a piece. Of course, the diversification in the gifts of the Spirit leads to a division of labor among believers that emphasizes one or another of these expressions of faith; but they are all expressions, ultimately, of the one Christian faith. This Reformed view reflects an Augustinian integration of faith and reason and opposes their cleavage in Thomism at one extreme and in Barthianism at the other.

Beginning with Faith. I close with a brief account of the approach of Henry Stob. In a series of articles on "Apologetics," Stob defines the function of apologetics in the same Augustinian spirit: "How then is Christianity to be vindicated and confirmed? There is no other way than by beginning with Christianity itself. Standing squarely in and on the Faith, one must begin with the decisive Christian affirmations, and then attempt to do three things" (no. 11, 9). Let us consider each of those three things.

The Priority of Faith. First, the apologist must "show, what is indeed a fact, that everyone does think and speak out of some faith" (no. 11, 9). Such primacy of faith harks back to Augustine, but Stob, like Le Cerf, reformulates it to apply universally to every religio-philosophical position, as Kuyper had already done. "The opposition of Christianity and other philosophies is not an opposition of faith and reason, but of rival faiths" (no. 11, 9). Those who think and philosophize apart from the leading of Christian faith do not think and philosophize apart from some *faith*. If human beings do not trust in the God who reveals himself, it does not follow that they do not trust in something else. We saw how Le Cerf expresses it: "One must believe in something to accept life." The religious term *unbelief* implies only the absence of *Christian* faith, not the lack of faith. Stob classifies these alternative faiths, each of which is opposed to authentic Christianity and constitutes therefore a source of attack upon it, under three heads: "There are rival *religious* systems—such as

Judaism, Mohammedanism, Hinduism, Buddhism, and the like. There are *defective Christian* systems—such as Modernism, Romanism, Adventism, and the like. And there are rival *philosophical* systems—such as Idealism, Materialism, Positivism, and the like" (no. 7, 25). The defenses of Christianity will differ, of course, according to the nature of the attack implicit or explicitly formulated from within these three alternative visions of life.

For all the priority of faith, however, we should not overlook the seriousness with which Stob takes reason. Although he rejects the idea of an autonomous reason unguided by any faith, he affirms one of the essential characteristics of reason, namely, that the truth of any belief implies the falsity of all its contraries and contradictions. Christian faith is *trust* in God, of course; it is also the affirmation of propositions—*that* God exists and *that* he is a being of a certain kind, *that* he has revealed himself in Scripture and incarnation, and *that* the universe and humankind are his creative handiwork. If these propositions are true, any beliefs that are logically opposed to them are false. As Stob states it:

> The setting forth of truth always involves the setting aside of error, just as the cultivation of crops always involves the removal of weeds. The positive and negative activities, though not coordinate, are yet mutually dependent and quite inseparable. Their togetherness is important. Unless a theologian and a farmer work both for and against something they work neither for nor against anything, and they fail in their calling. (no. 5, 9)

Thus, although beginning with faith, the Reformed apologist endeavors to think and speak with reason: "*projecting* the the Christian intellectual outlook, . . . *exposing* the falsity of nonChristian philosophies and world-views, . . . and *defending* Christian truth against attack" (no. 7, 9). Reason and reasoning are essential to faith, even though faith is their starting point.

Opening the Door to Philosophy. Second, the Christian apologist will "attempt to show that Christian faith provides a perspective upon the world that is fuller and deeper than that provided by any other faith, that it lights up man's total experience, and that in principle it accounts for every fact" (no. 11, 9). This apologetic objective opens the door to doing Christian philosophy. Systematic or dogmatic theology gathers the teachings of Christianity from all of the more specialized theological disciplines (biblical exegesis and biblical theology, church history, homiletics, liturgics, etc.) and sets them forth in a "totality view." Thus formulated systematically, "Christianity meets its maximum resistance. As a Totality it finds itself confronted by other Totalities" (no. 5, 9). At this point the apologist must step in to defend Christian teaching against its rivals.

Becoming a Philosopher.   Third, this Reformed defense of Christian teaching is, for Stob as for Le Cerf, technically part of dogmatic theology. Still, it requires philosophical argument, for it aims to show that Christian faith not only expresses itself in a theological system, but also "lights up man's total experience." The Reformed apologist will accordingly "attempt to show that reality does not validate but rather contradicts nonChristian interpretations, the reason for this being that this is a Christian universe which will not submit to nonChristian categories of ultimate explanation" (no. 11, 9). That part of the apologist's task is a philosophical task. In pursuing it, the apologist meets opponents in direct confrontation. The apologist is not, however, thereby offering "to try Christianity in the supposedly neutral court of a supposedly pure reason" but presenting "a special kind of witness to [his opponent] of the relevance of Christ. It is a special kind of testimony to the power of the Gospel to renew all minds and to disclose the deeper meaning of existence" (no. 11, 9). Hence the apologetic appeal is to *reality* itself, which "contradicts nonChristian interpretations" of it, even though such an appeal cannot be fully shared by the objector because he or she lacks the Christian faith.

No Evidentialist Apologetics.   Note that the Reformed apologist refuses to see this activity as "evidentialist apologetics." Stob sets himself explicitly against the Princeton approach (no. 7, 9 and 16); in fact, he rejects Warfield's very definition of apologetics. Warfield, it will be recalled, defined the function of apologetics as establishing "the ground on which theology...is possible," opposing it to apology, the purpose of which is only the "ancillary" one of giving a defense. Stob redefines *apologetics* as "a theoretical or scientific discipline," distinguishing it from *apology*, which "is an always particular defense of Christianity": "Apologetics is a science and as such concerned with the principles of defense. An Apology, on the other hand, results from the skillful and artistic application of such principles in concrete situations. Apologetics is related to Apology, therefore, as science is related to art, or as principle is related to practice" (no. 7, 9). In this reading, Warfield's claim that the basic beliefs of Christian theology must first be established by reason before that theology can begin and Stob's rejoinder that Christian theology cannot be thus independently established are differing claims *within apologetics* over the nature of a legitimate Christian *apology*. It is the function of apologetics, in this view, neither to establish nor to defend Christianity, but to determine whether either of these is appropriate and, if so, how to do it. Thus apologetics gives an account (Greek *logos*) of what it is for a believer properly to give a defense (Greek *apologia*) of his Christian faith. In the former, Christians address one another about the implications of their faith for reason and reasoning; in the latter, they address their unbelieving neighbor who raises objections to their faith. Although Stob's distinction is an obvious and sensible one, it is generally over-looked in the literature.

In summary, to defend Christian faith, according to Le Cerf and Stob, is to begin with and remain within the commitments and propositions of that faith. Such defense does not hesitate, however, where called for, to consider the commitments and propositions of the unbeliever's different faith. For the beliefs that the unbeliever holds may be inconsistent with themselves, and in any event, they will not, when put together, account for human experience and the existence of the universe as adequately as those of the Christian faith. Indeed, some of this human experience as well as aspects of the universe itself, which the unbeliever knows or can come to know, may not only count as evidence *against* some of that person's own antitheistic beliefs, but also may count as evidence *for* the theistic beliefs of Christian faith. Not that any arguments of natural theology for the existence of God constitute a basis for such faith or that apologetic defenses against objections to faith are sufficient to induce faith in those who raise the objections. Still, the confrontation of the unbeliever's beliefs with the ifs and thens of reason and reasoning is entirely appropriate and necessary, because it expresses not only the believer's witness to the objector for his or her sake but also the believer's own search for truth for its sake.

Epilogue

I have finished my account of the origin and significance of Reformed epistemology. Its central claim is the immediacy of our knowledge of God. We do not, in the first instance, know God by inference or testimony but by direct acquaintance with him. A closely related claim is that we cannot easily remain indifferent to the God whom we know by such direct acquaintance. Thus our knowledge of God is like our knowledge of every other fundamental kind of reality—physical objects, their properties and relationships, other persons, right and wrong, good and evil, and the elementary objects of logic and mathematics.

Furthermore, the claim is that everyone knows God in this way, not just the Christian believer. If someone does not believe in God, that is, does not trust in God as Christians do, this is not because one does not know God. All human beings by nature have what John Calvin calls an awareness of divinity. This awareness is not a vague and indeterminate perception; it includes, according to Calvin, the propositions that God exists, that he is just one being and not many, that he is majestic and ought to be worshipped, and that he is our creator. Although the fall has clouded over this natural awareness of God and led to the loss of faith in him, it has not eradicated this awareness. Christian faith does not alter this direct awareness of God but rather presupposes it, rejuvenates it, and enlarges it. For to hear and believe the Gospel is to hear and believe the word of God; it is thus to hear and believe God himself, the very God of whom all human beings are already naturally aware. And to hear and believe God's revelation is to hear and believe his own testimony about himself, the world he has made, ourselves, our origin and destiny.

If our knowledge of God consists primarily in a direct acquaintance with his presence in our minds, in our lives and in the universe, it does not follow, of course, that such knowledge arises apart from the inferences of reason or the testimony of other human beings. Indeed, this direct way of knowing God is as dependent on the inferential workings of reason and on human testimony as is the direct knowledge of anything else. As we cannot perceive sticks and stones without having taken the very names for them on the authority of countless other human beings who have lived before us, so we cannot become aware of God without having taken the names of God on the authority of countless other human beings, from the most ancient times down to our own. And as with sticks and stones, much of what we know about God we cannot know without making inferences either from what we are told (by other human beings or by God himself) or from what we see directly for ourselves. Like knowledge in general, so our knowledge of God is, in George Mavrodes' words, a large and intricate "web woven of experience, inference and testimony."

To understand Reformed epistemology and especially its center-piece, viz., its account of our knowlege of God, we studied epistemology itself. We began this study with Plato, the first great source of epistemological ideas. We rejected the austere theory he outlines in the *Republic* that knowledge is quite opposed to belief, that it consists in direct acquaintance with objects and in whatever follows logically from such acquaintance. We did acknowledge with Plato, however, the priority of such direct knowledge by acquaintance, especially for the knowledge of the Good, which is Plato's analogue for God; and there we also found the ultimate philosophical source of the Reformed claim for the immediacy of the knowledge of God. But the mistake of restricting knowledge to direct acquaintance and what reason can infer from such acquaintance is that this restriction excludes everything else we say we know on the testimony of others; thus it collides with the way we ordinarily use the term *know*. On this usage, we know considerably more than we know by our direct experience of the present moment (and the remembered experiences of our past) and what we can infer from these. We know an incalculable number of things we believe on the word of other human beings whom we trust.

Due recognition of this fact led us to accept the more generous framework for understanding knowledge, which we also found in Plato (*Theaetetus*), within which knowledge is not opposed to belief, but is a form of belief—justified true belief. We know any true proposition we believe that we have adequate justification to believe. Adequate justification, I argued, includes not only being able to infer what we believe from what we know by direct acquaintance, but also being able to trust other human beings for what they tell us, a point Plato quite ignores. Finally, adequate justification for belief includes direct acquaintance itself, a point Plato also overlooks. The great advantage of my justified true belief approach to knowledge lies in its capacity to incorporate within its scope not only direct acquaintance but also testimony and inference, and to do so without ruining the priority of direct acquaintance, without overlooking the importance of both inference and testimony, and without ignoring the complex interrelationships among all three.

From our study of Plato we turned to the Bible for its teaching on faith. Though the Bible does not offer a theory of knowledge, it provides an abundance of materials that support the Reformed claim regarding the immediacy of our knowledge of God. Its principle purpose is to call human beings to faith in God, the kind of faith of which Abraham is the ancient exemplar. The Bible sharply contrasts this faith with unbelief. Both faith and unbelief presuppose a direct acquaintance with the God whose word is either believed or rejected; the Bible simply takes this acquaintance with God for granted, from its very first verse to the end of its last book.

We then took up the monumental thought of St. Augustine, the first great thinker to synthesize the biblical theme of faith with Greek philosophical ideas. Following Plato's approach in the *Republic*, Augustine continues to distinguish sharply between knowledge and belief and to subordinate the latter to the former. Though belief is prior in the order of time, knowledge is prior in the order of desire. We have a deep desire to transform what we believe on authority into the knowledge of personal acquaintance. This relationship between faith and knowledge is expressed in the famous formula associated with Augustine's name, "faith seeking understanding." Augustine construes this relationship between faith and understanding in two quite different ways. In one, the understanding faith seeks is rational proof that God exists; in the other, the understanding faith seeks is deeper acquaintance with God himself whose existence the believer already knows by God's own presence in his or her mind. This second way, I argued, is the authentic Augustinian way of interpreting the formula, faith seeks to understand.

John Calvin reformulates Augustine's emphasis upon the direct knowledge of God, but without pursuing the Augustinian connection between faith and understanding. His main themes are the natural awareness of God, the corruption of this awareness in the fall, and its renewal by faith. Faith is hearing and believing the Gospel as God's own word to human beings; it arises from an inner testimony to the human mind by the Spirit of God himself. For Calvin, as for the Bible and for Augustine, all human beings live in the direct presence of God, the sense of which is renewed in the believer by faith but avoided and even suppressed in those who lack such faith by unbelief. Almost entirely missing in Calvin, however, besides the Augustinian theme of faith seeking to understand, is an account of how faith restores reason from its corruption by the fall, although he provides some hints for the development of such an account.

Finally we examined Alvin Plantinga's revival and reformulation of Calvin's ideas about our knowledge of God within the framework of a contemporary theory of knowledge as justified true belief. We explored especially his claim that belief in God can be a properly basic belief. Being a properly basic belief means that belief in God is among the foundational beliefs of a fully rational human being, just like self-evident, perceptual, and memory beliefs. As a properly basic belief, belief in God no more depends for its justification on evidence and argument than do those other beliefs. In accord with this claim about belief in God, Plantinga restates the long-standing Reformed objection to natural theology, an objection that is already all but explicit in Calvin himself.

With this historical account of the origins of Reformed epistemology and review of its present revival by Plantinga in hand, I tried in the closing chapter to distill the Reformed view of faith and reason through a study of Reformed apologetics. Just as there is a Reformed objection to natural theology, so there is a Reformed objection to the rational defense of faith, if by this is meant that the believer must offer a successful refutation of objections to belief in God in order to maintain the justification of that belief. The biblical charter for a rational defense of faith lies elsewhere, both in love for those who raise objections to faith and in love for the truth itself. St. Peter exhorts the believer to "be prepared to give a defense" of his faith out of love for those who are without it and the cultural mandate of Genesis warrants the believer's pursuit of the truth, which apologetics requires, for its own sake.

In the Reformed view, there is no inherent opposition between faith and reason as in certain other Protestant traditions and even in some Reformed thinkers like Karl Barth. Nor do faith and reason coexist peacefully side by side, in two different orders of nature and grace, as in the Thomist tradition. The mistake of Protestant fideism is to ignore or even to deny the rationality of belief in God; the mistake of Thomistic rationalism is to locate the rationality of belief in God in the proofs of natural theology. The Reformed antidote to both fideism and rationalism is its claim for the adequacy of a direct natural knowledge of God. This direct natural awareness of God is presupposed both by faith in the revelation of his word and by the inferences of reason to his existence. We can no more sensibly believe the report of someone who has been to Rome than we can sensibly infer the existence of Rome from propositional evidence, unless we first have the concept of what a city is. And we cannot have the concept of a city in our minds unless it originates there by our acquaintance with at least one city itself (or with its necessary components). Likewise, we can no more believe that God exists on someone else's (even God's) word for it than we can believe it as the conclusion of an argument, unless we first have the concept of what or who God is. And we cannot have that concept of God in our mind unless it originates there by our acquaintance with God himself. What faith (in testimony, both human and divine) and reason (inference and argument) *can* do for us, considerable as it is, is only to elaborate and extend what we already know by direct acquaintance with the fundamental things that exist—the world, ourselves, and God.

What Reformed epistemology has not developed is its own version of the Augustinian formula of faith seeking to understand. As Nicholas Wolterstorff points out in "The Migration of Theistic Arguments" (and as we saw earlier in Norman Kretzman's interpretation of the formula), St. Thomas and his followers mean by the formula the *transmutation* of belief into knowledge by way of reasoning and argument:

> A proposition about God is better demonstrated than taken on faith—better in the precise sense that 'seeing' something to be true is always better than taking it on testimony....
>
> In demonstrating the preambles we leave faith behind with respect to those preambles, we advance toward 'seeing.' We *transmute* believing into seeing, faith into vision. (71–72)

Wolterstorff argues that St. Anselm in his *Proslogion* earlier engaged in the same project (75–77). Karl Barth, in *Fides Quaerens Intellectum*, argues that Anselm there aims at an *intellectus fidei*, not a demonstration of God's existence that either supports or supplants his faith (19–21, 26, 39–40). Barth thinks Anselm is even less ambiguous about this point than Augustine and that he should be interpreted as a "descendent" of the Platonic line (not, therefore, as a precursor of St. Thomas) (57–59).

However it may be for Anselm, the transmutation model is not the correct model for interpreting Augustine. As I have argued, Augustine backs off his one proof for God's existence in *On Free Will* because it fails to give faith the vision it seeks. For Augustine, such vision must already be possessed. I went on to show that Augustine thought of such vision not only as the beatific vision in the next life but also as a vision that the believer has by divine illumination already in this life. Consequently, what the believer needs and seeks is not to gain a vision he does not have but to revive, correct, and enlarge a natural vision of God he already has. This Platonic way of describing the believer's quest is just what distinguishes Augustine's conception of the quest from that of Aquinas. Accordingly for Augustine, faith seeking understanding by reason does not seek to replace *itself* by knowledge, but to restore and deepen reason's own natural knowledge of God.

It seems that the medieval mind misdiagnosed the true starting point of the search for God. It thought, as did Augustine in one of his moments, that faith is the starting point. But faith is trusting God for the truth of what he reveals, and such faith presupposes knowing that it is God who reveals in the first place. So, knowing God is the real starting point of the search, whereas faith only rekindles this natural knowledge of God, while also adding to it the truths of revelation. What the believer then seeks is not, or not primarily, to transmute what he or she believes into knowledge by reasoning and argument, but to confirm and augment the knowledge of God already possessed. The inferences of reasoning can assist in this confirmation and augmentation, but they never produce the knowledge in the first place. Instead they presuppose it. Faith is not the presupposition of a knowledge of God that replaces it; knowledge itself is the presupposition of faith. Faith is the acceptance of what God, who is already known, reveals about those things that are not naturally known, because of the fall, about him, about ourselves, and about the world. Faith, as such acceptance of what God says, also, of course, renews what is already naturally known of God but resisted by the fallen mind.

This Platonic way of describing the relationship between faith and reason is essential to understanding the Reformed teaching on the natural awareness of God. We recognize the very name of God because we have the concept of God in our minds, and we have the concept in our minds because we are acquainted with God. In Plantinga's language, the belief in God (that is, the belief that he exists) is a "deliverance of reason itself" when reason is functioning properly. Faith and reason (in the sense of *reasoning*) both presuppose this natural direct knowledge of God; in other words, both faith and reasoning are rooted in an original acquaintance with God. This original acquaintance with God is the source of the Reformed view of the integration of faith and reason. Faith and reason neither oppose one another, nor coexist side by side with different roots (testimony and inference); they are rather two branches of the same tree, nourished by the one root of the natural awareness of God. The testimony of others to us about God and the reasoning about him of our own minds both appeal to, and must be evaluated by, and are finally to be incorporated into our own natural awareness of him.

This natural awareness of God may or may not be amended by God's speaking to us in his revelation, which is his testimony to us in the Bible and in the incarnation of Jesus Christ. If it is not, our beliefs about God and our knowledge of him will be seriously incomplete and even distorted and deformed; we will, in one significant way or another, resist the truth about God. If, however, our natural awareness of God is amended by his speaking to us in revelation, our beliefs about God will be significantly more complete and correct than they could be apart from that revelation; we will also eagerly seek to know more of the truth. We will, in virtue of our faith, seek to know God's love, mercy, justice, sovereignty, transcendence, majesty, and many other things, in a way we did not know them before. Of course our renewed natural and our new revealed beliefs will still be subject to all manner of incompleteness, distortion, and error; but something of utmost importance in our beliefs will now be fundamentally correct in a way it would not be apart from our hearing and believing God's word. Moreover, our noncognitive attitudes of worship, trust, obedience, and gratitude will be converted; they will affect both our walk with God and our walk with our fellow human beings. Faith in God will change our entire lives. These are the ideas that will characterize the Reformed version of faith seeking to understand.

In his little book, *Reason within the Bounds of Religion*, Wolterstorff works out his version of the Reformed view of faith seeking understanding for the pursuit of *scientia*, in its classic sense of the systematic pursuit of all knowledge for its own sake. Of fundamental significance for all scientific theorizing, he argues, is the role of what he calls *control beliefs*. Control beliefs are very general, deep, and pervasive beliefs of a philosophical-religious nature that consciously or unconsciously influence the development of science in all its subdivisions. Wolterstorff's thesis is "that the religious beliefs of the Christian scholar ought to function as *control* beliefs within his devising and weighing of theories" (70). He develops this thesis as an explicit alternative to the the "complementarist" approach of the Thomist and (what he calls) the *preconditionalist approach* of Augustine (31–32, 98). Wolterstorff's thesis envisions an *internal* connection between faith and reason, between religion and science, between religion and metaphysics (81–82). That kind of internal connection between faith and reason is the hallmark of a Reformed epistemology. It is often popularly expressed by Reformed people as their aiming at "a comprehensive world and life view." In so far as this comprehensive Christian world-view is an implication of Christian faith, it may conflict at specific points with other world-views not informed by that faith; but also, in so far as these other world views are true to the actual nature of the world, of human beings, and of God, Christian theorizing must take account of them and appropriate their ideas.

To take Wolterstorff's account of Christian theorizing as the essence of the Reformed version of faith seeking understanding would be a mistake, however; for this would imply, like the medieval transmutation model he rejects, that the formula applies only to the educated believer, trained in the liberal arts and sciences. Wolterstorff acknowledges that his focus is upon "the role of one's Christian commitment in one's practice of scholarship" (21), and he recognizes that the community of Christian scholarship exists within the larger community of all Christians. But that does not explain what the formula can mean for all the nonscholarly members of that community. So the Reformed conception of faith seeking understanding still needs further development, especially to discover how it integrates the faith and reason of every Christian.

Still, the implications of the Reformed view of faith and reason for philosophy and theology are reasonably clear. Reformed philosophy as well as Reformed theology are the products of an organic union of faith and reason. The natural knowledge of God formulated by reason will be renewed by a biblical faith in God that believes his revelation; it will also be newly responsive to the testimony and reasonings about God of other human beings, Christians and nonChristians alike. Of course there will be a division of labor. Reformed theologians will concentrate on articulating the content of divine revelation; Reformed philosophers will concentrate on articulating the meaning and significance of the proposition that God is the ultimate explanation of the universe. But every Reformed theologian will also be an apologist, more or less, and therefore more or less philosophical in his or her theologizing; the theologian will take critical account of those views of God held by others, not only by non-Reformed theologians but also by non-Christian theologians and philosophers of all kinds. In taking such account, the Reformed theologian will be especially assisted by Reformed philosophers. And every Reformed philosopher will be a theologian, more or less, taking critical account of what the theologians say. The philosopher will be especially assisted in this by Reformed theologians, but will also learn from non-Reformed theologians, for the object of their inquiry, no less than of the philosopher's, is God. God is just that one God who is the God of nature *and* of grace, who is Creator *and* Redeemer; he enlightens every mind with his truth, however that mind may be disposed or indisposed to receive or explore it. So Reformed theologian and Reformed philosopher alike, as St. Augustine before them (and before the modern distinction between theology and philosophy arose), will seek the truth about God wherever it may be found, each for a specialized purpose.

As an illustration of this organic relationship between faith and reason in the pursuit of truth, I conclude this Epilogue and my book with a brief outline of Plantinga's metaphysics. His metaphysics offers a fine parallel to his epistemology; it exemplifies the very integration of faith and reason that his epistemology expounds. I begin with his *Does God Have a Nature?* In this little book Plantinga crosses back and forth over the neat line some philosophers and some theologians try to draw between philosophy and theology, and certainly over the line some of them draw between natural and revealed theology. For that reason alone, his book is a model of Reformed philosophy, philosophy that ignores neither reason nor revelation but makes the most of them at once.

Christians believe, says Plantinga, that God is a "being of incomparable greatness"—"preeminent" in "love, justice, mercy, power and knowledge" (1). They also believe in his *aseity* and *sovereignty* and these are the two characteristics Plantinga wishes to explore. The core meaning of *aseity* is independent existence, the existence anything will have if it exists without depending for its existence and nature on anything else; that is, if it exists literally "from its own self alone." The core meaning of *sovereignty* is power, power over other things, including human beings.

Now what is the origin of these theological ideas? Were they "naturally discovered" or "supernaturally revealed"? Plantinga does not go into this question, but the answer is significant for the purpose of my review of his book. The answer is, of course, that these ideas were both naturally discovered by the ancient Greeks and revealed in the Scriptures of the ancient Hebrews and Christians. Actually, even among the Greeks, the ideas first appear not in philosophy but in religion, the natural religion of the ancient Greeks. What sets the Greek gods apart from human beings is their power and their immortality. If Zeus and the other Olympians are not quite all-powerful, their power over human beings is impressive enough, as Homer first testifies and Aeschylus and Sophocles later dramatize. They are also immortal, enjoying an existence independent of the dissolving powers of death.

Their power and their immortality are severely circumscribed by the fact that they were *generated* by earlier gods, who were generated by the earth itself, which was generated from the primeval chaos. Still, the concept of divinity, in ancient Greek religion, contains the seeds of sovereignty and aseity. In their reasoned search for the ultimate *archē*, the Greek philosophers pick up these originally religious ideas, refine them, and apply them variously (and mistakenly) to the elements and forces of nature, to numbers and Forms, to the soul, and to being itself. The explicitly theological culmination of this Greek development is Plato's Form of the Good, the natural theology of his *Timaeus* and his *Laws*, and the self-existent unmoved mover God of

Aristotle. Plato's Good, his demiurge, his other gods, and Aristotle's God—all of these approach, each in its own way, the "incomparable greatness" of the God of Christian faith.

Part of the incomparable greatness of the Christian God is that he is not the generative but the creative origin of all things other than himself. God is an uncreated creator; he is, therefore, both all-powerful and he exists *a se*. He is the sovereign ruler and lord of all he has made, including human beings; their destiny and the destiny of all things is in his hands. When Plantinga examines his all-powerfulness and his aseity, is he doing natural or revealed theology? It is actually impossible to discover in his discussion where one begins and the other ends; the two theologies merge into an integrated whole. To be sure, Christian theology today, whether done by philosophers or theologians, is difficult to conceive in any other way. It is the virtue of Reformed epistemology and metaphysics to recognize and exemplify that fact not with hesitation or apology but with gusto and aplomb.

Still, many theologians, under the spell of the modern distinctions, will turn away from Plantinga's book because, they will say, it is philosophy. Thus the modern academic conception of learning rears its multifarious head. But Plantinga's question is one that theologians can ignore only at their peril. The question is, What is the relationship between divine sovereignty and aseity and "abstract objects—the whole Platonic pantheon of universals, properties, kinds, propositions, numbers, sets, states of affairs and possible worlds" (3)? The question arises because these objects seem also to possess aseity. They, like God, have no beginning or end; also, like God, their nonexistence seems impossible. So how then are they related to God?

Plato first introduced abstract objects into philosophy with his doctrine of the Forms; he also gave the first answer to Plantinga's question. According to Plato, every individual entity, even a god, depends for whatever reality it has on the Forms that exist *a se* in a realm of their own. This dependence signals the inferior character of individual entities, whether they are stones, humans or gods. But Plato's answer must be quite mistaken from the point of view of the biblical revelation of a definite, individual, personal being who depends in no way on anything outside himself at all. Indeed, Plato's answer may even be contrary to the deepest instincts of the natural religion of the Greeks that preceded it. For although this religion in its more developed stages subjects the power of the gods to that of impersonal, abstract Fate (or Destiny), the relation of the original gods—earth, heaven, love—to Fate (or Destiny) is obscure. Be that as it may, there is no obscurity in the Bible; according to it, there is in the beginning absolutely nothing other than God.

As Plantinga notes, Augustine provides the distinctively Christian answer to the question. For Augustine, the Forms must be *"part* of God" (5). (That the Platonic Forms exist as ideas in God's mind is not original with Augustine; it can be found already in Philo [first century A.D.] and Albinus [second century A.D.].) Just as Reformed epistemology can be traced back to Augustine, so can Reformed metaphysics. But theistic philosophizing since Augustine has produced three other, different answers to the question. First, a very widely accepted proposal, classically set forth by Aquinas and captured by the doctrine of divine simplicity, is that God is identical with his nature. Second, nominalists propose, with the help of Occam's razor, to eliminate the existence of the whole realm of abstract objects *ab initio*, because they are the source of the problem in the first place. Third, universal possibilists, following Descartes, propose that abstract objects exist alright, but they exist only at God's behest; this proposal just ignores their intrinsically necessary character and thereby establishes both divine aseity and sovereignty totally unthreatened and supreme. To this list of proposals, Plantinga could have added twentieth century existentialist Neoplatonists (for lack of a better name) who, like Paul Tillich, interpret the personal God of the Bible as an anthropomorphic symbol of Being-Itself, thus recarving the same chasm Plato originally carved between the gods and the Good. Plantinga mentions Tillich, more as someone under the spell of Kant than of Plato, and also Gordon Kaufman, whose Kantian agnosticsm he discusses at some length (13–18).

Plantinga spends most of his time, however, arguing that the three earlier answers just specified will not work. He concludes that the truth of the matter lies in the original Augustinian approach, according to which the Forms (and all abstract objects) are ideas in the mind of God. He argues further that it is consistent with this approach to claim that God has a nature; that this nature is not identical with him; and finally that, although God does not really have control over his nature, properly understood, that implication is no threat to his sovereignty. For the properties (as abstract objects) that define God's nature still depend on him and are grounded in him; they depend on him because it is part of his nature to affirm them, even as he affirms himself.

Plantinga articulates this Augustinian answer more explicitly in his 1982 American Philosophical Association presidential address, "How to Be an Anti-Realist":

A proposition exists because God thinks or conceives it. For propositions, as I see it, are best thought [of as] the thoughts of God. You might think this idea compromises the necessary existence of propositions; but not so. For God is a necessary being who has essentially the property of thinking just the thoughts he does think; these thoughts, then, are conceived or thought by God in every possible world and hence exist necessarily. (70)

Thus the Forms (and all the other abstract objects that have multiplied in modern logic and mathematics) are ideas in the mind of God. Propositions are the thoughts of God! What a striking echo of St. Augustine's "Behold where God is: it is wherever the truth is known." Thus Reformed philosophy, as Plantinga models it, is more than a refashioned Augustinian epistemology; it is a rejuvenated Augustinian metaphysics.

Long before Augustine, Aristotle had already tried to bridge Plato's chasm by characterizing God both as an individual, living, and thinking being and as pure form. He went on to describe God as "thought thinking itself." Now the biblical God also (originally) thought only himself, there being nothing else (originally) for him to think. "In the beginning," however, God freely created a world that is not part of his own nature at all, with the consequence that he now thinks about something else that he did not think about before. The mystery—and disappointment—with which Greek natural theology ends is the divine thought thinking itself, entirely oblivious of us mortals. The mystery—and surprise—with which the biblical revelation begins is the divine power bringing forth *ex nihilo* the world in which, although it is not divine, not one sparrow is forgotten by the divine mind.

It was Augustine who gathered together all these Greek and biblical ideas about God and set forth the first fully developed Christian concept of God. Little did he realize what alternative answers to the question of Plato's Forms Western philosophy after him would produce. Little did he realize either that, having examined these answers and found them wanting, someone like Plantinga 1600 years later would articulate his classic answer afresh. Nor did Augustine realize that his concept of God and his theory of our knowledge of God would inspire, by way of John Calvin, an entire tradition that we can now call *Reformed epistemology*. The ultimate test of any epistemological theory is whether it invigorates and is invigorated by metaphysics, the heart of philosophy. It should be evident from my brief account of Plantinga's metaphysics that Reformed epistemology clearly meets that test. It should also be evident from my whole account of Reformed epistemology that its present vitality springs from ancient and hardy roots.

Works Cited

Alston, W. P. "Christian Experience and Christian Belief." In *Faith and Rationality: Reason and Belief in God*, ed. A. Plantinga and N. Wolterstorff. Grand Rapids, Mich.: Eerdmans, 1983.

———. "Concepts of Epistemic Justification." *The Monist* 68, no. 1 (January 1985): 57–89.

Anscombe, E. "What Is It to Believe Someone?" In *Rationality and Religious Belief*, ed. C. F. DeLaney. Notre Dame, Ind.: University of Notre Dame Press, 1979.

Anselm. *Proslogium*, trans. S. N. Deane. La Salle, Ill.: Open Court, 1958.

Aquinas, Thomas. *Basic Writings of St. Thomas Aquinas*, ed. A. C. Pegis. New York: Random House, 1945.

Aristotle. *Basic Writings*, ed. R. McKeon. New York: Random House, 1941.

Augustine. *Answer to Skeptics, Divine Providence and the Problem of Evil, The Happy Life*, and *Soliloquies*, trans. D. J. Kavanagh et al. In *Fathers of the Church*, vol. 1. New York: CIMA, 1948.

———. *On Christian Doctrine*, trans. D. W. Robertson, Jr. Indianapolis: Bobbs-Merrill, 1958.

———. *The City of God*, trans. G. G. Walsh. New York: Doubleday, 1958.

———. *On Christian Doctrine*, trans. D. W. Robertson. Indianapolis: Bobbs-Merrill Co., 1958.

———. *Confessions*, trans. J. K. Ryan. New York: Doubleday, 1960.

———. *Eighty-Three Different Questions*, trans. V. Bourke; *Literal Commentary on Genesis*, trans. J. H. Taylor. In *The Essential Augustine*, ed. Vernon Bourke. Indianapolis: Hackett, 1974.

———. *Expositions on the Book of Psalms*. In *Nicene and Post-Nicene Fathers of the Christian Church*, vol. 8, ed. P. Schaff. Grand Rapids, Mich.: Eerdmans, 1956.

———. *On Free Will; The Teacher; Of True Religion;* and *The Usefulness of Belief*. In *Augustine: Earlier Writings*, trans. J. H. S. Burleigh. Philadelphia: Westminster Press, 1953.

———. *Letters 83–130* and *131–164*. In *Fathers of the Church*, vols. 18 and 11, trans. W. Parsons. Washington D.C.: Catholic University Press: 1953.

———. *Retractations.* In *Fathers of the Church,* vol. 60, trans. M. I. Bogan. Washington, D.C.: Catholic University of America Press, 1968.

———. *Sermon 43.* In *Introduction to the Philosophy of St. Augustine: Selected Readings and Commentaries,* ed. J. A. Mourant, pp. 39–44. State College: Pennsylvania State University Press, 1964.

———. *On Nature and Grace; On the Predestination of the Saints; On the Trinity.* In *Basic Writings of Saint Augustine,* 2 vols., ed. W. J. Oates. New York: Random House, 1948.

Baillie, John. *The Idea of Revelation.* New York: Columbia University Press, 1956.

———. *Our Knowledge of God.* New York: Charles Scribner's Sons, 1939.

Barth, Karl. *Church Dogmatics,* vol. 2, pt. 1, trans. G. W. Bromiley and T. F. Torrance. Edinburgh: T. and T. Clark, 1957.

———. *The Doctrine of the Word of God,* trans. G. T. Thomson. Edinburgh: T. and T. Clark, 1936.

———. *Fides Quaerens Intellectum,* trans. I. W. Robertson. London: SCM Press, 1960.

Bavinck, Herman. *The Doctrine of God,* trans. W. Hendrickson. Grand Rapids, Mich.: Eerdmans, 1951.

Berkhof, Louis. *Systematic Theology.* Grand Rapids, Mich.: Eerdmans, 1949.

Berkouwer, G. C. *General Revelation.* Grand Rapids, Mich.: Eerdmans, 1955.

Bourke, Vernon. *The Essential Augustine.* Indianapolis: Hackett, 1974.

Brunner, Emil. *The Christian Doctrine of God,* trans. Olive Wyon. Philadelphia: Westminster, 1950.

Brunner, Emil, and Barth, Karl. *Natural Theology.* London: Geoffrey Bless, The Centenary Press, 1946.

Burnaby, John. *Amor Dei.* London: Hodder and Stoughton, 1960.

Burnyeat, Myles. "Wittgenstein and Augustine *De Magistro.*" In *Proceedings of the Aristotelian Society,* vol. 61. Oxford: Blackwell, 1987.

———. *The Skeptical Tradition.* Berkeley: University of California Press, 1983.

Callahan, J. F. *St. Augustine and the Augustinian Tradition.* Villanova, Pa.: Villanova University Press, 1967.

Calvin, John. *Commentary on Galatians and Ephesians.* Grand Rapids, Mich.: Eerdmans, 1948.

———. *Commentary on Philippians, Colossians and Thessalonians.* Grand Rapids, Mich.: Eerdmans: 1948.

————. *Concerning the Eternal Predestination of God.* London: James Clark, 1963.

————. *Institutes of the Christian Religion,* 2 vols., trans. F. L. Battles. Philadelphia: Westminster, 1960.

"Chapter and Verse." *Harvard Magazine* 92, no. 3 (January– February 1990), p. 54; 92, no. 5 (May–June 1990), p. 116.

Chisholm, R. *Theory of Knowledge,* 2d ed. Englewood Cliffs: Prentice-Hall, 1977.

Cornford, F. M. *Plato's Theory of Knowledge.* New York: Bobbs Merrill, 1957.

Cross, R. C., and Woozley, A. D. *Plato's Republic: A Philosophical Commentary.* New York: St. Martin's Press. 1964.

Crosson, Frederick. "Structure and Meaning in St. Augustine's *Confessions." Proceedings of the American Catholic Philosophical Association,* 1989.

Descartes, R. *Discourse on Method* and *Meditations of First Philosophy,* trans. D. A. Cress. Indianapolis: Hackett, 1980.

Dowey, Edward A. *The Knowledge of God in Calvin's Theology.* New York: Columbia University Press, 1952.

Evans, C. Stephen. "Kierkegaard and Plantinga on Belief in God." *Faith and Philosophy,* 5, no. 1 (January 1988): 25–39.

Friedlander, Paul. *Plato: An Introduction,* 2d ed. Princeton, N.J.: Princeton University Press, 1969.

Gilson, Etienne. *Christianity and Philosophy.* New York: Sheed and Ward, 1939.

————. *The Christian Philosophy of St. Augustine.* New York: Random House, 1960.

————. *God and Philosophy.* New Haven, Conn.: Yale University Press, 1951.

Hackforth, R. *Plato's Phaedo.* New York: The Liberal Arts Press, n.d.

Hodge, Charles. *Systematic Theology.* New York: Charles Scribner, 1872.

Hoitenga, D. J. "Faith and Reason in Calvin's Doctrine of the Knowledge of God." In *Rationality in the Calvinian Tradition,* ed. H. Hart et al. Lanham, Md.: University Press of America, 1983.

————. "Knowledge, Belief, and Revelation: a Reply to Patrick Lee." *Faith and Philosophy,* 8, no. 2 (April 1991).

The Holy Bible, trans. James Moffatt. New York: Harper Bros., 1946.

Holy Bible, Revised Standard Version. New York: Thomas Nelson, 1952.

Itard, J. *The Wild Boy of Aveyron.* New York: Appleton-Century-Crofts, 1962.

James, William. *The Will to Believe and Other Essays.* New York: Dover Books, 1956.

Keil, C. F., and Delitzsch, F. *Commentary on the Old Testament,* Pentateuch vol. 1 and Isaiah vol. 1. Grand Rapids, Mich.: Eerdmans, 1951, 1954.

Kenny, A. *Faith and Reason.* New York: Columbia University Press, 1983.

Kierkegaard, Sören. *Concluding Unscientific Postscript,* trans. D. F. Swenson. Princeton, N.J.: Princeton University Press, 1944.

―――. *Fear and Trembling,* trans. W. Lowrie. Princeton, N.J.: Princeton University Press, 1952.

Kirwan, C. *Augustine.* New York: Routledge, 1989.

Kretzmann, Norman. "Faith Seeks, Understanding Finds: Augustine's Charter for Christian Philosophy." In *Christian Philosophy,* ed. T. Flint. Notre Dame, Ind.: University of Notre Dame Press, 1990.

Kuyper, Abraham. *De Gemeene Gratie.* Amsterdam: Hoeveker and Wormser, 1902.

―――. *Principles of Sacred Theology,* trans. J. H. DeVries. Grand Rapids, Mich.: Eerdmans, 1954.

Le Cerf, Auguste. *An Introduction to Reformed Dogmatics,* trans. André Schlemmer. London: Lutterworth Press, 1949 (reprinted Grand Rapids, Mich.: Baker, 1981).

Lewis, C. S. "On Obstinacy in Belief." In *The World's Last Night.* New York: Harcourt, Brace and Co., 1960.

―――. "Religion: Reality or Substitute." In *Christian Reflections.* Grand Rapids, Mich.: Eerdmans, 1967.

Lewis, H. D. "History of Philosophy of Religion." In *Encyclopedia of Philosophy,* ed. P. Edwards. New York: Macmillan, 1967.

Locke, John. *Essay Concerning Human Understanding,* 2 vols. New York: Dover Books, n.d.

R. A. Markus. "St. Augustine on Signs." In *Augustine: A Collection of Critical Essays,* ed. R. A. Markus. New York: Doubleday, 1972.

Mavrodes, George. *Belief in God.* New York: Random House, 1970.

―――. *Revelation in Religious Belief.* Philadelphia: Temple University Press, 1988.

Moline, Jon. *Plato's Theory of Understanding.* Madison: University of Wisconsin Press, 1981.

Nash, Ronald. *The Light of the Mind: St. Augustine's Theory of Knowledge.* Lexington: University of Kentucky Press, 1969.

Newman, Cardinal John Henry. *Apologia Pro Sua Vita*. New York: W. W. Norton, 1968.

Parker, T. H. L. *Calvin's Doctrine of the Knowledge of God*. Grand Rapids, Mich.: Eerdmans, 1959.

Penelhum, Terence. *God and Skepticism*. Dordrecht, Holland: Reidel, 1983.

Plantinga, Alvin. "Coherentism and the Evidentialist Objection." In *Rationality, Religious Belief, and Moral Commitment*, ed. R. Audi and W. J. Wainwright. Ithaca, N.Y.: Cornell University Press, 1986.

———. *Does God Have a Nature?* Milwaukee, Wisc.: Marquette University Press, 1980.

———. "Epistemic Probability and Evil." *Archivo di Filosofia*, 56 (1988): 447–584.

———. "The Foundations of Theism: A Reply." *Faith and Philosophy* 3, no. 3 (July 1986): 298–313.

———. *God, Freedom, and Evil*. New York: Harper and Row, 1974.

———. *God and Other Minds*. Ithaca, N.Y.: Cornell University Press, 1967.

———. "How To Be An Anti-Realist." *Proceedings and Addresses of the American Philosophical Association* 56, no. 1 (September 1982): 47–70.

———. "Is Belief in God Properly Basic?" *Nous* 15, no. 1 (March 1981): 41–51.

———. "Is Belief in God Rational?" In *Rationality and Religious Belief*, ed. C. F. Delaney. Notre Dame, Ind.: University of Notre Dame Press, 1979.

———. "Justification and Theism." *Faith and Philosophy* 4, no. 4 (October 1987): 403–426.

———. *The Nature of Necessity*. Oxford: Clarendon Press, 1974.

———. "Reason and Belief in God." In *Faith and Rationality: Reason and Belief in God*, ed. A. Plantinga and N. Wolterstorff. Grand Rapids, Mich.: Eerdmans, 1983.

———. "On Reformed Epistemology." *The Reformed Journal* 32, no. 1 (January 1982): 13–17.

———. "The Reformed Objection to Natural Theology." *Proceedings of the American Catholic Philosophical Association*, 1980.

———. "Self-Profile"; "Replies." In *Alvin Plantinga*, ed. J. E. Tomberlin and P. Van Inwagen. Dordrecht, Holland: Reidel, 1985.

———. *Warrant: The Current Debate*. Forthcoming.

Plato. *The Dialogues of Plato*, 2 vols., trans. B. Jowett. New York: Random House, 1937.

——. *Five Dialogues*, trans. G. M. A. Grube. Indianapolis: Hackett, 1981.

——. *Phaedo*, trans. R. Hackforth. New York: Library of Liberal Arts, 1952.

——. *The Republic*, trans. F. M. Cornford. New York: Oxford University Press: 1963.

——. *The Republic*, trans. G. M. A. Grube. Indianapolis: Hackett, 1974.

——. *Timaeus*, trans. F. M. Cornford. Indianapolis: Bobbs-Merrill, 1959.

Plotinus. *Enneads*, trans. S. MacKenna and B. S. Page. New York: Pantheon Books, 1962.

Popkin, R. H. *The History of Skepticism from Erasmus to Spinoza*. Berkeley: University of California Press, 1979.

Price, H. H. *Belief*. London: Humanities Press, 1969

——. "Some Considerations about Belief." In *Knowledge and Belief*, ed. A. P. Griffiths. Oxford: Oxford University Press, 1973.

Prichard, H. H. *Knowledge and Perception*. Oxford: Oxford University Press, 1950.

Robinson, R. *Plato's Earlier Dialectic*. Oxford: Oxford University Press, 1953.

Russman, T. A. "'Reformed' Epistemology." *Thomistic Papers IV*, ed. L. A. Kennedy. Houston: Center for Thomistic Studies, 1988.

Sayre, Kenneth. "Marks of Distinction between Belief and Knowledge." Unpublished.

Sextus Empiricus. *Against the Logicians*, trans. J. Bury. Cambridge, Mass.: Harvard University Press, 1961.

——. *Outlines of Pyrrhonism*, trans. J. Bury. Cambridge, Mass.: Harvard University Press, 1961.

Stob, H. "Apologetics." *The Banner* 95, no. 5 (January 29, 1960): 9 ff; no. 7 (February 12, 1960) 9 ff; no. 11 (March 11, 1960): 9 ff.

Swift, Jonathan. *Battle of the Books*. Oxford: Oxford University Press, 1920.

——. *Gulliver's Travels*. New York: W. W. Norton, 1970.

Thucydides. *The Peloponnesian War*, trans. Rex Warner. New York: Penquin Books, 1982.

Van Hook, Jay M. "Knowledge, Belief, and Reformed Epistemology." *The Reformed Journal* 31, no. 7 (July 1981): 12–15.

Vos, Arvin. *Aquinas, Calvin and Contemporary Thought*. Washington D.C.: Christian University Press, 1985.

Vos, G. *Biblical Theology*. Grand Rapids, Mich.: Eerdmans, 1948.

Warfield, B. B. "Apologetics." In *Studies in Theology*. Oxford: Oxford University Press, 1932.

———. *Biblical Doctrines*. New York: Oxford University Press, 1929.

———. *Studies in Tertullian and Augustine*. Oxford: Oxford University Press, 1930.

White, N. J. D. *The Expositor's Greek Testament*, vol. 4, ed. R. Nicoll. Grand Rapids, Mich.: Eerdmans, 1951.

White, N. P. *Plato on Knowledge and Reality*. Indianapolis: Hackett, 1976.

Whitehead, A. N. *Process and Reality*. New York: The Humanities Press, 1929.

Wilson, John Cook. *Statement and Inference*, 2 vols. Oxford, Oxford University Press: 1926.

Wolterstorff, N. "Evidence, Entitled Belief, and the Gospels." *Faith and Philosophy* 6, no. 4 (October 1989): 429–459.

———. "Introduction." In *Faith and Rationality: Reason and Belief In God*, ed. Alvin Plantinga and N. Wolterstorff. Notre Dame, Ind.: University of Notre Dame Press, 1983.

———. "The Migration of Theistic Arguments: From Natural Theology to Evidentialist Apologetics." In *Rationality, Religious Belief, and Moral Commitment*, ed. R. Audi and W. J. Wainwright. Ithaca, N.Y.: Cornell University Press, 1986.

———. *Reason within the Bounds of Religion*, 2nd ed. Grand Rapids, Mich.: Eerdmans, 1984.

Index